PROMOTING THE WELL-BEING OF THE ELDERLY: A COMMUNITY DIAGNOSIS

ABOUT THE AUTHORS

Thomas T.H. Wan, Ph.D., who received his doctorate at the University of Georgia (1970), is presently Professor of Health Administration at the Medical College of Virginia, Virginia Commonwealth University. He has been on the faculty of University of Maryland Baltimore County and Cornell University, and has also served as a Senior Research Fellow of the National Center for Health Services Research. Dr. Wan's research has largely been concerned with the epidemiology of disabilities, health service issues in aging, evaluation of geriatric services, and the measurement of well-being. He has authored many publications on health services utilization, evaluation of health care outcomes, and the effects of life-changing experiences on the elderly. He is also the author of *Stressful Life Events, Social Support Networks and Gerontological Health: A Prospective Study* (Lexington, Mass.: D.C. Heath, 1982). Dr. Wan is currently involved in research on the impact of life change events on gerontological health.

Barbara Odell, M.A., is a Research Associate at the University of Maryland Baltimore County. Ms. Odell has been involved in several community studies that assess the needs of the elderly. She has a broad knowledge of interorganizational theory and its applications to community planning. Her background in the area of aging and health services includes research to determine the effects of life change events, particularly widowhood and retirement, on social participation and residential mobility.

David T. Lewis, Ph.D., is Professor and Chairman of the Sociology Department at the University of Maryland Baltimore County. He received his doctorate in sociology from Ohio State University and has previously taught at Miami University (Ohio). A social demographer, Dr. Lewis co-authored the book *Population Problems* with the late Dr. Warren S. Thompson.

PROMOTING THE WELL-BEING OF THE ELDERLY: A COMMUNITY DIAGNOSIS

THOMAS T. H. WAN, Ph.D.

Barbara Gill Odell, M.A.

David T. Lewis, Ph.D.

The Haworth Press
New York

The Haworth Press, 28 East 22 Street, New York, New York 10010

Library of Congress Cataloging in Publication Data

Wan, Thomas T. H.
    Promoting the well-being of the elderly.

    Includes bibliographies and index.
    1. Aged—Maryland—Baltimore County. 2. Aged—
Services for—Maryland—Baltimore County. I. Odell,
Barbara Gill. II. Lewis, David T.   III. Title.
HQ1064.U6M38   1982   362.6′09752′71   82-9209
ISBN 0-917724-38-0   AACR2
ISBN 0-917724-39-9 (pbk.)

Printed in the United States of America

Contents

List of Tables

Acknowledgments

While the authors are grateful to many who contributed to this book, special recognition is given to Timothy Fagan, Director of the Baltimore County Department of Aging and Carl Kuppe, Planner, of the same office, who initiated the Senior Needs Assessment Project (SNAP). Further, we recognize the substantial contribution made by the staff members who were involved in designing and collecting the SNAP data.

We also acknowledge the Duke University Center for the Study of Aging and Human Development for its contribution in the formulation of multidimensional functional assessment questionnaire from which several items of the SNAP schedule were adopted.

Appreciation must be expressed to Joyce Riley, M.A. for preparation of chapters 6 and 7 of this book and to Francine Meo for her patience and skills in typing numerous drafts as well as the final manuscript.

Preface

This book is intended primarily for social planners, policy makers, researchers, and graduate students and their teachers who face the difficulty of translating their passionate socially relevant concerns into planning directives based upon studies. The book demonstrates that comprehensive planning of social and health services for the elderly can be achieved through careful assessment of their level of well-being and an identification of the type and extent of their service needs and unmet needs in the community.

It is an intellectual challenge for researchers to undertake the difficult task of merging and reconciling the arts of social practice and the sciences of social research. This task, we believe, is accomplished by applying a needs assessment approach through which knowledge about the current status of the elderly is acquired and practical requirements for planned change for improving human services are specified.

In 1978, the Baltimore County Department of Aging took decisive action for future comprehensive planning by initiating the Senior Needs Assessment Project (SNAP). Findings of this project are detailed in this volume to illustrate the ways in which needs assessment techniques can be productively used to gain an understanding of a community.

Chapters 1 and 2 present a broad-based introduction to the concept of needs assessment and its application to the study population. Chapter 1 acquaints the reader with an understanding of needs assessment by answering three questions: What is needs assessment? Why is it important? How can needs be measured? This chapter also describes the components of needs assessment and the ways these components can be integrated into a coherent conceptual framework. Chapter 2 provides a general sociodemographic profile of the population studied according to their age, sex, and socioeconomic characteristics.

In Chapters 3, 4, and 5, the social, psychological, and physical well-being of the sample population are profiled. Chapter 6 describes such activities as leisure pursuits, voter registration, and volunteerism.

Chapter 7 adds to the profiles described in previous chapters by enumerating the perceived service needs of the population and service needs that are at this time unmet in Baltimore County.

Chapters 8 and 9 examine the variation in the use of health and social services, which is associated with differences in sociodemographic characteristics, knowledge of services available, access to transportation, and perceived economic well-being.

Chapter 10 brings together the physical, psychological, and social well-being dimensions profiled in chapters 3, 4, and 5 with the need dimension explored in chapter 7 in order to identify the frail elderly. The frail elderly are defined as persons who have poor physical, psychological, and social well-being, and who also have a higher level of service needs that are not being met. The use of social and health services by the frail elderly is examined in this chapter. In chapter 11, strategies for reducing the misuse of services and for improving the service delivery network in the future are recommended within the policy framework introduced in chapter 1, which includes the steps of planning, implementation, and evaluation.

It is generally acknowledged that research is a cumulative process. One study, such as in Baltimore County, cannot answer all our questions about effectively meeting the needs of the elderly. We do feel, however, that this book will be a significant contribution to local communities who are committed to improving their service delivery networks.

PROMOTING THE WELL-BEING OF THE ELDERLY: A COMMUNITY DIAGNOSIS

1

An Introduction to Needs Assessment

It is generally recognized by social planners and gerontologists that, no matter what the subject of inquiry, the collection of social facts that are pertinent to the development of plans or programs for the elderly should be systematic. Research activities that are organized to (1) identify the levels of health or well-being of the elderly, (2) determine their variations in perception of service needs, and (3) analyze the patterns of utilization of services are the important steps toward the formulation of comprehensive planning for health. One of the key approaches to promoting the well-being of the elderly is commonly known as needs assessment.

The major objectives of a needs assessment approach are fourfold: (1) to describe, both qualitatively and quantitatively, the nature, type, magnitude, intensity, and variability of human service needs; (2) to determine social, psychological, and physical functioning levels of community members; (3) to identify alternative modes of services or innovative service modalities; and (4) to recommend necessary actions for planned changes. There is a pressing need to search for a valid and comprehensive approach to assessing the needs of the elderly. The importance of needs assessment is stressed in the Older Americans Act, which requires Area Agencies on Aging to formulate an area plan to:

> provide for the establishment of a comprehensive and coordinated system for the delivery of social services within the planning and service area covered by the plan, including *determining the need for social services in such an area* (taking into consideration among other things, the number of older persons with low incomes residing in such areas), *evaluating the effectiveness of the use of resources in meeting such need and entering into agreements with providers of social services* in such areas, for the provision of such services to meet such needs. [emphasis added]

1

In order to ascertain the needs at the local level, several conceptual and methodological questions had to be addressed. In this introductory chapter, we clarify our conception of what is meant by needs assessment. What are its components? What are its anticipated outcomes for the community? How can a needs assessment approach be integrated into comprehensive planning of social and health services for the elderly?

NEEDS ASSESSMENT: ITS COMPONENTS AND OUTCOMES

The term *needs assessment* is used "to describe the systematic process of determining needs, both qualitative and quantitative. . . . The assessment leads to a description of the (population's) limitations and strengths which, in turn leads to the identification of service goals. The assessment also establishes baseline information that is used to evaluate (client) progress and effectiveness of service" (Katz et al., 1976, p. 225). This definition implies that there should be a balance between the needs of the population on the one hand and the services provided on the other. The term *unmet needs* has been used to describe needs for which there are no services available or accessible (Carr & Wolf, 1979).

Siegel, Attkisson, and Carson (1978) have noted that needs assessment does not merely imply the identification of needs but also a priority rating of needs on the basis of their importance to individual well-being. Establishing priorities of need has implications concerning the provision of services. Needs assessment can be an important tool in (1) describing demands for service, (2) setting clearly defined goals for providing services, (3) stimulating coordination of services on the local level, (4) establishing the relevance of existing services, (5) delineating groups "at risk," and (6) blending citizen participation (consumer preferences) with professional viewpoints in the planning process.

Needs assessment of the elderly has at least three components, which are the evaluation of physical, psychological, and social well-being. While the relevance of an individual's physical and psychological state to his or her use of services is fairly obvious, Palmore (1971) points out that social well-being is also an important factor. He says that "the need for frequent, cognitively stimulating and emotionally satisfying human interaction is one of the basic needs of man, the social animal" (p. 529). He further observes there is an interrelationship between areas of need. For example, living alone may be related to poor diet, which, in turn, may affect health needs. In another case, poor health may limit transportation options and lead to social isolation.

The Older Americans Resources and Services (OARS) survey identifies the need components more specifically as the assessment of social resources, economic resources, physical health, mental health, and the ability for self-care (Duke University Center for the Study of Aging and Human Development, 1978).

Regardless of the terms applied to the specific components included in needs assessment, it is certain that among older adults such assessment must aim to evaluate the various functioning dimensions of the *whole person*.

APPROACHES TO NEEDS ASSESSMENT

The three basic approaches to needs assessment are: (1) health and social indicators approach, (2) social area surveys, and (3) community group approach (Warheit, Bell & Schwab, 1979). The social indicators approach relies primarily on data collected by public agencies. Information on service needs is extracted from these data. For example, the "underservice" index developed by the Department of Health, Education and Welfare is derived from a composite of four major social indicators: (1) percentage of population below the poverty line, (2) the percentage of elderly population, (3) the infant mortality rate, and (4) the doctor-population ratio. This index describes the general level of health care needs in a community.

Social area surveys, on the other hand, require the collection of data for the specific purpose of examining needs for services in an area. One type of social area survey is the citizens' survey, which indicates the expressed needs of residents.

The third approach to needs assessment, the community group approach, while also dealing with information collected for a specific purpose, has a professional rather than a consumer emphasis. Techniques are employed to obtain the consensus of professional opinion on population needs (Delbecq, 1975; Delbecq et al., 1971). Delphi technique is one of the methods used more frequently to obtain a balanced and undistorted report of opinion. The Delphi method elicits the opinions of specialists through offering a sequence of questions, reordering feedback from them, and subsequently readministering questions for reassessment.

For the assessment of needs, we choose to employ a social area approach. This approach was selected for several reasons. First, analysis of public data as used in the social indicators approach yields limited information on needs for care. A community survey of senior citizens, however, enables us to probe specific problem areas of the elderly in our community. Second, there is a considerable debate in the literature as to whether professional viewpoints of need reflect the actual needs perceived by the elderly population (Keith, 1975; Riesenfeld et al., 1972; Avant & Dressel,

1976). In fact, comparing the service priorities of professionals and of elderly residents living in a model neighborhood area, Riesenfeld et al. (1972) noted older persons tended to favor a noninstitutional approach to service delivery favoring such supportive services as discount cards and transportation aids, while professionals tended to favor facility-based, direct service solutions to the elderly's problems. Further, Avant and Dressel (1976) present some disturbing findings that service providers with training in gerontology were in less agreement with consumer viewpoints on service provision to the aged than were the providers without such training.

While professional input is necessary in the planning of services, consumers' assessments of their own needs are crucial for the development of effective comprehensive planning for the elderly. Previous research (Wan, 1976; Keith, 1975) offers evidence that service systems should be based on the needs expressed by older persons themselves through such methods as survey interviews. Even though adult children may feel they understand their parents' needs, they may misinterpret their parents' desires. Clearly, of all the approaches to need assessments, "the citizens survey approach alone is capable of eliciting from individuals specific information about their own needs and utilization of services and about the needs and utilization patterns of their families" (Bell et al., 1976, p. 287).

Looking at six areas of need, Palmore (1971) in a study of 6,289 aged who were residents of low-income communities in the United States found:

1. *Dietary needs* were associated with age, living alone, and having comparably less education than others. Younger aged had somewhat more adequate diets than older aged. Dietary needs were also interrelated with housing and transportation needs.
2. *Housing needs* were found more among males, persons living alone, and persons with comparatively less education and less income than others.
3. *Medical needs* were found more often among men, nonwhites, and persons with less education and less income than others.
4. *Disability needs* occurred more often among men and persons of advanced age. Disability needs were related to having less income than others and living alone.
5. *Transportation needs* were related to having less income than others, living alone, being nonwhite, and being among the older aged.
6. *Isolation* was associated with women, advanced age, and being white. Unexpectedly, having a comparatively higher income level was also associated with isolation.

While Palmore's finding of a relationship between age and disability is supported by other studies (Berg et al., 1970), his finding that men have more disabilities is disputed (Berg et al., 1970). It has also been suggested that there is a relationship between living alone and disability (Berg et al., 1970).

Powers and Bultena (1974) speculate that social support provided by family and friends may be another factor affecting need for services. They hypothesized that social support may be a key factor explaining why the elderly they surveyed actually used social services less than they said they thought they would.

Access to care may influence unmet needs. Berg has noted in a sample of institutionalized and noninstitutionalized aged persons that inappropriate placements for service can result in underutilization. Further, client satisfaction with services may be another factor affecting use of services (Mayer & Timms, 1970), since dissatisfied clients may use services less than their needs require.

COMPREHENSIVE PLANNING FOR PROMOTING WELL-BEING OF THE ELDERLY: A CONCEPTUAL FRAMEWORK

In order to have effective planning for health, the following four steps are required: (1) assessment of the general well-being of the population, (2) determination of use of health and social services, (3) identification of the most frail elderly, and (4) incorporation of needs assessment findings into the planning process.

Assessment of General Well-being

First, local and area-wide planning agencies concerned with increasing services to the elderly in their own communities need precise data on the prevalence and distribution of health-related problems. The identification of which population groups have poor physical, psychological, or social functioning has some practical implications for planning. It addresses questions concerning the types of services needed, priorities of services, projected resources required, and the kinds of personnel who should be trained to give effective services to the community in the future.

The general well-being of the population can be described by indicators showing their available resources and needs for care. Assessment of social well-being in terms of the availability of such informal sources of care as children or other relatives is especially important in determining formal resources required. Pertinent indicators of social, psychological, and physical well-being include:

1. Social Well-being
   • Social support
   • Social activity
   • Living arrangement
   • Economic well-being
   • Sense of environmental well-being
2. Psychological well-being
   • Symptoms
   • Self-assessed psychological well-being
   • Life satisfaction
3. Physical well-being
   • Disability and impairment
   • Functional dependency
   • Self-assessed physical health
   • Nutritional status

The three dimensions of well-being are assumed to be conceptually distinctive. Empirically, they are not completely independent, since indicators of social, mental, and physical well-being are correlated (Wan, 1976).

As shown in Figure 1.1, the three areas of functioning may be independent or may overlap in one, two, or all three areas. For example, persons may have poor physical health but good psychological and social functioning, or may have poor psychological and physical health and yet have a strong social support system. The shaded area in Figure 1.1 represents the overlapping of all three well-being indicators. This area describes persons with good functioning in all the areas, a population who, we suspect, needs relatively few services, and persons with poor functioning in all the areas—the frail elderly—who should have the greatest number of needs for service. More detailed explanations of factors encompassed in the social, psychological, and physical dimensions of well-being are detailed in chapters 3, 4, and 5. The interrelationships between these dimensions are explored in chapters 10 and 11.

Utilization of Services

The second step is to investigate factors that contribute to utilization of services. Based upon the systems model developed by previous research (Andersen, 1968; Andersen & Newman, 1973; Wan & Soifer, 1974; Berki & Kobashigawa, 1976), a theoretical model is designed to explain varia-

tions in use of social and health services as the result of a three-stage sequence of predisposing, enabling, and need components. The propensity
or predisposition to use specific services may vary from person to person
because of differences in the personal, social, demographic, and
psychological characteristics. Enabling factors refer to conditions that
facilitate or impede the use of services by an individual who is predispos-
ed to seek care. These factors include family or individual resources,
knowledge about the service programs, transportation barriers, and community availability of specific programs. Assuming that both the predisposing and enabling conditions are met, the elderly must perceive the need
for services before they will use the services that are available. Chapters
8 and 9 examine use of health and social services in detail.

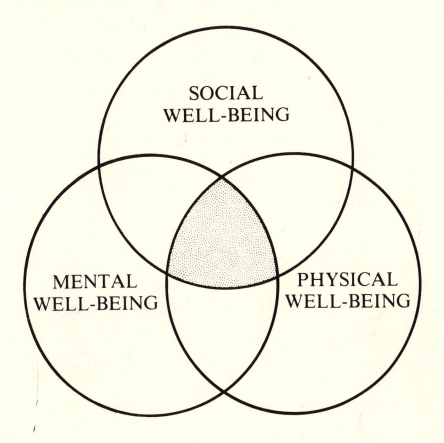

Figure 1.1. Relationships between Three Dimensions of Well-being

Definition of the Frail Elderly

The third step is to identify the characteristics of frail elderly in order to develop programs targeting on the population who have the most pressing needs for services. We define the frail elderly as those characterized by the presence of functional incapacities who also perceive the needs for service that are not being met.

Planning Processes

The practical application of needs assessment must be incorporated into planning processes (see Figure 1.2). Needs assessment is considered as an ongoing activity in the planning processes whereby information obtained from the assessment is fed back into each planning phase.

The four phases of the planning process outlined in Figure 1.2 are the (1) policy formulation phase, (2) strategic phase, (3) implementation phase, and (4) evaluation phase. When existing resources are limited, needs assessment may be particularly useful in priority setting in the policy stage. By knowing what the greatest needs of a specific community are, resources can be allocated more efficiently and planning can become more responsive to the personal characteristics of the population. In the strategic phase, needs assessment can contribute to the development of a comprehensive service plan. By discerning which service needs are held in common by specific population groups, natural links for coordination of services may become evident. In addition, understanding the needs of a community can contribute to more accurate estimations of manpower requirements and can help in deciding where to locate specific programs and facilities that are being planned. As shown by the evaluation phase, needs assessment

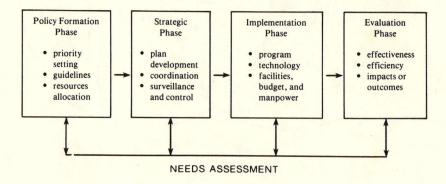

Figure 1.2. Planning Processes

can not only help planners to design future plans more clearly, but can also help to assess the effectiveness, efficiency, and outcome of what has already been done in the area of service delivery. Thus, surveying the needs of the elderly in a community can give perspective on past and present actions as well as contribute to planning for the future.

THE PRESENT STUDY

In response to the mandate of the 1973 Amendments to Title III of the Older Americans Act, which charges Area Agencies on Aging with the responsibility of identifying the needs of the elderly in their regions, the Baltimore County Department of Aging conducted a needs assessment survey of its elderly residents in the summer of 1978. The project of surveying older adults' needs was officially termed the Senior Needs Assessment Project or SNAP, as it can be called. The survey elicited Baltimore County residents' own opinions of their present well-being, their awareness of existing services, and their desires for additional assistance.

The older population of Baltimore County has been growing rapidly. While in 1970 there were 45,668 county residents 65 years and over, it has been estimated that in 1978 there were about 65,000 persons age 65 and over, a 42% increase in eight years (Commission on Aging, 1978). In order to keep pace with this growing elderly population who not only face aging-related problems but also spiralling inflation, there has been an expansion of social, recreational, and health-related services. At the time of the study, it was clearly imperative that the Department of Aging become aware of the present needs of the older population in its area of jurisdiction in order to efficiently plan the appropriate level and range of services for the future. Such awareness is required to carry out (1) a systematic analysis of the total older population's perceived and unmet service needs and (2) a comprehensive assessment of their use of social services.

In the analysis that follows of the Baltimore County elderly population, we examine the influence of the following factors on needs for service: (1) social and demographic characteristics of the elderly population, (2) the social, psychological, and physical well-being of the elderly population, (3) characteristics of the frail elderly, who, we expect, will exhibit a higher level of unmet needs, (4) use of health and social services, and (5) factors affecting unmet service needs and their interrelationship with social and health characteristics of the community's elderly. We examine these characteristics not only among the population as a whole but also for populations in each of five designated service areas in the county: Southeast, Southwest, North, Northeast, and Northwest. The use of area-specific analysis will help make area-wide planning more effective. We do not consider our effort in searching for all of the problems faced by our older citizens to be exhaustive, but we do believe that the results of this study will increase public and professional understanding of needs of the elderly in a large urban county in a mid-Atlantic state.

REFERENCES

Andersen, R. 1968. *A Behavioral Model of Families' Use of Health Services*. Research Series No. 25. Chicago: Center for Health Administration Studies, University of Chicago.

Andersen, R. and J. Newman. 1973. "Societal and Individual Determinants of Medical Care Utilization in the United States." *The Milbank Memorial Fund Quarterly*, 51:95–124.

Avant, W.R. and P.L. Dressel. 1976. "Comparative Perceptions of the Needs of the Elderly and Their Implications for Service Delivery: An Analysis of Metropolitan Community." Paper presented at Annual Meeting of the Gerontological Society in New York.

Bell, R.A. et al. 1978. "Service Mobilization, Social Indicator and Citizen Survey Approaches to Human Service Need Assessment" in *Evaluation of Human Service Programs*, edited by C.C. Attkisson et al. New York: Academic Press.

Berg, R.L. et al. 1970. "Assessing the Health Care Needs of the Aged." *Health Services Research* 36–59.

Berki, S.E. and B. Kobashigawa. 1976. "Socioeconomic and Need Determinants of Ambulatory Care Use." *Medical Care* 14:405–421.

Carr, W.S. and S. Wolf. 1979. "Unmet Needs as Socio-Medical Indicators." in *Socio-Medical Health Indicators*, edited by J. Elinson and A. Siegman. Farmingdale, N.Y.: Baywood.

Commission on Aging. 1978. Annual Report. Baltimore County Department of Aging.

Delbecq, A.L. 1975. *Group Techniques for Program Planning—A Guide to Nominal Group and Delphi Processes*. Glenview, Ill.: Scott, Foresman.

Delbecq, A.L. et al. 1971. "A Group Process Model for Problems Solving Identification and Program Planning." *Journal of Applied Behavioral Science* 7:466–492.

Duke University Center for the Study of Aging and Human Development. 1978. *Multidimensional Functional Assessment: The OARS Methodology*, Second Edition. Durham, N.C.: Duke University Center for the Study of Aging and Human Development.

Katz, S. et al. 1976. "Medical Perspective of Team Care" in *Long Term Care*, edited by S. Sherwood. New York: Spectrum.

Keith, P. 1975. "Evaluation of Services for the Aged by Professionals and the Elderly." *Social Services Review* 49:271–278.

Mayer, J. and N. Timms. 1970. *The Client Speaks*. London: Routledge and Kegan Paul.

Palmore, E. 1971. "Variables Related to Needs Among the Aged Poor." *Journal of Gerontology* 26:524–531.

Powers, E. and C. Bultena. 1974. "Correspondence Between Anticipated and Actual Uses of Public Services by the Elderly." *Social Service Review* 48:245–254.

Reisenfeld, M.J. et al. 1972. "Perceptions of Public Service Needs: The Urban Elderly and the Public Agency." *The Gerontologist* 12:185–190.

Siegel, L.M., C.C. Attkisson, and L.G. Carson. 1978. "Need Identification and Program Planning in the Community Context" in *Evaluation of Human Service Programs*, edited by C.C. Attkisson et al. New York: Academic Press.

Wan, T.T.H. 1976. "An Organizational Analysis of the Determinants of Unmet Service Needs for the Elderly." Paper presented at Annual Meeting of the American Sociological Association in New York.

Wan, T.T.H. 1976. "Predicting Self-Assessed Health Status: A Multivariate Approach." *Health Services Research* 11 (4):464–477.

Wan, T.T.H. and S.J. Soifer. 1974. "Determinants of Physician Utilization: A Causal Analysis." *Journal of Health and Social Behavior*. 15:100–108.

Warheit, G.J., R.A. Bell, and J.J. Schwab. 1979. *Needs Assessment Approaches: Concepts and Methods*. Washington, D.C.: U.S. Government Printing Office DHEW Publication Number (ADM) 79-472.

2

Descriptive
Characteristics of
the Population Studied

BACKGROUND OF THE SNAP POPULATION

In order to provide the Area Agency on Aging with baseline community data on human service needs, a survey instrument was developed by the staff of the Baltimore County Department of Aging in consultation with the Sociology Department of the University of Maryland Baltimore County. The survey instrument was reviewed by representative professionals in the area of aging and older residents in the county. After this review, the questionnaire was revised and pretested. It was then revised again to assure that the questions were understandable and unambiguous. Respondents were selected through neighborhood canvassing on the basis of a quota sample. A total of 1,300 persons were surveyed by trained interviewers during the summer of 1978. When incomplete questionnaires were discarded, a sample size of 1,182 persons resulted. These persons constitute the SNAP population referred to in this text.

In our analysis, careful attention is paid to responses reported within the five specific service areas that constitute Baltimore County. These service areas are geographic units used by the Department of Aging for planning and administrative purposes. Borders of designated service areas were drawn recognizing community boundaries and considering geographic factors and such existing county designations as census tracts, regional planning districts, and zoning areas. The five service areas are the Southwest (including Catonsville, Lansdowne, Woodlawn); Northwest (including Randallstown, Pikesville); North (including Towson, Ruxton, Chestnut Ridge, Timonium, Lutherville, Jacksonville, Sparks, Mt. Carmel,

Hereford); Northeast (including Parkville, Perry Hall, Rossville, Rosedale, Middle River, Windlass, Fork, Kingsville, Overlea); and Southeast (including Northpoint, Edgemere, Dundalk, Essex) (see Figure 2.1). The total number of usable interviews was distributed as follows: Southwest 34.3%, Northeast 27.2%, Southeast 18.7%, North 13.8%, and Northwest 5.9% (see Table 2.1)*. We speculate that the reason for these differences in representation by service area may have been due to differences in population density and willingness of residents to be interviewed. In areas where the Department of Aging was better known for its services, residents might have been more receptive to interviewers.

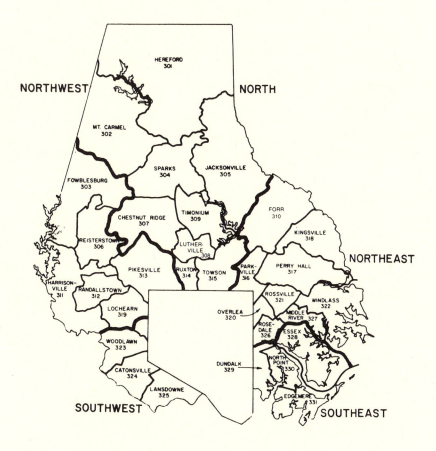

Figure 2.1. Base Map of Regional Planning District in Baltimore, Maryland

---

*Tables appear in Appendix D.

AGE AND SEX

Both age and sex distribution are indicators of the kinds of services need-ed in an area. Table 2.1 shows that approximately three-quarters of the elderly surveyed in Baltimore County are between the ages of 60 years and 74 years (the young-old), and one-quarter are age 75 years or older (the old-old). The old-old represent a group "at risk" of being higher users of health and social services because of needs resulting from advanced age. Over all, there is little difference in age distribution between the service areas. Slightly fewer persons over 75 years, however, were found in the Southeast (14.1%) and Northeast (18.9%) than the average for the coun-ty (22.1%).

As is true nationally, our sample was composed of almost twice as many females (63.2%) as males (36.8%). There appears to be a closer balance in the number of males and females in the Northwest area than in the other areas. This finding could be due to the smaller number (N=70) of persons sampled in this area.

Looking at the effect of increasing age on the distribution by sex, it is apparent that, generally, women survive in much larger numbers than do men. In the 75-and-over group, some service areas (Southwest, Nor-thwest, Southeast) have well over twice as many women as men. It is in-teresting, however, that our sample of the Northeast area has roughly the same proportion of men and women above 75 years of age.

MARITAL STATUS

Variation in marital status may also be an indication of variations in the support people require through formal services. Research has demonstrated that in addition to providing continuity with earlier life and economic sup-port, spouses can be an important source of help to each other in times of failing health by providing nursing care as well as psychological sup-port (Shanas, 1968; Stehouwer, 1965). As shown in Table 2.2, 53.8% of the respondents of our total sample were married, with more than 50% being married in each of the service areas. The Northwestern service area had the highest proportion of married elderly (65.7%), while the Northeast area had the lowest proportion (50.3%).

Clearly, while about half of the population studied do have spouses whose help they can draw upon in times of need, the other half do not have this source of support in their later years. Over a third (37.1%) of our respondents were widowed. The widowed with an average age of 72 years tended to be somewhat older than respondents who were married or separated or divorced (average age = 67 years) or those who were single (average age = 70 years). Based on our data on sex distribution, we found that the majority (84%) of the widowed respondents were females. A small proportion of respondents in each service area either had never married or were separated/divorced. The proportion of those never married was lowest in the Northwest area (1.5%) and highest in the North (6.7%) area. Also, the proportion of separated and divorced persons is somewhat lower in the Northwest area and in the Northeast. It may be that the more even balance between men and women sampled in the Northwest area accounts for some of the differences noted, since in this age group most men are married and most women are not.

SOCIOECONOMIC STATUS

Information on socioeconomic status is widely used to indicate a standard of living. Socioeconomic status is generaly considered to have three components: education, occupation, and income.

Educational level has been previously related to needs for service. Those with less education have less knowledge of available resources and, consequently, have more unmet needs.

Respondents of the Southeast service area display notably lower educational levels than those in other service areas (see Table 2.3). About half of this population (50.2%) have only nine years of schooling or less as compared with only 13.5% in the North area. In the remaining four service areas (excluding the Southeast area), less than one-third of the respondents fell into this category (less than nine years of education). Also, when comparing number of high school graduates by service area, the Southeast had fewer graduates than the other service areas, 15.8% compared with at least 25% in the other areas. While the Northeast area appeared to have the least educated population, the North area respondents appeared to have the most education. When we compare the percentages of those with college education, we find that the North area had the highest proportion of college-educated persons (28.8%), while the Southeast had the lowest (2.7%).

Table 2.4 categorizes the longest occupation that the respondent has held. In studying the elderly, we can assume that the occupation held the longest is the one that strongly influences friendships, values, and orientation to work. Occupations reported were grouped into twelve categories similar to those employed by the U.S. Bureau of the Census. The table shows the largest single occupational group among our respondents was clerical workers (20.7%) followed by professionals (18.2%). This percentage no doubt reflects the higher proportions of females to males represented in our sample. The smallest groups were those employed in agricultural work (farmers, farm managers .7% and farm laborers .9%).

For the purposes of analysis, it is convenient to divide the designated twelve occupations into white-collar and blue-collar workers. White-collar workers include those in professional, managerial, sales, and clerical positions. Blue-collar workers include craftspersons, mechanics, transport equipment operators, laborers, service workers, and household workers. Agricultural workers (farmers and farm laborers) are considered separately. As a rule, white-collar workers are considered to have more prestige and to receive higher incomes than blue-collar workers. Their work is also less physically demanding (Mills, 1956). Looking at Table 2.4 in this way, it is apparent that the majority of respondents (60.9%) in the total sample are considered to be employed in white-collar occupations. Only slightly over a third (36.2%) are blue-collar workers, and about one percent (1.4%) are agricultural workers.

Examination of occupational distribution by service area reveals some differences in occupational experience. While approximately three-quarters of the respondents in the Northwest (74.3%) and North (77.2%) areas were employed in white-collar occupations, less than half of our respondents in the Southeast area (39.3%) were so employed. Moreover, blue-collar workers were one-quarter or less of those sampled in the North (19.6%) and Northwest (25.6%) areas, but they were more than half (54.3%) of those sampled in the Southeast area.

Further, although 20.4% of the sample in the Southeast area are classified as laborers, this is true for only 3.7% in the North and 7.1% in the Northwest area. Similarly, while professionals made up 33.1% and 25.7% of the occupations reported in the North and Northwest areas, respectively, less than 10% of the sample reported they were professionals in the Southeast area (9.5%).

Unfortunately, the amount of one's income is not asked in this survey. Source of income, however, is reported. Table 2.5 shows that 84% of the total sample do not derive their income from employment. Fully 78.6% received Social Security benefits and 42% received income from assets. A surprisingly small percentage of respondents receive Supplemental Security Income (SSI) (2.5%), unemployment compensation (1.6%), or contributions from relatives (4.3%).

There were few variations in source of income by service area. Considerably more respondents in the North area obtained income from savings (69.3%) and assets (57.7%) than in other areas. More persons also received contributions from relatives in the North area (6.1%) and in the Northwest (5.7%) than in the Southwest, Northeast, and Southeast. On the other hand, a greater proportion of respondents in the Southeast area received Supplemental Security Income (5.4%) and disability payments (12.7%) than the rest of the county.

From this information, a profile tends to emerge that describes greater economic insecurity in the North, where persons have more savings and assets, and less economic security in the Southeast, where more income is derived from formal income supplements (i.e., disability payments, SSI).

EMPLOYMENT STATUS

In recent years, much attention has been given to the problems of the retired elderly who must live on a fixed income while coping with the rising costs of such basic needs as food, housing, and medical care. Differences in work status may also reveal variation in the amount of available time to engage in recreational activities.

Approximately seven-tenths of our sample were retired, as shown in Table 2.6. Less than one-tenth did not report their work status. We suspect that some of the respondents may have been concealing a secondary source of income that may supplement, in some small way, retirement benefits. Only a small portion of the total sample were classified as unemployed (1.4%). Unemployed is defined as not working but actively seeking employment.

Looking at our sample by employment status, we find that 71.3% of the sample were retired. The respondents in the Southwest had the highest proportion of retired (78.1%), while fewer respondents were retired in the Southeast area (64.3%). Relatively more respondents were employed full time in the Southeast area (9.5%) and in the North area (9.2%). Given our information on occupational orientation and age, we may speculate on the reasons why some respondents have not retired. Respondents in the Southeast area may be continuing to work either because they are somewhat younger than the population sampled in other areas or because they are in predominantly blue-collar occupations and may not have sufficient resources to retire. Although the North area has a higher proportion of people aged 75 and over than three of the other areas studied (Northwest, Northeast, and Southeast), this area may have fewer retired people because more of its respondents are engaged in professional occupations, which are generally less physically demanding, thereby allowing them to continue to work. The relatively high percentage of "unknown", and the variation of this percent by area (14.3% to 23.1%), makes us less confident than we would like to be about the degree to which our percentages reflect the actual distribution among the employment status categories.

RESIDENCE

Adequate shelter constitutes a basic human need. Homeownership and length of tenure may both affect perception of the need for improvements in housing and the desire to move. Homeownership may further be an indirect indicator of financial well-being.

In our total sample, as shown in Table 2.7, almost 70% of the respondents were homeowners, with about 60% reporting their mortgages paid and only 7.7% still making payments on their homes. One-quarter of the respondents were paying their own rent, while another 5.6% had their rent provided from others. Those who had their "rent provided from others" could have been receiving supplements from such formal sources as the federal government or from such informal sources as family.

Homeownership and rental status do differ by service area. As observed, approximately 60% of the sample fully owned their homes and about 25% were renters. There are more homeowners with their mortgages paid in the Northeast (64.6%), Northwest (64.3%), and Southwest (61.8%). The area with the fewest homeowners with their mortgages paid is the North (46.6%). The North area and the Northwest both have more persons who report they are still making payments on their homes than other areas. The fact that the North service area has the highest percent of renters and respondents still making mortgage payments and the lowest percent with their houses paid for should not be seen as evidence of lower economic status than the other areas. The North has high levels of educational attainment and the highest proportion of professionals and managers, making it likely that the respondents from this area have expensive houses bought later in life and the ability to retire to the many apartment complexes found in the area. The Northwest area had substantially fewer renters than other areas.

It is interesting that the Northwest (8.6%) and North (9.2%) areas had more respondents who reported that their rent was provided by others than other areas. This may be due to the availability of senior citizen housing or to families who supplement rent in these areas.

Our findings that over half of all the respondents were homeowners whose mortgages were paid are supported by data on length of residence. These data support national findings that residential mobility among the elderly is low. As Table 2.8 shows, half of our total sample (50.4%) had lived in their present homes for twenty or more years. Less than five percent (4.7%) had moved within the past year, a figure somewhat lower than the national average of 10% (U.S. Department of Commerce, 1978).

There are, however, some variations in mobility by service area. The proportion of persons having moved within the past year was somewhat higher in the Southeast area (9.0%) as compared with other areas. We suspect many of the variations in the length of residence by service area may be due to variations in terms of peak suburban development between areas. For instance, more residents in the North and Northwest areas have been in their homes for ten to fifteen years as compared with the Southwest, Northeast, and Southeast. This period corresponds to the expansion of suburban developments in this area. The Southwest area, a more established residential and very slowly growing area, shows the highest percentage of residents of twenty or more years (61.1%).

SUMMARY

The five service areas reveal significant difference in their demographic profiles and socioeconomic status. If, as we believe, differences in these characteristics are related to different service needs, then the delivery of services to these areas must also be varied. For this reason, it is necessary to take into account these factors in our analysis of use of services.

As a whole, the population studied has characteristics indicative of a comfortable standard of living. At least 60% of the total population were homeowners with their mortgages paid and 70% were white-collar workers. Most of those studied had lived in their homes for many years, half having lived in their homes for twenty years or more.

Still, there is a segment of the study population for whom planning of comprehensive services needs to be targeted. Over one-third of the population studied were widowed. Most of these were female. One-quarter of those studied were age 75 or over. Almost one-third had completed only nine years of schooling or less. These groups—the widowed, the old-old, and those without much formal schooling—may have fewer resources, greater need for services, and less knowledge of and access to care than the rest of the sample.

An examination of specific areas shows that the service areas studied do differ in character. In particular, we noted a contrast between the Southeast and the more affluent North and Northeast service areas. Major area-specific variations are summarized as follows:

- Disproportionately large numbers of the older residents in the Southeast area had a lower educational level and were more likely to be blue-collar workers and recipients of formal assistance in the form of Supplemental Security Income than those in other areas.
- More older residents of the North and Northwest have achieved a higher educational level and were more likely to be professionals and managers than those in other areas. They were more likely to supplement their incomes with their own savings and assets.

- Fewer of the workers in the blue-collar Southeast area are retired than in other areas.

In the next chapter, we assess the social well-being of the elderly in Baltimore County through a consideration of their economic and environmental well-being and the social supports available to them.

REFERENCES

Mills, C.W. 1956. *White Collar*. New York: Oxford University Press.

Shanas, E. et al. 1968. *Old People in Three Industrial Societies*. New York: Atherton.

Stehouwer, J. 1965. "Relations between Generations and the Three Generation Household in Denmark." in *Social Structure and the Family: Generational Relations*, edited by Ethel Shanas and Gordon Streib. Englewood Cliffs, N.J.: Prentice-Hall.

U.S. Department of Commerce, Bureau of the Census. 1978. "Geographic Mobility: March 1975–March 1977." *Current Population Reports*. Washington, D.C.: Government Printing Office.

3

The Social Well-being of the Elderly

Included under the rubric of social well-being are the social support networks, self-assessed economic well-being, and environmental well-being. We analyzed the daily lives of our respondents by finding out who they talk to, who talks to them and who listens to them, how they cope economically in times of inflation, and what fears they have. Furthermore, we examined the extent to which the elderly perceive the availability of social supports in crisis situations. In short, we wanted to know how secure the older adults feel about themselves and their communities. This provides pertinent information for the planning of social service programs aimed toward achieving the optional level of well-being of the elderly.

SOCIAL SUPPORTS AND NETWORKS

In recent years, research on social support has demonstrated that the presence of strong social support contributes to positive adjustment in later life (Wan & Weissert, 1981); Lin et al., 1979). Support has been defined as "enduring personal ties to a group of people who can be relied upon to provide emotional sustenance, assistance and resources in times of need" (Caplan, 1974). It has been speculated that personal ties provide feedback reinforcing values and feelings of self-worth as well as providing material aid when such stressful life changes as widowhood, unemployment, retirement, and failing health occur.

There is also evidence that the presence of such supportive persons as kin or friends reduces the effects of stressful events on physical and mental health (Nuckolls, Cassel, and Kaplan, 1972; Caplan, 1974; Gore, 1978; Myers, Lindenthal & Pepper, 1975). More relevant to the experience of

21

the elderly have been findings that social support mitigates the negative effects of involuntary job loss (Gore, 1978), widowhood (Parker in Cobb, 1976; Burch in Cobb, 1976; Lowenthal & Haven, 1968), and retirement (Lowenthal & Haven, 1968; Palmore et al., 1979). In fact, Lowenthal and Haven (1968) state that such role losses are ameliorated by the presence of a confidant. Besides, social support has been related to the use of health services. It has been observed that such support plays an important role in preventive health, behavior (Langlie, 1977), compliance with treatment regimens (de Araujo et al., 1973), and rehabilitation (Smith, 1979). Experiencing a high degree of companionship in marriage (Pratt, 1972), living in extended-family settings (Murdock & Swartz, 1978), and having friends (Langlie, 1977) have been associated with greater knowledge of and use of health services.

There are many ways of measuring the presence or absence of social support. Several variables have been considered in previous studies as measures of social support, including the availability of kin (Finlayson, 1976; Horwitz, 1978; Palmore et al., 1979), frequency of interaction with kin and non-kin (Langlie, 1977; Lin et al., 1979), living arrangements (Brody et al., 1978; Eaton, 1978; Murdock & Swartz, 1978), and presence of marital bonds (Pratt, 1972; Eaton, 1978). In our study of Baltimore County, three indicators of social support were used: living arrangement, social networks, and perception of human resources.

Living Arrangement

Living arrangement indicates whether or not there are other persons within the household who might be able to give support. The percentage of elderly living alone in Baltimore County (26.6%) is far lower than what the data from the U.S. Bureau of the Census (1979) indicates. As shown in Table 3.1*, about one-quarter (26.6%) of our sample lived alone; three-quarters did not. There appears to be considerable variation in living arrangement between service areas and by sex, age, and marital status. Retirement status was not related to living arrangement.

To be more specific, between 25% and 30% of respondents lived alone in the Southeast, Northeast, North, and Southwest areas while only 11% lived alone in the Northwest. As could be expected, most of those living alone were females who were 75 or over. Younger males (60–74 years) were least likely to be living alone. Also, those who were widowed, separated/divorced, or never married were more apt to live alone. It should be noted, however, that such single marital status does not presume a solitary living arrangement. While approximately half of those who were unmarried lived alone, half did not.

---

*Tables appear in Appendix D.

Social Network

Children are often an important component of the social network for the aged. Next to spouse, respondents list their children as people they expected to provide them with help during a health crisis (Riley & Foner, 1968). Old people living alone are particularly likely to call on children for aid during illnesses. The absence of children may indicate the need for social support services.

Turning to Baltimore County, eighty percent of our sample (80.4%) had children (see Table 3.2). Fewer respondents reported having children in the North service area (73%) than in the Southeast (79.2%), Southwest (80%), Northwest (82.9%), and Northwest (84.8%). It may be that the higher socioeconomic status of the North area to some degree explains this variation, since higher status has been related to lower fertility. Males, nonretired persons, and persons who did not live alone were more likely to say they had children.

While the existence of children may be a source of support and comfort, the proximity of children affects the actual amount of physical aid that can be given. Children who live near their parents are more likely to be available to give help when needed. According to our data, in Table 3.3, 83% of those sampled had at least one child within one hour's driving distance, a finding similar to findings of other studies. Shanas (1962) found 84% of her sample of 1,700 noninstitutionalized elderly had at least one child living nearby. In our sample, older males were somewhat less likely to have children living nearby than the other three age and sex categories.

Looking at friendships, which is one aspect of the social network, our sample seemed to be socially well-connected. Fifty-five percent knew six or more persons well enough to visit them in their homes (Table 3.4). This finding qualifies the prevailing notions about social isolation among the elderly. Careful inspection of the data, however, shows that older females knew fewer persons whom they might visit (39.7%) than younger males (63.7%), younger females (54.6%), and older males (53.4%). People without spouses (widowed, never married, separated/divorced) also knew fewer persons.

Social Supports

The term social support implies any person (spouse, kin, or friends) who provides support in times of crisis by offering such aid as nursing, meals, or positive feedback that reinforces a positive identity. The existence of such resources was sought by the questions:

- Do you have someone you can trust and confide in?

- Is there someone who would give you any help at all if you were sick or disabled?
- Is there someone who would take care of you as long as you needed help?

Almost all of our respondents (95.9%) had someone they could trust or confide in (Table 3.5). As might be expected, married persons (97.3%) were more likely to have someone to trust and confide in than widowed (94.5%), separated/divorced (95.7%), and never married (91.8%) persons.

The majority of the respondents (92%) reported that they would have someone to take care of them if they were sick or disabled. Those who were least likely to be helped were older, female, widowed, not retired, and living alone.

It is interesting that the never married, who were less likely to report having a confidant, were more likely to say they had someone who would help in times of sickness than other marital status groups (Table 3.6). Such differences in responses imply that older persons' definitions of persons they can confide in and persons who can be relied on for help are not synonymous.

While it seems that people in our sample have persons to confide in and persons who would give them help, the picture of availability of aid changes somewhat when the time period over which help would be offered is considered. Only 70% of the total sample have someone who would give them help indefinitely (Table 3.7). Residents of the North area were the most likely to feel they have someone who would give them help indefinitely, while those in the Southwest area (66.7%) were least likely. Males, particularly younger males (60-74 years), and persons married, retired, or not living alone more often said that they had a source of help for an indefinite period.

In short, the elderly population of Baltimore County appears to be well endowed with informal sources of social support. The majority do not live alone, have children, and believe that they have informal resources to call upon in crisis. We should caution, however, that these findings do not minimize the critical needs of those without such supports. Our data indicate that being female, 75 and over, and widowed places an individual in multiple jeopardy of being without available social supports. This group clearly requires formal supportive services.

ECONOMIC WELL-BEING

In recent years, the economic well-being of the elderly has been one of our society's major social concerns. The economic consequences for society of a growing elderly population, early retirement, inflation, rising health care costs, pension equity, and public assistance costs have been publicly debated (Schultz, 1976).

By and large, most observers conclude that the economic well-being of the older population is gradually improving. Whether this trend will continue is still unclear. In 1978, the median income of family heads was $9,156 for males and $8,777 for females. The median income for nonfamily heads was $4,123 for males and $3,762 for females (U.S. Bureau of the Census, 1979). Males clearly have greater incomes than females in comparable situations. In addition to these apparent sex differences and perhaps compounding them considerably, the economic status of older persons varies with sociodemographic indicators as well.

Schultz notes, "Lumping all the aged population together seriously distorts the reality of the situation, in this case the economic reality" (1976, p. 11). He suggest that the following distinctions must be considered in examining economic status: (1) retirement status, (2) race, (3) marital status, (4) age, (5) living arrangement, and (6) taxation laws in effect in an area (i.e., property tax relief, etc.). These attributes contribute to diversity in sources and amount of income, for instance, whether income is primarily derived from salary, pension, assets, or other sources.

Current national statistics tend to underline these distinctions. Looking at age, those under 65 are more likely to derive their income from employment than Social Security. Married persons also have more sources of income and higher income than nonmarrieds. Census data from 1976 show that while 39% of married persons 65 years and older received more than one pension, this was true of only 20% of nonmarrieds. Further, fully 44% of persons who are not married received all their income from Social Security or public assistance as compared with only 21% of married persons (Grad & Foster, 1976).

Although income is clearly an important indicator of economic well-being, evidence suggests that individuals' assessment of their financial situation is not dependent upon income alone (Hansen et al., 1976; Peterson, 1973; Youmans, 1976). Variations in income do not clearly reveal differences in wealth. Low income is not always indicative of low satisfaction with economic situations. Thompson and Streib (1958) report one-half of the older persons they studied who had annual incomes below $1,800 had no sense of economic deprivation. Satisfaction with income may be influenced by age and social status. In one study, younger men (60-74 years) with higher incomes experienced greater subjective economic deprivation than older men (75 years) whose incomes were lower (Youmans, 1976). This seeming inconsistency may be due in some degree to differences in tastes and expectations based upon life experience. Feelings of relative financial deprivation in comparison with previous life style and in comparison with peers may influence how people assess the adequacy of their incomes (Liang & Fairchild, 1979; Peterson, 1973). Peterson (1973) has observed that retirees tend to assess their previous economic situation as more favorable than their present situation and anticipate less financial adequacy in the future than at present.

It is noteworthy that subjective assessments of economic well-being do not always conform to standard economic indicators, such as the Retired Couples Budget prepared by the Department of Labor Statistics or the Poverty Index developed by the Social Security Administration (Peterson, 1973). Such discrepancies lead us to conclude that official measures of economic well-being do not always reflect actual perception of needs. Nonetheless, personal perceptions of financial adequacy may affect the purchase of food, clothing, and health services and influence decisions regarding participation in recreational activities. Therefore, in addition to objective measures of financial resources, it is important to understand how older persons view their economic well-being.

The Baltimore County Needs Assessment survey looked at several dimensions of self-assessed economic well-being. Questions were asked concerning the adequacy of resources to meet emergencies, the need for financial assistance, the ability to purchase "extras," and the respondents' feelings about economic security in the future.

Table 3.8 summarizes responses along the above dimensions. An examination of the total sample shows that only about one-quarter (23.6%) report they *do not* have financial problems, and half think they have enough money for future needs. Almost one-quarter admit they do have difficulty buying little "extras" and smaller proportions of our senior citizens said they faced critical financial difficulties. Almost one-fifth (18.4%) say they need financial assistance, 15% have insufficient funds to meet emergencies, and 7% cannot take care of their own needs. Considering these responses, it is indeed surprising that only 4.8% of our sample feel they are worse off financially than others their age. It appears that public attention given to the economic plight of the elderly has convinced many that they are no worse off than others their age.

The variations observed among service areas are fairly consistent. Substantially more respondents in the Southeast area reported financial difficulties in almost all the economic categories than those in the other areas. One-quarter of these residents reported they had insufficient financial resources for emergencies and that they needed financial assistance. Conversely, respondents in the North area seem to be comparatively better off. For example, only 8.6% of respondents in the North area said they did not have funds for "luxuries" as compared with 34.8% in the Southeast. Moreover, 2.5% of those in the North area said they could not take care of their own needs as compared with 13.1% in the Southeast area. Clearly, the Southeast should be a target area for increasing the residents' awareness of the availability of financial supplements. It is interesting that while the North area seems better off in terms of present status, fewer respondents in this area thought they had enough money for future needs. It may be that the reason for this seeming inconsistency lies in subjective definition of "enough." Residents of the North area may support a life style more demanding of financial resources and also may be more aware of the possible financial difficulties in the future than older persons in other service areas.

Tables 3.9 through 3.15 focus upon variations in self-assessed economic well-being according to several sociodemographic characteristics. On the whole, these tables indicate that those who feel less secure about their financial well-being are more likely to be female, the young-old (60–74 years) (Table 3.9, 3.13, 3.14), divorced (Tables 3.9–3.14), widowed (Tables 3.9, 3.10, 3.11, 3.13), and, to a lesser extent, those living alone (Tables 3.9, 3.10, 3.13, 3.14). Table 3.10 describes differences in the need for financial assistance among marital status categories. It appears that while 38% of divorced/separated persons and 20% of the widowed need financial assistance, this is true for only 11.5% of people never married and 16.2% of married persons. It should also be noted that in response to this question the young-old (60–74 years) appeared to feel they needed financial assistance more than those over seventy-five.

Inflation was said to be the biggest financial problem (Table 3.15) for 19.4% of the population. The other problems reported were buying food (9.4%) and paying for housing (7.7%). The areas of least financial difficulty were buying clothing (0.5%) and paying for entertainment (0.6%). Obviously, these were areas where the elderly felt they could most easily economize, while food and housing are essentials that cannot be done without.

Turning to the respondents' assessment of their future economic status (Table 3.14), it can be seen that 13.6% of the sample said they did not have enough money for future needs. The high percentage of persons not responding to this question (30.9%) raises serious questions about what conclusion may be drawn from this table. A high level of nonresponse may indicate that in these uncertain times of high inflation, many persons hesitate to make judgements concerning their financial status in the future. Nonetheless, one may note that the young-old (60–74 years) and nonretired persons seem to feel less secure about having money to meet future needs.

Feelings About Retirement

Blau (1961) has observed that in our achievement-oriented society "retirement deprives the older individual of the run of common experience that is shared by people who work" (p. 437). Loss of the work role may entail the loss of a satisfying identity, a reorganization of existing roles as spouse, friend, etc., as well as a change in other social relations (Cavan, 1962). Considering the magnitude of life change involved, it is surprising that our evidence (Table 3.16) tends to show that the disruptive effects of retirement are less than what might be expected. Streib and Schneider (1971) also noted no indications of increased feelings of uselessness or increased awareness of aging among the retired elderly men they studied. Nonetheless, there is some evidence that suggests women may have more difficulty getting used to retirement than men (Atchley, 1975; Fox, 1977). Occupational and work history variations between men and women, as well as differences in retirement benefits, may account for some of these differences.

Individuals' feelings about retirement in general are no doubt influenced by their personal adjustment to the fact of being retired or anticipated adjustment to it. Research has demonstrated that the circumstances under which retirement occurs may be a key factor in such adjustment. Several factors have been cited as influencing adjustment to retirement including health status (Kinnel, Price & Walker, 1978; Barfield & Morgan, 1978), preretirement feelings toward the event (Glasmer, 1976), and type of retirement—voluntary, or involuntary (for example, due to mandatory laws, poor health). Persons whose health is good, who have a positive preretirement attitude, or who retired voluntarily are more satisfied with their retirement than persons who have poor health, have negative feelings about retiring, or were involuntarily retired.

Several sociodemographic characteristics (sex, marital status, income and education) also have been associated with attitudes toward retirement. Married people and those who have higher income or educational levels have been shown to be more positive in their evaluation of retirement (Barfield & Morgan, 1978; Kimmel, Price & Walker, 1978).

The SNAP survey assessed attitudes toward retirement among the total sample. Persons who were working, retired, and who had never worked were included. While for some respondents, actual experience may have affected their feelings toward retirement, for others, vicarious experience (spouse's retirement) or anticipatory socialization may have colored their views. Data in Table 3.16 show that about half of our sample expressed positive feelings toward retirement (52%), about 22% had negative attitudes. Those who were already retired were more positive in their assessment of retirement (60.4%) than the nonretired (32.4%). It is interesting to note that nearly one-third of the nonretired refused to respond to this question. This may be an indication of their anxiety about retiring.

Males and females differed in their feelings about retirement. Irrespective of work status, males were more positive in their feelings about retirement than females, a finding supported by previous research (Fox, 1977; Atchley, 1975). Females, regardless of age, displayed more ambivalence toward retirement than males. It should be noted that a much larger percentage of females than males did not respond to this question, perhaps indicating females' lack of direct experience with this event.

According to Table 3.16, age made little difference in feelings about retirement. Younger men (30%) were somewhat more negative in their feelings about retirement than older men (20%), but more older men (9.17%) than younger men (4.6%) did not answer. This may have been because younger men are anticipating the occurrence of this event while older men have already experienced retirement and adjusted to it. Older women were far more ambivalent about retirement (20%) than younger women (11.3%). Older women, however, may have had less direct experience with retirement than succeeding cohorts of younger women. For these women, time has also served to decrease any strong feelings held at the time of their spouse's retirement.

SENSE OF ENVIRONMENTAL WELL-BEING

The concept environmental well-being encompasses attitudes about crime, personal safety, and membership in the community. Any discussion of the effects of crime on the elderly must address two issues: (1) victimization and (2) fear of crime. Conklin (1976) employed the terms direct and indirect victimization to distinguish between actual victims of crime (direct victims, i.e., those who were attacked, robbed) and those whose behavior and attitudes were influenced by the occurrence of crimes in their community (indirect victims).

A paradoxical relationship exists between victimization and fear among older adults. While the elderly are less often the victims of crime, particularly violent crimes (Cook and Cook, 1976; Hindelang, 1976; Antunes et al., 1977), fear of crime is more prevalent in this age group than in others (Harris, reported in National Council on the Aging Report, 1975; Adams & Smith, 1976). In fact, the U.S. Select Committee on Aging noted "fear of crime is a pervasive and serious problem for older Americans; the quality of life for senior citizens is diminished by fear." (1977).

Clearly, the consequences of crime for this age group are serious. Victimization and fear may increase isolation by reducing social activity (Sundeen & Mathieu, 1976) or encouraging persons to move from a lifelong home to another location (Beaver, 1979). One study found that 62% of the people interviewed stated they would not walk outside because of fear,

25% avoided certain areas in their neighborhods, and 54% avoided certain areas of the city because they felt unsafe (Rifai, 1977).

Looking at direct victimization, the elderly are more likely to experience such predatory crimes as robbery or larceny than such violent crimes as assault or rape (Antunes et al., 1977). Older persons who are in relatively better health and of higher socioeconomic status are less often the victims of crime (Kahana et al., 1977).

While the prevalence of crime would not appear to justify the fear reported, it has been suggested that the location of crimes (Antunes et al., 1977), their nature (Antunes et al., 1977), and the deprivations experienced in health and economic losses relative to other age groups (Cook et al., 1978) may explain this attitude. For example, older persons who are the victims of violent crime are more likely to be attacked in or near their homes than other age groups. This violation of personal space may contribute to fear. Further, elderly are more likely to be victimized by stangers and youth, a victimization pattern that might escalate fears (Antunes et al., 1977). Finally, Cook et al. (1978) have noted that medical bills incurred by the elderly as results of attack represent a substantial part of their monthly income. Besides, their losses as a group are higher than other groups over age thirty-two. Thus, in comparison with middle-aged persons, the deprivation elderly experience is substantially greater.

Previous studies have noted that fear of crime is higher among women, blacks, and urban residents (Brown, 1975; Clemente & Kleiman, 1976). Fear is also higher among persons in age-heterogeneous neighborhoods (Gubrium, 1974), and in areas where ties to the community are lower (Sundeen and Mathieu, 1976). It appears that living in an age-homogeneous area or having social supports available (neighbors who can be called upon for help) may reduce fear.

Table 3.17 summarizes Baltimore County older residents' perception of their environmental well-being. Table 3.17 shows residents' attitudes toward their community, their perceptions of its safety, and their actual experience as victims of crime or harassment. Attitudes toward one's community are indicative, albeit indirectly, of fears experienced and how these fears affect behavior. Three-quarters of those sampled feel a part of their neighborhood and 93% like living in their neighborhood. Residents of the Northwest (60%) are somewhat less likely to report that they feel a part of their neighborhood than those of other areas, particularly the North (79.8%) and Northeast (80.1%). Furthermore, more residents of the North (95.7%) and Northeast (96.6%) state that they like living in their neighborhoods than residents in other areas. Looking at attitudes toward neighborhood by selected demographic characteristics (Tables 3.18 and 3.19), it is apparent that males, particularly males between 60 and 74 years, felt themselves to be a part of their neighborhood more than older males or females. Also, those who, we presume, had more extensive social ties (the married, not retired, and those not living alone) were more likely to feel a part of their neighborhood.

There were few differences on the basis of the above characteristics in reports of liking one's neighborhood, although older males and females (≥ 75 years) did tend to like their neighborhood slightly more than younger respondents (Table 3.19).

We might suspect that persons who felt a part of, and liked their community, perceived that social supports were available in their neighborhood that might tend to reduce fears. Overall, a very high percentage (96.3%) of the residents reported that they felt their neighborhood was a safe place to live (Table 3.17). There was little variation in this attitude between service areas. A further analysis of this question indicated that responses did not vary substantially by age, sex, marital status, retirement status, or living arrangement (Table 3.20). Interestingly, all persons who had never married felt their neighborhood was safe. This is one of many examples of the strength of never-married persons in coping with their environmental and personal circumstances that we found in our data. It will be remembered that the never-married also were least likely to report the need for financial assistance.

Responses in Table 3.17 suggest that older residents feel less safe waiting for a bus or walking alone at night than in the day. While almost 90% (88.3%) felt safe waiting alone for a bus during the day, only half as many (43.5%) felt the same about this activity at night. Residents of the Northeast and Southeast areas felt safer about nighttime activities than residents of other service areas. On the other hand, residents of the Southwest and Northwest tended to feel less safe about nighttime activity. There was little variation among areas concerning the safety of daytime activity.

In order to see whether fears were cumulative, we constructed an index of fear by summing (1) fear of walking outside during the day, (2) fear of walking outside at night, (3) fear of waiting for a bus during the day, and (4) fear of waiting for a bus at night. Scores ranged from zero (lowest) to four (highest). We might assume that fear would more directly affect the behavior of those with high fear than those with low fear; that is, persons with high fear would take more precautions against crime. According to our findings, age, sex and area of residence explain some of the variations (12%) in fear among the elderly in Baltimore County. Marital status, retirement status, and living arrangement (whether the respondent lived alone) did not contribute to differences in fear response.

Surprisingly, younger males (60-74 years) experienced the greatest level of fear of crime, while older females (≥ 75 years) had the least. This may be because younger males are more often in situations where crimes are more apt to occur. They are more likely to leave their homes for work or to go out socially and to be more aware of news media items that could heighten fears. Older females, on the other hand, may choose to stay home more often and may be more isolated from fearful situations. Our results tend to pose a contradictory relationship between attitude toward neighborhood and fear. Although younger males were more likely to report that they felt part of their community, they were also likely to report high levels of fear. Apparently, associations within the community serve to increase awareness of potential victimization rather than decrease it.

Turning to direct victimization, almost twenty percent (19.5%) of those sampled had been victims of crime at some time in their lives (Table 3.17). Fewer residents of the Southeast area (12.7%) said they had been victims of a crime than residents of other areas. A higher percentage of victimization was reported in the Southwest (24.4%) and Northeast (20.8%). Table 3.21 shows the distribution of crime victims by demographic characteristics. Victims tended more often to be males between 60 and 74 years of age and persons who were never married. Separated/divorced persons were least often victims. There were no differences in victimization on the basis of retirement status or living arrangement.

Harassment, while not a crime, is also a problem faced by the elderly. Harassment may include being teased, disturbed by noise, or subjected to other forms of bothersome behavior. Seventeen percent of our sample reported they had been bothered by children or teenagers (Table 3.17). Southeastern residents (25.8%) reported they had been bothered by children or teenagers more than residents of the Northwest (18.6%), Southwest (15.5%), Northeast (15.2%), and North (13.5%).

Environmental well-being also encompasses feelings of membership in the community. Ageism is a term coined by gerontologists to refer to discrimination against individuals simply on the basis of their age (Crandall, 1980, p. 8). Very few of the SNAP population felt they were treated unfairly because of their age (6.2%) (Table 3.22). Persons who were separated/divorced clearly felt more discrimination than other marital groups. Older females (≥ 75 years) reported feeling the least age discrimination.

In conclusion, although we might assume that victimization, feelings of safety, and feelings about one's neighborhood are interrelated, it appears they are not closely related in this sample. While almost one-fifth of our sample had been victims of crime, residents generally liked and felt safe in their neighborhoods, and few felt treated unfairly because of their age (see Table 3.22). Looking for policy implications, we can surmise that fear of crime on the streets at night is most likely to limit activity of the elderly. Such programs as escort services or group transportation to sponsored nighttime activities should be considered.

HOUSING

Evaluation of housing is related to the residents' perception of amenities offered within their community (Carp, 1966, 1975; Hamovitch & Peterson, 1969; Clemente & Kleiman, 1976). It has been postulated that the importance of community environment, and we may include housing here, increases as physical mobility declines. As a person ages, therefore, there is an increasing dependence on the community (and therefore housing) for the fulfillment of physical, psychosocial, and health needs (Carp, 1972).

Several factors that reflect the quality of neighborhood environment have been associated with the satisfaction with housing. Among these are perceived safety and security (Carp, 1966, 1975; Clemente & Kleiman, 1976; Toseland & Rasch, 1978), nearness of shopping and laundry facilities (Hamovitch & Peterson, 1969), and access to medical personnel (Hamovitch & Peterson, 1969). The importance of the presence of friends in the area and perceived similarity to neighbors for residential satisfaction has been debated (Lawton et al., 1978; Rosow, 1967). In the preceding section of this chapter, we attempted to tap some of the foregoing aspects through our description of attitudes about the community.

Such characteristics of housing as its size relative to needs and its general pleasantness have been shown to be more relevant to the older peoples' perception of the adequacy of their housing than such items as number of steps or type of dwelling unit (single family home, apartment, etc.) (Lawton et al., 1978).

Considering the relevance of housing environment to the health and well-being of older persons, it is understandable that both government and private industry have attempted to provide a variety of alternative housing arrangements. While most elderly (households headed by a person age 65 or over) own their own homes (U.S. Department of Housing and Urban Development, 1977), other options available include a growing number of age-segregated housing units, so-called congregate housing, and retirement communities. These housing communities vary widely in the spectrum of services they offer, ranging from reduced rents to such broad-based supportive services as meals, laundry, and housekeeping services. While Lawton (1978) has observed that tenants in such congregate housing display less physical competance, this is likely due to selective factors of admission to such rental units rather than the nature of the units themselves.

At the time of the SNAP survey, there was only one federally supported congregate housing unit for the elderly operating in Baltimore
County, so the present analysis will not focus upon residents of such housing arrangements. For the most part, our respondents were residents either
of privately owned dwellings or apartments.

In its Annual Housing Survey of adequacy of housing, the U.S.
Bureau of the Census uses two criteria: (1) *physical adequacy*, that is, the
availability of heating, plumbing, bathroom and kitchen facilities, structural soundness, design of the unit, and its maintenance and (2) *affordability*, the relationship of housing costs to personal income. The Census
Bureau approximates that housing costs should consume approximately
one-quarter of the monthly budget. To these criteria may be added a third
suggested by Heumann (1978): How well does housing meet the functional
abilities of the individual? For instance, How well does a two-story house
meet the needs of an elderly person who has difficulty climbing stairs?

Analysis of data from both the 1973 and 1976 national housing
surveys (Struyk, 1977; U.S. Department of Housing and Urban Development, 1979), shows that the elderly (household head   65 years) are only modestly less well housed than the population as a whole. Approximately 90% of housing units for the elderly, as for the nation as a whole, were
without flaws. Older persons were more likely to own their own housing
(83%) and to live in older housing than the younger population (U.S.
Department of Housing and Urban Development, 1979).

According to the U.S. Bureau of the Census, of the 14.8 million elderly
households in 1976, 45% consisted of two people, 33% of women alone,
10% of men alone, and 12% in which either a husband or a wife was absent. Elderly couples tended to have better housing than elderly living alone
or living in family situations with a spouse absent.

Looking at affordability, older persons had to spend a greater proportion of their cash income to obtain unflawed housing than the general
population. In 1976, 42% of elderly households had to spend over one-
fourth of their incomes to obtain unflawed housing as compared with 20%
of the general population. Caution is necessary, however, when drawing
implications from these figures. Elderly may have savings or assets, which
were not included in the survey, which may compensate, to some extent,
for the proportion of income expended.

Our data on the physical adequacy of housing in Baltimore County
compare favorably with national standards. It should be noted, however,
that our data were not directly comparable to that of the U.S. Bureau of
the Census. While census data report only those households headed by a
person 65 years or over, our data include older persons living in their own
or other households where the household head may be over 60 but under
65 years of age. As described earlier, the majority of residents (60%) are

homeowners with their mortgages paid. As shown in Table 3.23, the majority (66%) lived in single-family detached homes. An additional 11% lived in single family townhouses and about 15% lived in commercial apartments. Less than 2% of the sample lived in trailers.

Fully 90% of respondents in the Northwest area lived in single-family detached homes. A higher percentage of residents in the Southwest and Southeast areas lived in single-family townhouses. Moreover, a greater number of respondents in the Southwest, North, and Northeast lived in commercial apartment complexes than in the Northwest and Southeast. These differences may be indicative of variations in the available housing in these areas. One difference between the areas that should be underlined is that while almost 10% of older respondents in the Southeast lived in trailers, almost no respondents in the other service areas lived in this type of structure. This probably reflects differences in local housing and building codes.

Data from the U.S. Bureau of the Census indicate that the elderly's housing was only slightly more flawed than that of the general population. Older persons had a higher proportion of plumbing (2.6%), kitchen (2.9%), and sewage (2.4%) flaws than the rest of the population (general population: plumbing 2.6%; kitchen 1.8%; sewage 1.3%). Older men who live alone had a higher proportion of kitchen and plumbing flaws than other elderly. It is possible that this finding may reflect a greater tolerance for kitchen deficiencies among older single men due to lack of use. Although rural elderly represent a very small proportion of the older population in our study, they tended to have more structural flaws in their housing than urban households.

Tables 3.24 and 3.25 describe, to some extent, the physical adequacy of existing housing. Table 3.24 shows that 97% of SNAP respondents had private kitchen facilities. Only 1.4% reported sharing a kitchen with other households, and a negligible 0.1% reported having no kitchen at all. It is noteworthy that a somewhat higher percentage of residents of the Northwest (4.3%) and Southeast (3.6%) said they shared a kitchen. There were no substantial differences in the likelihood of having a private kitchen associated with sex, marital status, retirement status, or living arrangement.

Table 3.25 shows a similar pattern of findings with respect to private or shared bathroom facilities. Almost all of our sample (97.9%) reported having a private bathroom. As we observed with kitchen facilities, residents in the Northwest and Southeast were somewhat more likely to share bathroom facilities with another household than were residents in other service areas. Overall, however, we can conclude that almost all of the county residents interviewed had private bathrooms and kitchen facilities. Although our data are not directly comparable, we feel it is safe to assume that the Baltimore County elderly population is at least as well off, if not better off, than the elderly population in the country as a whole with respect to these facilities.

Nonetheless, merely having kitchen and bathroom facilities does not mean that these facilities are entirely adequate. Rather than assess specific facilities, we attempted to assess general adequacy through questions and interviewer observations of the need for repairs in the respondent's building. Table 3.26 reveals respondents' assessments of whether their buildings were in need of repairs, either inside or outside. As shown, twenty-eight percent of respondents said their building needed repairs. More persons in the Southwest (31.8%), Northwest (30.0%), Northeast (26.7%), and Southeast (30.8%) indicated needing repairs than in the North (16%). Fewer separated and divorced persons said they needed repairs than the married, never married, or widowed. Differences in other categories were not substantial.

To give another perspective on housing, we also considered interviewers' observations of housing condition (Table 3.27). The interviewers were generally more positive about housing condition than the respondents. Still, it should be emphasized that interviewers' observations of housing were limited to what they could see. Interviewers reported that 12.5% of housing needed some work, while 1% needed extensive repairs. Interviewers observed that housing in the Southwest, Southeast, and North areas was in greater need of some or extensive repairs than housing in the other two areas. They reported that dwellings of older males, never-married persons, retirees, and persons living alone were in greater need of extensive work.

These data generally support national census data, particularly with respect to older males. The fact that older males did not report needing repairs more than other groups, while our interviewers reported they needed such repairs, tends to confirm our earlier suspicions that older males might not perceive, and therefore underreport, needed repairs. It may be that older males are less fussy about their housing. Likewise, it is interesting that separated and divorced persons reported needing less repairs (Table 3.26) than our interviewers' observations indicate.

Other than physical adequacy, such considerations as the kind of housing and number of rooms may contribute to satisfaction with housing. The majority of those sampled (83.3%) said they were very satisfied and another 12% were somewhat satisfied with their present housing (Table 3.28). Only about 3% were either somewhat dissatisfied or very dissatisfied. Dissatisfaction with housing was highest in the Southwest (3.8%) and Southeast (5.4%) areas. Separated or divorced persons were significantly more dissatisfied than other marital status groups, even though they reported less need for repairs. Our data suggest that divorc-ed/separated persons are dissatisfied with the kind of housing they lived in rather than its physical adequacy.

Table 3.29 examines the satisfaction of the respondents with respect to whether the size of housing meets their present needs. About 17% of the sample said their houses were either too small or too large for their needs. A larger percentage of respondents in the Northwest area (20%) tended to feel their houses were too large than those of the respondents in other areas. Comparatively more residents in the Southwest and Southeast felt their houses were too small; however, differences in this category were not great. Persons who were married, widowed, or never married said their houses were too large, while divorced persons tended to feel their housing was too small. These differences may suggest some desire to bring housing into line with present life style for older married couples, widowed, and never-married persons. Divorced persons, on the other hand, may still yearn for the housing of their former married years. Elderly living alone thought their housing was too large. This finding may be the result of living in housing that was appropriate in previous "family years."

Our data tend to suggest that the housing picture for the elderly in Baltimore County is brighter than in some other parts of the country. Many residents are homeowners, most have private kitchen and bathroom facilities, and most are relatively satisfied with their housing. The fact that 27.9% (Table 3.26) report need for some repairs in their housing indicates that home maintenance services are needed.

SUMMARY

The social world of the elderly has many dimensions. In this chapter, we explored housing, environmental quality, economic situation, and availability of social supports in order to assess the level of social well-being of the elderly. We suspect that persons who "feel good" about the degree of support they receive are undoubtedly better prepared to deal with environmental contingencies such as neighborhood problems and hous-ing deterioration. Persons who feel comfortable about their economic well-being are more likely to make repairs and improvements in their housing, which may enhance their satisfaction with their homes. Clearly, feeling that one has economic and social resources enables one to cope with his or her environment. Our data from the Baltimore County survey suggest that our elderly are at least as "well off" as national samples. Still, analysis of social well-being by specific demographic characteristics (age, sex, marital status, retirement status, and living arrangement) pinpoints some specific groups who are in need of formal as well as informal social supports. Our major findings are briefly summarized as follows:

Social Support

- Most (three-quarters) lived with someone (spouse or families), while one-quarter lived alone.
- Most had someone who could be called upon to provide help during illness. Fewer, however, had a source of help who would provide care for an indefinite period.

Economic Well-being

- Most of the respondents reported that they were managing independently without need of formal economic assistance. Only 15% reported they had insufficient funds to meet emergencies. Nonetheless, it is apparent there was an economic pinch being felt by a substantial number of citizens. Many reported some financial problems. Only half reported they were sure they had enough money for future needs.
- The picture of economic well-being varied substantially between the five service areas. Residents of the Southeast area reported the greatest need for financial assistance and were less secure in their assessments of their economic well-being.
- Females, young-old (60–74 years), unmarried persons, nonretired persons, and those living alone were less secure about their financial well-being than other corresponding groups.
- About half the sample expressed positive feelings about retirement. Those who were retired felt more positive about retirement than those who were not retired. It may be that nonretired persons were less positive in their projections about this event or that retired persons tended to overcome their resistance to retirement to obtain consistency between their feelings about retirement and their own experience.

Environmental Well-being

- Most felt themselves to be a part of, and liked living in, their neighborhood.
- While most felt safe walking in their neighborhoods or waiting for the bus during the day, fewer felt safe undertaking these activities at night.

- Younger males (60–74 years) had greater fear of crime than the other age and sex groups studied. We suspect this fear may be, at least in part, due to higher levels of activity outside the home (assisting friends, going to work, etc.) leading to greater exposure to what are perceived as more threatening environments.

Housing

- Most lived in low-density, single-family detached homes.
- Almost all housing had private kitchen and bathroom facilities. Almost one-third of their housing was perceived, however, to need *some* or *extensive* repairs. Interviewers felt the homes of older males, retirees, and persons who lived alone were in greatest need of repairs.
- Only a small proportion of respondents were dissatisfied with their present housing.

Although our findings tend to present a positive picture of the social well-being of the elderly, the potential need for long-term care and supportive services is apparent. While most of the elderly had someone they could rely upon for short-term care during illness, those sampled were less sure of their resources for help during a long illness. It appears such supportive services as home maintenance and repair programs are also needed. That home maintenance is tied to economic resources is suggested by the fact that residents in the service area having the lowest educational level, the highest number of blue-collar residents, and reporting the greatest need for financial assistance also said they needed home repairs most frequently.

This chapter has attempted to translate the elderly's assessments of their social world into potential needs for service. The following chapter probes the psychological dimension of well-being by exploring older persons' attitudes toward life and their views of themselves. An understanding of this dimension may influence our assessment of the various needs for services required by the elderly.

REFERENCES

Social Support

Brody, E.M. 1978. "Community Housing for the Elderly. The Program: The people, the Decision-Making Process and the Research." *The Gerontologist* 18:121-218.

, Gerald. 1974. *Support Systems and Community Mental Health*. New York:
avioral Publications.

ney. 1976. "Social Support as a Moderator of Life Stress." *Psychosomatic
ne* 38:300–311.

G.P. et al. 1973. "Life Change, Coping Ability and Chronic Intrinsic
" *Journal of Psychosomatic Research* 17:359–363.

78. "Life Events, Social Supports and Psychiatric Symptoms: A
analysis of the New Haven Data." *Journal of Health and Social Behavior*
19:230–234.

Finlayson, A. 1976. "Social Networks as Coping Resources." *Social Science and
Medicine* 10:47–103.

Gore, S. 1978. "The Effect of Social Support in Moderating the Health Consequences of Unemployment." *Journal of Health and Social Behavior*
19:157–165.

Horwitz, A. 1978. "Family, Kin and Friends. Networks in Psychiatric Helpseek-
ing." *Social Science and Medicine* 12:297–304.

Langlie, J.K. 1977. "Social Networks, Health Beliefs and Preventive Health
Behavior." *Journal of Health and Social Behavior* 18:244–260.

Lin, N. et al. 1979. "Social Support, Stressful Life Events and Illness: A Model and
Empirical Test." *Journal of Health and Social Behavior* 20:108–119.

Lowenthal, M.F. and C. Haven. 1968. "Interaction and Adaptation: Intimacy as
a Critical Variable." *American Sociological Review* 33:20–30.

Murdock, S.H. and D.F. Swartz. 1978. "Family Structure and Use of Agency Services: An Examination of Patterns Among Elderly Americans." *The Gerontologist* 18:475–481.

Myers, J.K., J.J. Lindenthal, and M.P. Pepper. 1975. "Life Events, Social Integration and Psychiatric Symptomology." *Journal of Health and Social Behavior*
16:421–427.

Nuckolls, K.B., J.K. Cassel, and B.H. Kaplan. 1972. "Psychosocial Assets, Life
Crisis and Prognosis of Pregnancy." *American Journal of Epidemiology*
95:431–441.

Palmore, E. et al. 1979. "Stress and Adaptation in Later Life." *Journal of Gerontology* 34:841–851.

Pratt, L. 1972. "Conjugal Organization and Health." *Journal of Marriage and The
Family* 2:85–95.

Riley, M.W. and A. Foner, eds. 1968. *Aging and Society Vol. 1: An Inventory
of Research Findings*. New York: Russell Sage Foundation.

Shanas, E. 1962. *The Health of Older People: A Social Survey*. Cambridge: Harvard University Press.

Smith, R.T. 1979. "Rehabilitation of the Disabled: The Role of Social Networks
in the Recovery Process." *International Rehabilitative Medicine* 1:63–72.

U.S. Department of Commerce, Bureau of the Census, 1979. *Statistical Abstract*.
Washington, D.C.: Government Printing Office.

Wan, T.T.H. and W.G. Weissert. 1981. "Social Support Networks, Patient Status,
and Institutionalization." *Research on Aging* 3:240–256.

Feelings About Retirement

Atchley, R.C. 1975. "Dimensions of Widowhood in Later Life." *The Gerontologist* 15:176–178.

Blau, Z. 1961. "Structural Constraints on Friendship in Old Age." *American Sociological Review* 26:429–439.

Barfield, E.C. and J.N. Morgan. 1978. "Trends in Satisfaction with Retirement." *The Gerontologist* 18:19–23.

Cavan, R. 1962. "Self and Role in Adjustment During Old Age." in *Human Behavior and Social Process*, edited by A. Rose. New York: Houghton Mifflin.

Fox, J.H. 1977. "Effects of Retirement and Former Work Life on Women's Adaptation to Old Age." *Journal of Gerontology* 32:196–202.

Glasmer, F.D. 1976. "Determinants of a Positive Attitude Toward Retirement." *Journal of Gerontology* 31:104–107.

Kimmel, D.C., K.F. Price, and J.W. Walker. 1978. "Retirement Choice and Retirement Satisfaction." *Journal of Gerontology* 33:575–585.

Streib, G. and G. Schneider. 1971. *Retirement in American Society*. Ithaca: Cornell University Press.

Environmental Well-being

Adams, R. and T. Smith, 1976. "Fear of Neighborhood." *National Opinion Research Center Report 127C on the Social Change Project*. Chicago: National Opinion Research Center.

Antunes, G.E. et al. 1977. "Patterns of Personal Crime Against the Elderly—Findings from a National Survey." *The Gerontologist* 17:321–327.

Beaver, M.L. 1979. "The Decision-Making Process and Its Relationship to Relocation Adjustment in Old People." *The Gerontologist* 19:567–574.

Brown, E. 1975. Fear of Assault Among the Elderly. Paper presented at the Annual Meeting of the Gerontological Society. Louisville, 1975.

Clemente, F. and M. Kleiman. 1976. "Fear of Crime Among the Aged." *The Gerontologist* 16:207–210.

Conklin, J.E. 1976. "Robbery, Elderly and Fear: An Urban Problem in Search of Solution." in *Crime and the Elderly: Challenge and Response*, edited by J. Goldsmith and S. Goldsmith. Lexington, Mass.: D.C. Heath, Lexington Books.

Cook, F.L. and Cook, T.D. 1976. "Evaluating the Rhetoric of Crisis: A Case Study of Criminal Victimization of the Elderly." *Social Service Review* 50:632–636.

Cook, F.L. et al. 1978. "Criminal Victimization of the Elderly: The Physical and Economic Consequences." *The Gerontologist* 18:338–349.

Crandall, R.C. 1980. "The Environments of the Aged." in *Gerontology: A Behavioral Science Approach*, edited by Richard Crandall. Reading, Mass.: Addison-Wesley.

Gubrium, J. 1974. "Victimization and Three Hypotheses." *Crime and Delinquency* 20:245–250.

Hindelang, M. 1976. *Criminal Victimization in Eight American Cities*. Cambridge, Mass.: Ballinger.

Kahana, E. et al. 1977. "Perspectives of the Aged on Victimization, "Ageism" and Their Problems in Urban Society." *The Gerontologist* 17:121–129.

National Council on Aging. 1975. *The Myth and Reality of Aging in America*. Washington, D.C.: National Council on Aging.

Rifai, M. 1977. "Implications for Crime Prevention." *Police Chief* 44:48–50.

Sundeen, R.A. and J.T. Mathieu, 1976. "The Fear of Crime and Its Consequences Among Elderly in Three Urban Communities." *The Gerontologist* 16:211–219.

U.S. Congress, House Select Committee on Aging, 94th Cong., 1977. *In Search of Security: A National Perspective on Elderly Crime Victimization*. Washington, D.C.: Government Printing Office.

Economic Well-being

Grad, S. and K. Foster. 1979. "Income of the Population Aged 55 and Older, 1976." *Social Security Bulletin* 42:16–32.

Hansen, G.D. et al. "Older People in the Midwest: Conditions and Attitudes" in *Older People and Their Social World*, edited by A.M. Rose and W.A. Peterson. Philadelphia: Davis.

Liang, J. and T. Fairchild. 1979. "Relative Deprivation and Perception of Financial Adequacy Among the Aged." *Journal of Gerontology* 34:746–759.

Peterson, D.A. 1973. "Financial Adequacy in Retirement: Perceptions of Older Americans." *The Gerontologist* 12:379–383.

Schultz, J.H. 1976. *The Economics of Aging*. Belmont, California: Wadsworth.

Thompson, W.E. and G.F. Streib. 1958. "Situational Determinants: Health and Economic Deprivation in Retirement." *Journal of Social Issues* 14:18–34.

U.S. Department of Commerce, Bureau of the Census. 1979. *Statistical Abstract*. Washington, D.C.: Government Printing Office.

Youmans, E.G. 1966. "Objective and Subjective Economic Disengagement Among Older Rural and Urban Men." *Journal of Gerontology* 21:439–441.

Housing

Brody, E.M. 1978. "Community Housing for the Elderly. The Program: the People, the Decision-Making Process and the Research." *The Gerontologist* 18:121–218.

Carp, F.M. 1966. *A Future for the Aged: Victoria Plaza and Its Residents*. Austin: University of Texas Press.

———1972. "Mobility of Old Slum-dwellers." *The Gerontologist* 12:57–65.

———1975. "Impact of Improved Housing on Morale and Life Satisfaction." *The Gerontologist* 15:511–515.

Clemente, F. and M. Kleiman. 1976. "Fear of Crime Among the Aged." *The Gerontologist* 16:207–210.

Hamovitch, M. and J.E. Peterson. 1969. "Housing Needs and Satisfaction of the Elderly." *The Gerontologist* 9:30–33.

Heumann, L.F. 1978. "Planning Assisted Independent Living Programs for the Semi–Independent Elderly—Development of Descriptive Models." *The Gerontologist* 18:145–152.

Lawton, M.P. et al. 1978. "The Lifespan of Housing Environments for the Aging." *The Gerontologist* 20:56–64.

Rosow, I. 1967. *Social Integration of the Aged*. New York: Free Press.

Struyk, R.J. 1977. "The Housing Situation of Elderly Americans." *The Gerontologist* 17:130–139.

Toseland, R. and J. Rasch. 1978. "Factors Contributing to Older Persons Satisfaction With Their Communities." *The Gerontologist* 18:395–402.

U.S. Department of Housing and Urban Development. 1977. *How Well Are We Housed? 4. The Elderly*. Washington, D.C.: Government Printing Office.

4

The Psychological Well-being of the Elderly

A casual review of the kinds of supportive services developed under the auspices of the Older Americans Act indicates the importance that has been given to maintaining the psychological well-being of older populations. Social services to encourage continued activity, counseling to facilitate adjustments to changes experienced in later life, and health-related services have been developed on the basis of extensive research that details the correlates of a healthy psychological state. In this chapter, the psychological well-being of our study population is examined with respect to overall life satisfaction, self-report of psychological symptoms, and self-assessed emotional health.

RELATED RESEARCH

Concept of Psychological Well-being

The concept of psychological well-being is difficult, if not impossible, to measure. While mental health can be assessed by psychiatric diagnosis and psychological evaluation of symptoms, the general concept of psychological well-being is diverse and multidimensional in its nature. For this reason, psychological well-being has been measured along several theoretical constructs that are indicative of one's attitude toward life in the past, present, and future. Both objective measures such as symptomology and subjective assessments of mental health have been used to assess the state of an individual's psychological health. Although one might question the validity of subjective assessments of mental health, since such assessments presuppose the ability to judge one's own state, previous research shows that self-ratings have been found to be valid and reliable (Andrews & Withey, 1973; Bradburn, 1969; Robinson & Shaver, 1973; Wan, 1976).

Most studies have examined psychological well-being in terms of life satisfaction and morale. Life satisfaction has been defined by Cantril (1965) as "an assessment of the overall conditions of existence as derived from a comparison of one's aspirations to one's overall achievements." Similarly, Neugarten, Havighurst, and Tobin (1961) define life satisfaction as congruence between desired and achieved goals. Gerontologists have emphasized life satisfaction as an important indicator of psychological well-being. Perhaps this is because the elderly have the vantage point from which to examine their lives after many chapters have been completed. Morale, on the other hand, is indicative of emotional health at the present time.

Several approaches have been used in assessing both *life satisfaction* and *morale*. For instance, Spreitzer and Snyder (1974) and Rose (1955) used only a single-item measure—the question, "How satisfied are you with your life?" There have been, however, some criticisms of this approach on the grounds that this single-item approach cannot account for the varied components of the psychological state. The comparative approach to assessment of well-being is frequently employed to portray the dynamic qualities of life satisfaction and morale. Not only are people asked their present state, but they are also asked to compare their present state with their life at some previous time or with other persons their own age. In this way, indicators yield relative measures of well-being that take into account, at least to some extent, the influence of age and life experiences. Larson (1978) has pointed out in her review of the literature that the measures assessing long-term satisfaction show higher associations with actual state (e.g., Edwards & Klemmack, 1973; Harris, 1975) than single-item measures dealing just with the present time (e.g., Clark & Anderson, 1967; Kutner et al., 1956; Palmore & Luikart, 1972).

Another approach to the psychological assessment describes well-being as a multidimensional concept (Neugarten, Havighurst & Tobin, 1961; Cavan et al., 1949; Kutner et al., 1956). The Life Satisfaction Index developed by Neugarten, Havighurst, and Tobin (1961) or some variant of it has been widely used in this approach (Bultena & Oyler, 1971; Cutler, 1973; Edwards & Klemmack, 1973; Bull & Aucoin, 1975). Neugarten's index uses five dimensions: zest versus apathy; resolution and fortitude; congruence between achieved and desired goals; positive self-concept; and mood tone.

In an attempt to unravel the complex nature of psychological well-being in terms of the SNAP population, our analysis made use of all three approaches to assessing psychological well-being.

Correlates of the Psychological Well-being

Through the use of the various approaches to psychological well-being described above, correlates of a healthy mental state have been found. These correlates include demographic factors (sex, age, socioeconomic status), health and life change factors (e.g., retirement, widowhood), and activity level.

A majority of studies (Neugarten, Havighurst & Tobin, 1961; Palmore & Luikart, 1972; Bradburn, 1969; Clemente & Sauer, 1976) using a single time as a point of reference found that male and female elderly report they are equally satisfied with life. Nevertheless, Spreitzer and Snyder (1974) using a longitudinal analysis discovered that males' life satisfaction increased after age 65 while females' declined. Studies of the effects of age on life satisfaction are inconclusive. The bulk of evidence indicates that life satisfaction appears to decline with advancing age (Alston & Dudley, 1973; Blau, 1973; Phillips, 1967; Wessman, 1956). Gurin, Veroff, and Feld (1960) offer some explanation for this association, stating that the elderly view their lives much more pessimistically than the young. There is, nevertheless, some evidence offered by the findings of Clemente and Sauer (1976) who report that life satisfaction increases with age. They found that persons 40 years and over reported higher life satisfaction than did younger groups. A few studies (Palmore & Luikart, 1972; Edwards & Klemmack, 1973) add further to the controversial relationship between age and life satisfaction by suggesting that the two factors are not related. Edwards and Klemmack's (1973) study reported that the relationship between age and satisfaction with life was eliminated when they controlled for socioeconomic status (SES). Thus, SES may be a key factor in determining the relationship between life satisfaction and age. It may be that differences in SES in the populations studied may account for some of the observed variations in the relationship of age to life satisfaction. Also, differences in measurement techniques employed to assess life satisfaction may account for variations in findings.

In fact, various studies have identified SES as a critical factor in predicting life satisfaction (Kutner et al., 1956; Hansen & Yoshioka, 1962; Thompson, Streib & Kosa, 1963; Marshall & Eteng, 1970; Edwards & Klemmack, 1973; Alston & Dudley, 1973; Cantril, 1965; Gurin, Veroff & Feld, 1960; Chatfield, 1977). Summarizing the trend of the findings, Chatfield (1977) found that individuals with higher family incomes showed higher Life Satisfaction Index scores and concluded that "while a low income does not necessarily mean low satisfaction, a high income is associated with greater life satisfaction, i.e., an older person is unlikely to be relatively unhappy (compared to other older people) with a high income."

The findings concerning the relationship of marital status to psychological well-being also clearly indicate that higher levels of well-being are associated with being married (Campbell, Converse & Rodgers, 1976; Edwards & Klemmack, 1973; George & Maddox, 1977; Gurin, Veroff & Feld, 1960; Robinson & Shaver, 1973; Wessman, 1956). Gurin, Veroff, and Feld (1960) have explained this relationship by arguing that "living alone presents a major psychological problem for many adults in our society."

Some evidence suggests that experiencing changes in marital and retirement status is associated with lower levels of well-being. Persons who are married or who were never married have higher levels of well-being than persons who are separated, divorced, or widowed (Warr & Livieratos, 1978; Kutner et al., 1956; Pihlblad & Adams, 1972; Neugarten, Havighurst & Tobin, 1961). Particularly relevant to the elderly, there have been findings suggesting that widowhood is associated with a decline in psychological well-being for men and women (Riley & Foner, 1968; Lopata, 1970). Lopata, in studying widows of Chicago explained this decrease in life satisfaction for women by arguing that widowhood deprived a woman of personal companionship and diminished her self-concept to the degree that her identity was based on her husband's goals and achievements.

Some studies have also associated retirement with a reduction in life satisfaction (Riley & Foner, 1968; Spreitzer & Snyder, 1974), finding that the working elderly have higher life satisfaction than the retired. Varying explanations for this finding have been proposed. One explanation treats those who continue to work as a select group. Men who remain in the labor force are healthier, better-adjusted and, in general, have more advantages than men who are retired (Riley & Foner, 1968). Another interpretation focuses upon income losses experienced with retirement, stating that loss of income is more devastating than the loss of the worker role (Chatfield, 1977). We should point out, however, that the effects of retirement on life satisfaction are still open to debate. Some researchers have found that gloomy expectations of life satisfaction in retirement are more negative than actual experience and that there is no decrease in life satisfaction consequent to retirement (Streib & Schneider, 1971; George & Maddox, 1977).

Finally, poor health and declining health have also been tied to lower morale and life satisfaction (Streib & Schneider, 1971; Palmore & Kivett, 1977; Wolk & Telleen, 1976; Bull & Aucoin, 1975; Spreitzer & Snyder, 1974; Edwards & Klemmack, 1973; Toseland & Sykes, 1977; Markides & Martin, 1979).

In summary, a number of factors have been associated with psychological well-being, including sociodemographic variables descriptive of the characteristics of the population, and life change variables indicating changes in status that the sample population may have experienced. Our analysis of the SNAP population considered the relevance of several of the above factors to psychological well-being. Variations in psychological well-being were examined by age, sex, marital status, retirement status, and living arrangement.

FINDINGS FROM THE SNAP DATA

We began our empirical inquiry into the components of psychological well-being by investigating older persons' perception of the quality of their lives in general. Selected social and demographic correlates of overall general life satisfaction were examined. Life satisfaction was probed by the single-item question, "Taking everything into account, how would you describe your satisfaction with life in general?" Table 4.1* presents the proportion of elderly who reported varying levels of life satisfaction. A large majority (71.2%) of the study population were satisfied with their lives. Respondents from both Southwest and Southeast had relatively lower life satisfaction as compared with those of other areas. There is an apparent difference between males and females in life satisfaction, irrespective of age. Males were more likely than females to be satisfied with their lives. The married (75.5%) were more satisfied with their lives than their counterparts, with divorced and separated respondents least satisfied (61.7%). Retirees (72.7%) were just slightly higher in satisfaction than nonretirees (67.3%).

In sum, we find that those with greater overall life satisfaction were most likely to be characterized as being male, age 75 and older, married, or retired. While our findings from the SNAP population corroborate previous research with respect to age and sex (Spreitzer & Snyder, 1974; Campbell, Converse & Rodgers, 1976; Edwards & Klemmack, 1973; George & Maddox, 1977; Gurin, Veroff & Feld, 1960; Robinson & Shaver, 1973; Wessman, 1956), the other findings from the SNAP data, which indicate that retirees and those over 75 years have higher life satisfaction, contradict previous findings (Riley & Foner, 1968; Spreitzer & Snyder, 1974; Alston & Dudley, 1973; Blau, 1973; Phillips, 1967; Wessman, 1956). Such a contradiction may be explained by the fact that few studies have attempted to look at the differences in life satisfaction between those elderly who are 60 to 74 years old and those who are 75 years or over. It may be that beyond a certain point, such as age 75, life may take on a slightly

---

*Tables appear in Appendix D.

different perspective as one moves toward acceptance of his/her aged status. Those retired in the SNAP study may be better off economically and therefore more able to deal with retirement than the populations sampled in other studies.

Life Satisfaction

In order to further assess the perception of the quality of life, the elderly were asked whether they generally found their life exciting, pretty routine, or dull. The majority (59.1%) found their life to be routine, only 7.9% found life dull, while 32.3% found their lives exciting (see Table 4.2). Those who were most likely to have a dull life were respondents of Northwest area, females aged 75 and older, separated/divorced, retirees, and persons living alone. On the other hand, older persons who found life to be exciting were also more likely to be residents of the Northwest, persons under 75 years, and those who were never married. It may be speculated that the majority of those under 75 may have more physical capability and more adequate financial resources to engage in a variety of social and recreational activities that could make life exciting. Residents of the Northwest had more financial resources, which could contribute to their viewing life either as exciting because they could afford more diversions or dull because they had more exciting experiences earlier in life.

The never-married may find life exciting for other reasons. Living independently all their lives, they no doubt have greater adaptability in coping with the problems of aging and have found ways to entertain themselves without depending on others. It should be noted that this group is also least likely to find life to be dull. Further, they do not have to anticipate such role losses as loss of spouse or a diminution of the parent role as do persons who are married or have been married. Probably for these reasons they continue to find life exciting in their later years.

Psychological Symptoms or Worriment

A short psychiatric evaluation schedule, which has been employed by the Center for Aging and Human Development (Pfeiffer, 1975), was adapted to measure the presence or absence of fifteen psychological symptoms. This index was used to identify the magnitude of depressive moods of the elderly. Symptoms were elicited by such questions as:

- "Is your daily life full of things that keep you interested?"
- "Is your sleep fitful and disturbed?"
- "Are you being plotted against?"

- "Are you troubled by your heart pounding and by a shortness of breath?"

For the entire listing of questions asked see Appendix B.

Overall, our results indicate an average of 2.5 psychological symptoms reported out of a possible 15, on this depression scale. A one-way analysis of variance was performed to determine the effect of each of the selected social and demographic factors on the level of psychological well-being. Data in Table 4.3 indicate that the effects of area, age and sex, and marital status on the number of symptoms reported were statistically significant. Respondents from Southeast and Northwest areas reported relatively greater number of symptoms than did those from other areas. More males than females had a better state of psychological well-being. Those who were divorced or widowed had poorer psychological status than their counterparts. The effects of retirement status and living arrangement on the reporting psychological symptoms were negligible.

Further insight into perception about psychological status can be gained by examining how often an individual worries about things. The data in Table 4.4 show that more than one-half (57.2%) of the study population were often worried about things, 27% were very often worried, and 30.1% were fairly often worried. Males, divorced, and separated persons were least likely to "worry about things." Differences in worrying between males and females should be highlighted. Females were much more likely either to be worried often or to hardly ever experience worry than males. This may be because females who are widowed in old age often must handle such new sets of problems as managing financial resources and dealing with home maintenance, which they did not have to deal with at earlier points in their lives. We suspect women may also have more concerns about the problems of their grown children and other members of their extended family. The characteristics of those who report they worry very often were almost matched with those who reported more frequent psychological symptoms.

Self-assessed Emotional Health

Psychological well-being may also be gauged by self-assessments of emotional health. Such self-assessments appear to be more meaningful when they are asked within a comparative framework, as in asking respondents to compare their present mental health with their health five years ago or to compare their mental health with others of the same age cohort.

Table 4.5 shows respondents' self-ratings of their present emotional health as compared with the emotional state five years before. As the table shows, 84% of the population rated their present state as better or about the same as it was five years ago. Fifteen percent (15.3%) perceived a decline in their emotional health over the previous five years. Females, particularly those 75 and over, widowed persons, and persons living alone were most likely to perceive their emotional health as declining. The recency of widowhood or the adjustments associated with widowhood may help to explain the fact that one-fifth of the widowed perceived a decline in their emotional health. By comparison, the unmarried, who do not face these adjustments, were least likely to have perceived a decline in emotional health. Clearly, counseling and other services offering emotional support are appropriate for the widowed to facilitate adjustment to new responsibilities and emotional deprivation that may result from the loss of a spouse.

It is interesting that while the widowed perceived a decline in their own emotional health they did not view their state as worse than others of their age (Table 4.6). Table 4.6 shows self-ratings of emotional health as compared with others in a similar age cohort. As displayed, fully 77.2% of the SNAP population rated their emotional health as good or better than others their age, 19.9% rated their health as fair, and 2.7% said their health was poor. Although there were no extreme differences in emotional health according to sociodemographic characteristics or service areas, it should be observed that persons in the Southwest and Southeast and separated/divorced persons were slightly more likely to feel their emotional health was poor as compared with others of their cohort.

SUMMARY

In this chapter, we have attempted to identify the complex, multidimensional concept of psychological well-being through an analysis of overall life satisfaction, psychological symptoms, and emotional health. Single-item, comparative, and index approaches were employed to discern various dimensions of well-being. Our findings indicate that, in general, the SNAP population has a high level of psychological well-being. Fully 70% of the study population were satisfied with their present life. Only an average of 2.5 psychological symptoms were reported out of a possible 15 symptoms as shown by the depression scale. The majority of respondents rated their emotional health as good and better than it was five years ago. Nevertheless, there was variation in the report of a healthy state by selected sociodemographic characteristics and by service area. Our findings indicate the following:

- Males and married persons had higher levels of life satisfaction, fewer psychological symptoms, and higher levels of emotional health than females, particularly older females and persons who were widowed, separated, or divorced. Persons who had experienced a change in their marital status were more likely to have poor psychological well-being than persons who had not experienced a change.

- Unmarried persons had the highest level of psychological well-being. This may be because unmarried persons do not experience many of the role losses associated with advanced age such as loss of the spouse role or a diminution of the parent role, or because unmarrieds have increased coping ability to deal with problems resulting from a lifetime of independent living.

- The effects of retirement and living arrangement on psychological well-being are inconclusive. While retired persons demonstrated greater life satisfaction and tended to worry about things less than the nonretired, the retired tended to report slightly more psychological symptoms than their counterparts. There was no real difference between nonretired and retired persons in their ratings of emotional health. Although persons who lived alone showed lower levels of life satisfaction than persons who lived with a spouse or others, and tended to find life a bit more dull, living alone was only slightly related to the presence of psychological symptoms and did not have a bearing on rating of poor emotional health at the present time. Persons who lived alone were more likely to have experienced a change in their emotional health for better or for worse as compared to five years ago. Time adjustment to widowhood or divorce may be reflected in this finding.

- Variation by service area was observed along the three dimensions of psychological well-being. Residents of the Southeast area reported lower levels of psychological well-being. They reported lower levels of life satisfaction, greater number of psychological symptoms, and were more likely to feel that their emotional health had declined during the past five years than respondents in other areas.

The above findings strongly imply the need for supportive services aimed at older females (≥ 75 years), those who have changed marital status, and those living in the Southeast service area. It is apparent from our analysis that circumstantial (i.e., marital and retirement status) and environmental factors (living arrangement, service area) are related to psychological well-being. The next chapter explores the relationship of these factors to physical well-being.

REFERENCES

Alston, J. and C. Dudley. 1973. "Age, Occupation, and Life Satisfaction." *The Gerontologist* 13:58–61.

Andersen, N.E. 1967. "Effects of Institutionalization on Self-Esteem." *Journal of Gerontology* 22:313–317.

Andrews, F. and S. Withey. 1973. *Developing Measures of Perceived Life Quality: Results from Several National Surveys.* Ann Arbor: Institute for Social Research, University of Michigan.

Blau, Z. 1973. *Old Age in a Changing Society.* New York: Franklin Watts.

Bradburn, N. 1969. *The Structure of Psychological Well-Being.* Chicago: Aldine.

Bull, C. and J. Aucoin. 1975. "Voluntary Association Participation and Life Satisfaction: A Replication Note." *Journal of Gerontology* 30:73–76.

Bultena, G. and R. Oyler. 1971. "Effects of Health on Disengagement and Morale." *Aging and Human Development* 2:142–148.

Campbell, A., P. Converse, and W. Rodgers. 1976. *The Quality of American Life.* New York: Russell Sage Foundation.

Cantril, H. 1965. *The Pattern of Human Concerns.* New Brunswick: Rutgers University Press.

Cavan, R. et al. 1949. *Personal Adjustment in Old Age.* Chicago: Science Research Associates.

Chatfield, W. 1977. "Economic and Sociological Factors Influencing Life Satisfaction of the Aged." *Journal of Gerontology* 32:593–599.

Clark, M. and B. Anderson. 1967. *Culture and Aging.* Springfield, Illinois: Charles C. Thomas.

Clemente, F. and J. Sauer. 1976. "Life Satisfaction in the United States." *Social Forces* 54:621–631.

Cutler, S.J. 1973. "Voluntary Association Membership and Life Satisfaction: A Cautionary Research Note." *Journal of Gerontology* 28:96–100.

Edwards, J.N. and D.L. Klemmack. 1973. "Correlates of Life Satisfaction: A Reexamination." *Journal of Gerontology* 28:497–502.

George, L.K. and G.L. Maddox. 1977. "Subjective Adaptation to Loss of the Work Role: A Longitudinal Study." *Journal of Gerontology* 32:456–462.

Gurin, G., J. Veroff, and S. Feld. 1960. *Americans View Their Mental Health.* New York: Basic Books.

Hansen, G. and S. Yoshioka. 1962. *Aging in the Upper Midwest: A Profile of 6,300 Senior Citizens.* Kansas City, Mo.: Community Studies.

Harris, L. and Associates. 1975. *The Myth and Reality of Aging in America.* Washington, D.C.: National Council on Aging.

Kutner, B. et al. 1956. *Five Hundred Over Sixty: A Community Survey on Aging.* New York: Russell Sage Foundation.

Larson, R. 1978. "Thirty Years of Research on the Subjective Well-Being of Older Americans." *Journal of Gerontology* 33:109–125.

Lopata, H.Z. 1970. "The Social Involvement of American Widows." *American Behavioral Scientist* 14:41–48.

Markides, K.S. and H.K. Martin. 1979. "A Causal Model of Life Satisfaction Among the Elderly." *Journal of Gerontology* 34:86–93.

Marshall, D. and W. Eteng. 1970. "Retirement and Migration in the North Central States: A Comparative Analysis: Wisconsin, Florida, Arizona." *Population Series #20.* Madison: Department of Rural Sociology, University of Wisconsin.

Neugarten, D., R. Havighurst, and S. Tobin. 1961. "The Measurement of Life Satisfaction." *Journal of Gerontology* 16:134–143.

Palmore, E. and V. Kivette. 1977. "Change in Life Satisfaction: A Longitudinal Study of Persons Aged 46–70." *Journal of Gerontology* 32:311–316.

Palmore, E. and C. Luikart. 1972. "Health and Social Factors Related to Life Satisfaction." *Journal of Health and Social Behavior* 13:68–80.

Pfeiffer, E. 1975. "Short Portable Mental Status Questionnaire." *The Journal of the American Geriatrics Society* 23:433–441.

Phillips, D. 1967. "Social Participation and Happiness." *American Journal of Sociology* 72:479–88.

Pihlblad, C. and D. Adams. 1972. "Widowhood, Social Participation and Life Satisfaction." *Aging and Human Development* 3:323–330.

Riley, M.W. and A. Foner, eds. 1968. *Aging and Society. Vol. 1: An Inventory of Research Findings.* New York: Russell Sage Foundation.

Robinson, J. and P. Shaver. 1973. *Measures of Social Psychological Attitudes.* Ann Arbor: University of Michigan Survey Research Center.

Rose, A. 1955. "Factors Associated with the Life Satisfaction of Middle Class, Middle Aged Persons." *Marriage and Family Living* 17:15–19.

Spreitzer, E. and E. Snyder. 1974. "Correlates of Life Satisfaction Among the Aged." *Journal of Gerontology* 29:454–458.

Streib, G. and C. Schneider. 1971. *Retirement in American Society: Impact and Process.* Ithaca: Cornell University Press.

Toseland, R. and J. Sykes. 1977. "Senior Citizens Center Participation and Other Correlates of Life Satisfaction." *The Gerontologist* 17:235–241.

Wan, T. 1976. "Predicting Self-Assessed Health: A Multivariate Approach." *Health Services Research* 11:464–477.

Wan, T. and B. Livieratos, 1978. "Interpreting a General Index of Subjective Well-Being." *Health and Society (Milbank Memorial Fund Quarterly)* 56:531–556.

Wessman, A. 1956. A Psychological Inquiry Into Satisfaction and Happiness. Unpublished Ph.D. dissertation. Princeton University.

Wolk, S. and S. Telleen. 1976. "Psychological and Social Correlates of Life Satisfaction As a Function of Resident Constraint." *Journal of Gerontology* 31:89–98.

5

The Physical Well-being of the Elderly

Our present understanding of the relationship between aging and physical health has been fraught with misconceptions and inconsistencies. On the one hand, Americans use such cliches as "you're as old as you feel," while, on the other hand, we believe that advanced age is associated with increased frailty.

In the past two decades, the health of the aged has been one of the major concerns of legislators, practitioners, and health-care planners. Hickey (1980) has noted that health status in old age has an impact on individual and societal levels. On the individual level, health status measures an individual's capability to maintain independent functioning and autonomy. Declining health may alter life style, limit the range of personal choices, restrict social roles, and strain personal economic resources. On the societal level, the health of the elderly has implications for the allocation of social and health resources. Prolonged disability among the elderly not only may limit their social participation but also may require the provision of a broad range of health-care and social services. Clearly, the health of elderly individuals affects their needs for service, and the society's provision of services affects the health status of elderly individuals.

Information on physical health of the study population is presented in this chapter. Physical health measures include the nature and type of physical impairment, the level of physical disability, the degree of functional dependency in terms of activities of daily living, and the self-perception of physical health. Social and demographic differentials in physical well-being are also examined.

RELATED RESEARCH

Correlates of Physical Well-being

The task of summarizing literature concerning the physical well-being of the elderly is complicated by the heterogeneity of the aged population and by the interrelationship between health status and functional capacity. Any analysis of the physical well-being of the elderly must proceed along the two dimensions of actual physical status and of functional limitations imposed by chronic illness. Previous studies on physical dysfunctioning show that there is no substantively meaningful correlation between a major disabling condition and the degree of functional dependency; the condition is not a strong predictor of the severity of disability (Wan, 1975; Haber, 1970). Furthermore, persons having the same condition are not necessarily incapacitated to the same extent. Thus, the ability to engage in daily living activities is determined by a complex relationship between a pathological condition and a variety of personal, social, demographic, and environmental factors.

The complexity of the interrelationship between health status and functional limitation is apparent when profiling the physical well-being of the elderly population. Fully 86% of the United States population over 65 years report having multiple chronic conditions, yet only 33% say they have trouble getting around by themselves, 38% report requiring assistance, and 29% are confined to their home (Harris, 1978; Kovar, 1977). The two most prevalent chronic conditions are arthritis, being present in 38% of the elderly population, and vision and hearing impairments, found in 49% of the population (Harris, 1978).

Differentials in health and disability status by sociodemographic attributes further complicate the picture of physical well-being. Age, sex, education, socioeconomic status, race, and urban-rural residence have been associated with various indicators of health status and functional impairment or disabilty. It is a well-documented fact that mortality, prevalence of chronic disease, and physical impairment all increase with age (Kovar, 1977; Haber, 1970; Wan, 1975). Higher reporting of poor health and chronic disability is found among the poor, the unmarried, the less educated, and rural residents (Jaffe, Day & Adams, 1964; Wan, 1974; Nagi & Riley, 1968; Namey & Wilson, 1972; Palmore, 1971; Wilder, 1972; Morgan et al., 1962; Swisher, 1970; Wan, 1972; McCoy & Brown, 1978; Urban Institute, 1979). In addition to being related to chronic disability, the above variables are also associated with greater severity of disability, particularly with those disabilities that limit the ability to work. It appears that lower levels of education restrict the job opportunities available to persons who also have functional limitations. Living in rural or smaller nonurban communities may also limit jobs available to persons with physically handicapping conditions.

Sex differentials in health and functional capacity have been presented in many studies. For example, national statistics reveal that women on the average live 7.7 years longer than men (Kovar, 1977). Although some research shows that women had lower mortality rates than men, they report more illness then men (Verbrugge, 1976; Fillenbaum, 1979). Sex differentials, however, have been disputed by other studies that find no significantly consistent differences in reported health status between men and women (Larson, 1978; Maddox & Douglass, 1974: Verbrugge, 1981).

The results of the 1970 National Health Interview Survey indicate that relatively the same proportion of men (12.4%) and women (11.3%) report some limitations in activity due to a chronic condition (Wilder, 1972). There are conflicting reports, however, concerning severity of disability. Haber (1968, 1971) observed that women were more seriously disabled. On the other hand, Sullivan (1971) noted more men had long-term disabilities than women. Such discrepancies in the literature may be due to varying definitions of what constitutes disability. It may, nonetheless, be fair to conclude that, at the present time, disabilities have more serious implications for men than for women with regard to work opportunities because men are more often engaged in physical labor at their work. As Marden and Burnright (1969) observe "disruptions in life that are produced by withdrawal from labor force and by developing medical difficulties are relatively more important for males." In the future, as women continue to acquire varied work roles, differences in the implications of disability for men and women may decrease.

In addition to the above demographic factors, other variables have also been suggested as contributors to variations in health status among the elderly, such as living arrangement (Shuval, Antonovsky & David, 1970), neighborhood stability (German et al., 1978), the occurrence of life-change events such as widowhood and retirement (Maddison & Viola, 1968; Wan, 1979; Holtzman, Berman & Ham, 1980), and the social-psychological factor of health anxiety (McCrae, Bartone & Costa, 1976; Blazer & Houpt, 1979).

Assessment of Physical Functioning

Given the complexity of assessing physical well-being and the diverse number of factors associated with well-being, it is necessary to measure physical health along several dimensions. The physical state of the population and its ability to function can be ascertained by separately assessing health status and functional capacity. Health status and functional capacity may be measured through self-assessments and clinical appraisals. Among the elderly, self-assessments of health and functioning level have been shown to be relatively accurate evaluations of actual clinical state (Friedson & Martin, 1963; Maddox, 1962, 1964; Maddox & Douglass, 1973; Meltzer & Hochstim, 1970; Suchman, Phillips & Streib, 1958; U.S. Department of HEW, 1977; Wan, 1976). Since this is the case, self-assessments have been preferred in research.

Health status may be ascertained by single questions or by asking the respondents to compare their present physical state with their health five years ago or with others of the same age. Such comparative measures add a time perspective to single questions of self-assessed health.

Numerous scales have been developed to access individual functional capacity (i.e., Meer & Baker's Stockton Geriatric Rating Scale; Lawton & Brody's Physical Self-maintenance Scale; Gurel, Linn, & Linn's PAMIE Scale).

One of the most widely used methods of accessing capacity for self-maintenance is the Activities of Daily Living scale (ADL) developed by Katz and his associates (1963). The ADL focuses upon five areas of activity: bathing, dressing, feeding, continence, and transferring. Transferring describes the ability to move from place to place; continence refers to the ability to refrain from the urge to defecate or urinate. The advantages of the ADL are that it is an efficient and relatively accurate measure when administered either by professional or lay interviewers. The ADL, while giving a profile of performance, does not give an indication of motivation to perform. This may be a key factor as yet untapped in assessments of functional performance. A further development in performance assessment has been the use of the Instrumental Activities of Daily Living index (IADL) (Lawton & Brody, 1969). The IADL measures capacity to perform tasks necessary to maintain independent living. Although the IADL measures physical performance, it is also indicative of the ability to perform social roles. Thus, in some respects it also reflects social well-being.

Nutritional Studies

The causes of poor nutrition among the elderly can be summarized under two headings (Exton-Smith, 1977, p. 6). There are external factors, which include insufficient funds to purchase food, lack of help, or inadequate facilities for food preparation; and such unfavorable social circumstances as isolation, loneliness, and lack of knowledge or concern about good nutrition. The internal conditions (those factors relating to the individual's physical well-being) that can produce poor nutrition include impaired appetite associated with constitutional disease, difficulty with chewing (may be due to missing teeth or ill fitting dentures), physical disability, and mental disturbances.

According to the Subcommittee on Aging (1973) approximately one-third to one-half of the health problems of the aged can be associated with poor nutrition and inadequate diet. There is some indication that there is a decline in nutrient intake among some elderly, especially those who are housebound, disabled, or over 75 years (Gillium & Morgan, 1955; Stanton & Exton-Smith, 1970; Berger, 1976; Exton-Smith, Stanton & Windsor, 1972).

A longitudinal study following a small sample of elderly females found that a nutritious diet in old age is usually maintained if the person remains physically fit and active (Stanton & Exton-Smith, 1970). However, disability was found as the most likely cause of declining nutritious eating by the elderly. In an earlier, larger longitudinal study, Gillium & Morgan (1955) reported a decline in a nutritious diet with age, especially after the age of 75 years.

Obesity is a major health problem of the elderly and is often related to poor diet. It is estimated that between 30% and 60% of the elderly can be classified as overweight or obese (Sherwood, 1970; Osborn, 1970; Howell, 1974). Differences between sexes and among socioeconomic statuses have been noted. Those of lower socioeconomic status are more likely to be overweight, and women are more frequently overweight than men. It is important to recognize that being overweight is not synonymous with being well-nourished.

Malnutrition is also a problem for some elderly. Older persons are frequently found to have diets low in calcium, iron, and vitamins A and C (Berger, 1976). When the diets of low-income elderly were compared with those of families of all ages with similar incomes, the diets of the elderly were found to be less adequate with respect to calories, protein, thiamin, and riboflavin (Guthrie, Black & Madden, 1972). It appears that low income compounded by old age increases the risk of malnutrition.

Malnutrition has also been associated with social isolation. The elderly can be victims of social isolation through widowhood, death of friends and peers, close family members living too far away, and decreased mobility. Sherwood (1970) found that the higher the level of social interaction the greater and more varied was the nutritional intake. Another study revealed isolated or lonely people are not as likely to eat a nutritious diet regardless of the availability of adequate food (Pelcovitz, 1972).

The physical health status of the SNAP population is analyzed in terms of physical impairment, functional dependency, self-perception of health, and nutritional status.

FINDINGS FROM THE SNAP DATA

Physical Disability and Impairment

An analysis of the SNAP data shows that a small proportion (8.8%) of all the elderly had physical disabilities due to paralysis, missing limbs, or broken bones (Table 5.1).* The distribution of disability by area ranged markedly from 5.5% in the North to 12.7% in the Southeast area. Eighteen percent (one-tenth) of all elderly had vision impairments (74% having poor vision even with glasses; 9.2% having difficulty in seeing; 1.5% being blind). Fifteen percent of the elderly had hearing impairments (including 8.5% having poor hearing; 1.5% being deaf, and 4.9% using hearing aids). Age and sex accounted for the only apparent differences in disability rates (Table 5.2). The young-old appeared to have higher disability rates than the old-old, and males had more disability than females.

It is reasonable to believe that due to performance demands of different social roles, disability may have varying impacts upon elderly persons depending upon what things they want to do. In the total study population, 47.5% reported no disabilities, 31.1% were moderately disabled, and 15.4% reported severe levels of disability (Table 5.3). The widowed had a slightly higher proportion with a moderate disability than other marital status groups. This may be because those in our sample who were widowed were an average of five years older than those in the sample who were married, separated, or divorced and an average of two years older than those who were single. There were no differences in the level of physical disability between the retired and nonretired, and negligible differences between persons living alone and those living with others.

In the present analysis, two measures of functional dependency are used. One is a revised measure of Katz et al. (1963) Activities of Daily Living (ADL) index, indicating primary sociobiological dysfunctions in terms of problems in grooming, walking, bathing, dressing, transferring, and feeding. The other measure is the Instrumental Activities of Daily Living (IADL) scale adapted from Lawton & Brody (1969). This scale measures the extent to which an individual needs human assistance in carrying out activities such as telephoning, traveling, shopping, preparing meals, doing housework, and taking medication.

Data in Table 5.4 show only 8% of the total population surveyed having at least one ADL dysfunction and 27.1% needing human assistance in performing IADL functions. Correlation analysis of the relationship between sociodemographic variables and ADL scores reveals that age was positively and educational level was negatively associated with both ADL and IADL scores. The older people become or the lower their educational

---

*Tables appear in Appendix D.

level, the greater the need for human assistance in physical and social functioning. The elderly who lived alone appeared to be more independent than those who lived with others, especially in performing ADL functions. Neither differences in marital status nor retirement status were associated with differences in functional dependency.

Detailed information concering ADL and IADL activities is in Tables 5.5 and 5.6. When we look at the variation in functional dependencies by service areas (Table 5.5), a pattern emerges that shows a small proportion of respondents needing assistance in performing instrumental activities in the North and a high proportion in the Southeast area.

The information on IADL activities shows that older males were more likely than other sex and age subgroups to be dependent upon assistance for all the IADL activities, except for traveling and shopping (Table 5.6). The widowed had a substantially higher proportion of need for help in traveling, shopping, and doing housework than their counterparts. More retirees than the nonretired were likely to need assistance in preparing foods and doing housework.

Overall, there was a small percentage of the elderly having dependencies in ADL activities; it ranged from 0.5% in feeding to 5.1% in bathing. A higher percentage of older females needed help in walking, transferring, bathing, and grooming than other sex and age subgroups. The widowed were especially more likely to be dependent in grooming, walking, and bathing than other subgroups. Although retired persons were more functionally dependent than the nonretired, the difference in percentages is insignificant. Those who lived with others had a lower proportion in need of help for the ADL activities than those living alone.

Perception of Physical Health

When the elderly were asked how their health compared with that of others of the same age, it was found that more than three-fourths of the respondents reported having either excellent or good health, while only 4.7% reported that their health was poor (Table 5.7). It is interesting to note that respondents of the Southeast area had the largest proportion of persons who ranked their health as poor. A second self-assessed health question was asked in which respondents were to compare their health today with that of five years ago (hereafter referred to as *comparative health*). Data in Table 5.7 show that 13.5% had improved health, 63.6% maintained the same health level, and 22.9% had a decline in self-assessed health over the five-year period. Respondents from both Southwest and Southeast areas had a relatively higher percentage of persons who thought their health was worse than five years earlier.

The information on social differentials in self-assessed health is presented in Table 5.8. Nearly one-third of the study population said their health was excellent. There is considerable variation in self-assessed health among the marital status categories. Never-married persons are more likely to report excellent health and much less likely to report poor health than other marital status groups, adding to their profile of strength that we have traced in relation to psychological social well-being. Separated/divorced persons are less likely to report excellent health and more likely to report poor health.

High proportions of older males and retirees also reported having excellent health. This may, in part, reflect survivorship of older males and retirees—males who are well may be enjoying retirement, and males who are sick are likely to be extremely sick and may have retired due to health. Persons who live alone either have excellent health, which enables them to maintain independent functioning, or have experienced severe health deterioration. The latter may be unable to care for themselves without supportive services.

The distribution of persons who perceived themselves as declining in health over the past five years was irregular in the four age and sex subgroups (Tables 5.9). Widowed persons were more likely than married, never married, or separated/divorced persons to report a worsening in their health. No apparent differences in comparative health between retired and nonretired persons was found. Persons living alone were more likely than those living with others to experience a decline in health.

Nutritional Status

To examine nutritional status as a component of physical well-being, the SNAP population was questioned about their diet; how many meals they had each day; whether they needed special diet; whether they took vitamins or mineral supplements; and whether they prepared their own food. The results are presented in Tables 5.10 through 5.12. The vast majority (89.2%) of those surveyed felt they had a "good" diet (Table 5.10). However, self-assessment is not a very accurate way to derive the nutritional status of a population since many who have "poor" diets may fail to recognize the fact. Others may not wish to admit having a poor diet.

When examining the respondents' own assessments of their diet by characteristics of the population (Table 5.11), the largest variation was between those living alone and those living with others. Those living alone (83.1%) less often said they had a "good" diet compared with those living with others (91.4%). This may be related to the factor of social isolation discussed previously.

Among the elderly in the sample, 70% said they consumed three or more meals per day. Among the service areas, the Southeast had the lowest proportion (58.3%) having at least three meals a day (Table 5.10). The Southeast also had the smallest percentage assessing their diet as "good". When questioned regarding the use of vitamin and mineral supplements, 38.3% (Table 5.10) of those queried responded affirmatively. The Southeast area had the lowest rate (33.5%) of those using vitamin tablets, while the Northeast area had the highest rate of supplement users (42.9%). Considering food preparation, about 60% of the respondents were responsible for the preparation of their own main meal of the day (Table 5.10). Caution is merited, however, in interpreting this statistic since preparation of meals does not mean the preparation of nutritious meals. As programs such as Meals on Wheels have demonstrated, some elderly might have better diets if meals were prepared for them. Surprisingly, older males and females (≥75 years) were less likely to be on a special diet than younger males and females (60-74 years). Slightly more persons who were separated or divorced were likely to be on a special diet. When examining the need for special diet by service area (Table 5. 10), we find that the North area had fewer people on special diets and the Southeast had the most on special diets.

The Southeast stands out as an area with special nutrition needs. This area had the smallest proportion of elderly who assessed their diet as "good." It was the area with the lowest rate of persons consuming at least three meals a day and had the highest rate of those on a special diet.

SUMMARY

Our inquiry into the physical well-being of the SNAP population proceeded along four dimensions: clinical symptoms, functional limitations, self-reported health, and nutritional status. In examining the concept of physical well-being, it was emphasized that actual clinical states alone do not indicate the extent of functional capacity or perception of health. Yet, these latter factors are extremely important in determining the particular supportive service requirements needed by the various subgroups in the population. Our overall findings in the areas of physical disability, functional dependency, self-perceived health, and nutritional status indicate:

1. While only a small portion of the total SNAP population (8.8%) suffered disabilities from paralysis, missing limbs, or broken bones, a larger proportion (15.4%) reported a severe level of disability from other causes. Older respondents (≥75 years) and those who were widowed reported more disabilities than comparable groups.

2. Although less than one-tenth (8%) of the SNAP respondents

reported at least one area of ADL dysfunctioning, almost one-third (27.1%) said they had difficulties performing IADL tasks. Thus, while only a relatively small proportion of persons had problems with personal self-maintenance (i.e., grooming, bathing, feeding), a considerably larger group had difficulty with such tasks necessary for independent living as telephoning and shopping. These persons needed assistance from others. Respondents who were older, had comparatively fewer years of education, or who were widowed were more apt to have functional limitations.

3. In subjective assessments of their own health as compared with others of their own age groups, the majority of respondents (75%) rated their health as being as good as their peers. Only a small proportion (5%) rated their health as poorer. Married persons were more likely to say their health was good while separated/divorced persons more often reported having poorer health.

4. There was substantial variation between service areas in physical well-being. A greater proportion of residents of the Southeast said they had functional limitations, and a larger percentage perceived a decline in their health over a five-year period than the respondents in other areas.

5. In general, the overall nutritional status of Baltimore County elderly appears to be adequate. The majority are eating what they consider a "good" diet and are consuming three or more meals a day. Well over half of the elderly population are still able to prepare their own meals. It should be noted, however, that considerably fewer residents of the Southeast service area had three meals a day and that the Southeast had the highest rate of those on a special diet.

Our results suggest directions for future planning. First, there appears to be a need for additional assistance in performing such tasks necessary to maintaining independent living as preparing meals, telephoning, and shopping. While not all of those who reported needing such assistance may require formal supportive services, it seems reasonable to suspect that many could benefit from such services if only to relieve the regular care providers in the home. Second, respondents from the Southeast area seem to be at a higher risk of becoming functionally dependent and requiring institutionalization in the future. They were also the least likely to consume three meals per day. This area may require a greater allocation of resources for providing comprehensive services. Finally, the fact that older persons and persons with lower levels of education are more likely to be disabled suggests that supportive and maintenance services in all areas of the county should be targeted at these people.

REFERENCES

Blazer, D. G. and J. F. Houpt. 1979. "Perception of Poor Health in the Healthy Older Adult." *Journal of the American Geriatrics Society* 24:330-334.

Berger, Ruth. 1976. "Nutritional Needs of the Aged. Pp. 113-122 in *Nursing and the Aged,* edited by I. M. Burnside. New York: McGraw-Hill.

Exton-Smith, A. N., B. R. Stanton, and A. C. M. Windsor. 1972 *Nutrition of Housebound Old People.* London: King Edward's Hospital Fund.

Exton-Smith, A. N. 1977. "Nutritional Problems of Elderly Populations." Pp. 1-20 in *Nutrition of the Aged.* Calgary: University of Calgary.

Fillenbaum, G. G. 1979. "Social Context and Self-assessments of Health Among the Elderly." *Journal of Health and Social Behavior* 20:45-51.

Friedson, H. and H. Martin. 1963. "A Comparison of Self and Physicians' Health Ratings in an Older Population." *Journal of Health and Human Behavior* 4:179-183.

German, P. S. et al. 1978. "Health Care of the Elderly in Medically Disadvantaged Populations." *The Gerontologist* 18:547-555.

Gillium, H. L. and A. F. Morgan. 1955. "Nutritional Status of the Aging." *Journal of Nutrition* 55:265.

Gurel, L., M. W. Linn, and B. S. Linn. 1972. "Physical and Mental Impairment of Function Evaluation in the Aged: The PAMIE Scale." *Journal of Gerontology* 27:83-90.

Guthrie, H. A., K. Black, and J. P. Madden. 1972. "Nutritional Practices of Elderly Citizens in Rural Pennsylvania." *The Gerontologist* 12:330-335.

Haber, L.D. 1968. "Disability, Work and Income Maintenance: Prevalence of Disability, 1966." *Social Security Bulletin* 31:14-23.

Haber, L. D. 1970. "Age and Capacity Devaluation." *Journal of Health and Social Behavior* 11:167-182.

Haber, L.D. 1971. "Disabling Effects of Chronic Disease and Impairment." *Journal of Chronic Diseases* 24:469-487.

Harris, L. and Associates, Inc. 1978. *Fact Book on Aging: A Profile of America's Older Population.* Washington, D.C.: National Council on Aging, Inc.

Hickey, T. 1980. *Health and Aging.* Monterey, Calif.: Brooks/Cole.

Holtzman, J. M., H. Berman, and R. Ham. 1980. "Health and Early Retirement Decisions." *Journal of the American Geriatrics Society* 28:23-28.

Howell, S. C. 1974. "Nutrition Education in Relation to Aging." Pp. 265-283 in *Learning for Aging,* edited by S. Grabowski and W. Donason. Washington, D.C.: Adult Education Association.

Jaffe, A. J., L. H. Day, and W. Adams. 1964. *Disabled Workers in the Labor Market.* Totawa, N. J.: Bedminster.

Katz, S. et al. 1963. "Studies of Illness in the Aged: The Index of ADL—A Standardized Measure of Biological and Psychosocial Function." *Journal of the American Medical Association* 185:914-919.

Kovar, M. G. 1977. "Health of the Elderly and the Use of Health Services." *Public Health Reports* 92:9-19.

Larson, R. 1978. "Thirty Years of Research on the Subjective Well-Being of Older Americans." *Journal of Gerontology* 33:109-125.

Lawton, M. P., M. Ward, and S. Yaffe. 1967. "Indices of Health in an Aging Population." *Journal of Gerontology* 22:334-342.

Maddison, D. and A. Viola. 1968. "The Health of Widows in the Year Following Bereavement." *Journal of Psychosomatic Research.* 12:297-306.

Maddox, G. L. 1962. "Some Correlates of Differences in Self-Assessment of Health Status Among the Elderly." *Journal of Gerontology* 17:180-185.

———— 1964. "Self-Assessments of Health Status: A Longitudinal Study of Selected Elderly Subjects." *Journal of Chronic Disease* 17:449-460.

Maddox, G. L. and E. B. Douglass. 1973. "Self-Assessment of Health: A Longitudinal Study of Elderly Subjects." *Journal of Health and Social Behavior* 14:87-93.

———— 1974. "Aging and Individual Differences: A Longitudinal Analysis of Social, Psychological and Physiological Indicators." *Journal of Gerontology* 29:555-563.

Marden, P. and R. Burnright. 1969. "Social Consequences of Physical Impairment in An Aging Population." *The Gerontologist* 9:39-46.

McCoy, J. L. and D. L. Brown. 1978. "Health Status Among Low-Income Elderly Persons: Rural-Urban Differences." *Social Security Bulletin* 41:14-24.

McCrae, R. R., R. T. Bartone, and P. T. Costa. 1976. "Aging, Anxiety and Self-Reported Health." *International Journal of Aging and Human Development* 7:49-58.

Meer, B. and J. Baker. 1966. "The Stockton Geriatric Rating Scale." *Journal of Gerontology* 21:392-403.

Meltzer, J. and J. Hochstim. 1970. "Reliability and Validity of Survey Data on Physical Health." *Public Health Reports* 85:1075-1086.

Morgan, J. N. et al. 1962. "The Economic Position of the Disabled." in *Income and Welfare in the United States,* edited by J. N. Morgan et al. New York: McGraw-Hill.

Nagi, S. Z. and L. E. Riley. 1968. "Coping with Economic Crisis: The Disabled on Public Assistance." *Journal of Health and Social Behavior* 9:317-327.

Namey, C. and R. W. Wilson. 1972. "Age Patterns in Medical Care, Illness, and Disability." *Vital and Health Statistics Series.* Series 10. No. 70.

Osborn, M. O. 1970. "Nutrition of the Aged." Pp. 235-259 in *The Daily Needs and Interests of Older People,* edited by A. M. Hoffman. Springfield Ill.: Charles C. Thomas.

Palmore, E. 1971. "Variables Related to Needs Among the Aged Poor." *Journal of Gerontology* 26:524-531.

Pelcovitz, J. 1972. "Nutrition to Meet the Human Needs of Older Americans." *Journal of the American Dietetic Association* 60:297-300.

Sherwood, S. 1970. "Gerontology and the Sociology of Food and Eating." *Aging and Human Development* 1:61-68.

Shuval, J. T., A. Antonovsky, and A. M. David. 1970. *Social Functions of Medical Practice.* San Francisco: Jossey-Bass.

Stanton, B. R. and A. N. Exton-Smith. 1970. *A Longitudinal Study of the Dietary of Elderly Women.* London: King Edward's Hospital Fund.

Subcommittee on Aging of the Committee on Labor and Public Welfare and The Special Committee on Aging, U.S. Senate, 1973. 93rd Congress, 1st session.

Post-White House Conference on Aging Reports, 1973. Washington, D.C.: Government Printing Office.

Suchman, E., B. Phillips, and G. Streib. 1958. "An Analysis of the Validity of Health Questionnaires." *Health and Human Behavior.* 36:223-232.

Sullivan, D. T. 1971. "Disability Components for an Index of Health." *Vital and Health Statistics.* Series 2, No. 42, July.

Swisher, I. G. 1970. "Family Income of the Disabled." *Social Security Survey of the Disabled: 1966.* Report No. 13, Social Security Administration, October.

The Urban Institute. 1979. "Health Status and Use of Medical Services." *Health Policy and the Elderly Series.* Washington, D.C.: Government Printing Office.

U.S. Department of Health, Education and Welfare. 1977. *A Concurrent Validational Study of NCHS General Well-Being Schedule.* DHEW Pub. No. (HRA) 78-1347. Hyattsville, Md.: Public Health Service.

Verbrugge, L. 1979. "Females and Illness: Recent Trends in Sex Differences in the United States." *Journal of Health and Social Behavior.* 17:387-403.

Verbrugge, L. 1981. "Sex Differences in Longevity and Health of Older People." in *Leading Edges: Recent Developments in Social and Psychological Aging.* Bethesda, Md.: National Institute on Aging.

Wan, T. T. H. 1972. "Social Differentials in Selected Work Limiting Chronic Conditions." *Journal of Chronic Diseases* 25:365-374.

———— 1974. "Correlates & Consequences of Severe Disabilities." *Journal of Occupational Medicine* 16:234-244.

———— 1975. "Age and Severity of Disability." *Review of Public Data Use.* 3:29-32.

———— 1976. "Predicting Self-Assessed Health Status: A Multivariate Approach." *Health Services Research* 11:466-477.

———— 1979. "Impacts of Major Life Change Events on Gerontological Health: A Longitudinal Study." Paper presented at the annual meeting of the Gerontological Society, Nov. 4-7, New York.

Wilder, C. S. 1972. "Time Loss from Work Among the Currently Employed Population." *Vital and Health Statistics.* Series 10, No. 71, April.

6

Activities
of the Elderly

In this chapter, we cover three specific areas of activities in which the elderly may take part: voter registration, volunteerism, and leisure activities. These three areas of activity were chosen to give a selective picture of the elderly's interest in participating in political affairs, helping in their community, and filling their leisure time. Certainly, these three areas do not exhaust the list of activities in which older persons engage. However, information on these areas was readily obtainable and is useful to program planners. As we indicated in chapter 1, doing needs assessment often requires a compromise between a desire for information and the costs involved in obtaining that information. The information contained in this chapter is particularly relevant to planners of recreational programs for the elderly who need to know what types of activities the elderly engage in and to those involved in programs that attempt to put to use the talents of older persons through volunteer activities.

RELATED RESEARCH

There has been much research concerning the relationship of activity to life satisfaction in old age. Disengagement theorists have generally proposed that activity is inversely associated with well-being (Cumming & Henry, 1961). According to this theory, the elderly who reduce their involvement in the social world around them by gradually relinquishing their social roles are happier than those who attempt to maintain these roles in old age. While disengagement theory has generated much research on the relationship between activity and psychological well-being, most research has not supported the hypothesized relationship. Instead, the literature tends to support the "activity theory," which asserts that activity is positively associated with well-being. Substantial research has shown that those who continue with their recreational and social activities have higher morale than those who do not (Lemon, Bengston & Peterson, 1972; Anderson, 1967; Kutner, 1956; Zborowski & Eyde, 1962; Maddox, 1965). There have been some qualifications in the literature of the proposed relationship between activity and well-being. For instance, there is reason to believe that the type of activity is more relevant to well-being than activity in general (Lemon, Bengston & Peterson, 1972). Moreover, Cutler (1973) argues that the relationship between activity and life satisfaction is an artifact of health and socioeconomic status. His study found that individuals who choose to participate in activities are healthier and have higher socioeconomic status. Further, Hoppa and Roberts (1974) note that level of activity is relative to the activity needs of the individual. While persons with higher levels of participation needs are adversely affected by low levels of participation, persons with low level participation needs are not adversely affected by few opportunities for participation.

Voting and Volunteerism: An Overview

Looking at voter registration we know that while the elderly constitute 17% of all registered voters nationally (U.S. Department of Commerce, Bureau of the Census, 1978), around 90% of those sixty-five and over are registered to vote (U.S. Department of Commerce, Bureau of the Census, 1975). Although they do not participate in voting at the same rate as middle-aged voters, they are more politically active than younger age groups (Crandall, 1980, p. 466).

It has been estimated that 22% of persons 65 and over engage in volunteer work (Crandall, 1980, p. 367). This is a significantly lower proportion than those 18 to 64 years of age (35%). There is, however, an additional 4% to 10% of the elderly who would like to do volunteer work. Participation in volunteer work by the elderly has been associated with those with higher incomes, more education, being white, and being employed (Harris & Associates, Inc., 1975).

Doing volunteer work can be very important to older persons at a time in their life when they are experiencing major role losses through retirement and departure of children from the household (Foner, 1972, p. 451). Many are able to draw upon skills learned through a lifetime of experience and can make a meaningful contribution to the community. This ability to contribute in a meaningful way can help establish and maintain a feeling of selfworth and a satisfactory level of prestige in the community (Crandall, 1980, p. 368).

FINDINGS FROM THE SNAP DATA

Voter Registration

Over three-quarters of the SNAP population stated they were registered voters. Table 6.1* gives the distribution of voter registration by sociodemographic characteristics. When we look at the variation for voter registration by service area, we find significant differences. Approximately three-quarters of the sample were registered to vote, with the North area having the highest rate of voter registration (87.7%) and the Southeast having the lowest (69.7%). The difference between these two areas is what we might expect based on the socioeconomic differences we have already reported. Men were more likely to be registered to vote than women, and married persons much more than other marital groups. It has been found that men in both age categories vote more frequently than women (Crandall, 1980, p. 446). Foner (1972) suggests women often stop voting when they are widowed because this was an activity they usually did with their husbands. Slightly more retired persons were registered than those still working. There was no variation in percent registered to vote associated with living arrangement.

Volunteerism

When questioned about their participation in volunteer work (Table 6.2), the SNAP population was below the average for other study populations of elderly (Crandall, 1980). However, in their desire to engage in volunteer work, they were above the average (Table 6.3).

There were some variations among service areas in the proportion involved in volunteer work. The North had the highest rate (19.6%), while the Southeast had the lowest rate (10.9%) (Table 6.2). Although the Southeast had the fewest persons engaged in volunteer work, it was the area with the highest percentage of those stating they would like to do volunteer work (Table 6.3). Since higher levels of education and income have been associated with doing volunteer work, the variation between the North and Southeast is not unexpected. The North has been shown as an area with a better educated and a more affluent elderly population, while the Southeast reported the lowest levels of education and economic security.

As might be expected, younger males and females (60–74 years) were more likely to do volunteer work than their older counterparts (Table 6.2).

---

*Tables appear in Appendix D.

Separated and divorced persons stand out as the group least likely to do volunteer work of all the categories in the table (Table 6.2). However, they showed the most interest in becoming active in volunteer work (21.3%) (Table 6.3). There was little variation by living arrangement or retirement status, although those not retired did show slightly more interest in becoming involved in volunteer work than those retired. If the results of Table 6.3 are a true reflection of interest, there is a significant pool of the aged available for volunteer work. This matter certainly deserves some attention.

Leisure Activities

To ascertain how the elderly spend their leisure time, SNAP participants were read a list of eight activities and asked how often they engaged in each of them: often, sometimes, or never. These activities included reading; going out to the movies, plays, concerts, or club meetings; going for walks; playing cards; gardening; working on a hobby; or playing sports. For clarity and simplicity of presentation only those who cited that they participated in the activity "often" were included in Table 6.4. The activity cited as often enjoyed in spare time was reading magazines or books (65.5%), followed by gardening (44.5%), and working on a hobby (42.6%). The activities least frequently cited as often enjoyed in spare time were going to movies, plays, or concerts (5.1%) and playing sports (7.7%).

As would be expected, younger males (60–74 years) were most likely to participate in playing sports while females were more likely to enjoy working on a hobby. Younger males and females (60–74 years) gardened more than older males and females (≥75 years). Younger males and females (60–74 years) were also more likely to go out to the movies and concerts than their older counterparts. Younger women (60–74 years) participated in meetings and enjoyed card playing more than older groups. The percent reporting most often participating in each activity dropped with advancing age for both males and females.

Considering marital status, those persons separated/divorced more often enjoyed such solitary activites as reading, going out to movies, and going for walks. Widowed persons preferred club meetings and working on hobbies as a leisure activity more than other marital groups. Married persons enjoyed gardening and playing sports.

There was not much variation between retired and not retired or those living alone or with others in choosing activities. Surprisingly, working persons participated in a hobby more frequently than retired persons. Also, persons living alone enjoyed going to meetings and working on hobbies more than persons living with others.

Variations between service areas is also included in Table 6.4. Persons in the Northwest more often enjoyed going to movies, plays, concerts, club meetings, and playing sports than other areas of the county. The Northeast indicated a preference for gardening and working on hobbies.

SUMMARY

The majority (78.3%) of the SNAP population are registered voters. A higher proportion of males and married persons are registered than other groups. Only a small percentage of the elderly are engaged in volunteer work (15.7%), but again, as many reported a desire to be a volunteer (15.8%). The willingness to participate in volunteer work demonstrated by the SNAP population could provide a ready resource for service of volunteer workers.

Most appeared to spend their leisure time in activities that can be done alone such as reading (65.5%), gardening (44.5%), or work on hobbies (42.6%). Activities least enjoyed in spare time were those that were expensive, namely, going to the movies, plays, or concerts (5.1%) and those that required physical stamina such as playing sports (7.7%).

REFERENCES

Anderson, N.E. 1967. "Effects of Institutionalization on Self-Esteem." *Journal of Gerontology* 22:313–317.

Crandall, R.C. 1980. *Gerontology. A Behavioral Science Approach.* Reading, Mass.: Addison-Wesley.

Cumming, E. and W.E. Henry. 1961. *Growing Old.* New York: Basic Books.

Cutler, S. 1973. "Volunteer Association Participation and Life Satisfaction: A Cautionary Research Note." *Journal of Gerontology* 28:96–100.

Foner, A. 1972. "The Polity." in *Aging and Society, Vol. 3: A Sociology of Stratification.* edited by M.W. Riley, M. Johnson, and A. Foner. New York: Russell Sage Foundation.

Harris, L. and Associates, Inc. 1975. *The Myth and Reality of Aging in America.* Washington, D.C.: National Council on Aging, Inc.

Hoppa, M.E. and G.D. Roberts. 1974. "Implications of the Activity Factor." *The Gerontologist* 14:331–335.

Kutner, B. et al. 1956. *Five Hundred Over Sixty.* New York: Russell Sage Foundation.

Lemon, B., B. Bengston, and J. Peterson. 1972. "An Exploration of the Activity Theory of Aging: Activity Types and Life Satisfaction Among In-Movers to a Retirement Community." *Journal of Gerontology* 27:511–523.

Maddox, G. 1965. "Fact and Artifact: Evidence Bearing on Disengagement Theory from the Duke Geriatrics Project." *Human Development* 8:117–130.

U.S. Department of Commerce, Bureau of the Census. 1975. "Voter Participation in November, 1974." *Current Population Reports*. Washington, D.C.: Government Printing Office.

————1978. *Statistical Abstracts of the United States*. Washington, D.C.: Government Printing Office.

Zborowski, M. and L.E. Eyde. 1962. "Aging and Social Participation." *Journal of Gerontology* 17:424–430.

7

Older Peoples'
Perceptions
of Service Needs

In the introductory chapter, the general concept of need was discussed, which included dietary, housing, medical, disability, transportation, and social needs. Need is a primary determinant of which services should be provided. In the preceding three chapters on physical, psychological, and social well-being, we have attempted to draw a general picture of the dimensions of service needs reported by the sample population. In this chapter, the perceived health and social service needs of older people are specifically addressed. We identify the differentials in perceived and unmet service needs and the effects of social factors on service needs.

With several studies suggesting that elderly consumers of services and professional providers do not always agree on service priorities (Keith, 1975; Riesenfeld et al., 1972), it was felt that this examination of consumer viewpoint would prove useful in pinpointing what potential recipients of services feel to be their service priorities.

The eighteen specific service needs used in this study are divided into three broad categories: "Personal Care Needs;" "Health Care Needs;" and "Miscellaneous Needs;" which included recreation, housing, employment, nutrition, and information and referral needs. Two separate analyses were performed for the purpose of (1) revealing the differentials in perceived needs for specific services and (2) determining the relative importance of selective sociodemographic factors that could affect the variation in perception of service needs by using Multiple Classification Analysis (MCA).[1]

---

[1]For those unfamiliar with Multiple Classification Analysis (MCA), MCA is an analytic technique that examines the effect of a predictor variable on a dependent variable when the predictor is taken by itself, and also examines the predictor's effect after adjustments are made for intercorrelations with other predictors (Andrews, Morgan & Sonquist, 1967). For a complete description of Multiple Classification Analysis and guidelines for interpreting MCA results, the authors suggest that the reader carefully examine Appendix C before continuing with this chapter.

Because the availability of transportation affects the ability of the elderly to use services they need, transportation is discussed in a separate subsection of this chapter.

FINDINGS FROM THE SNAP DATA

Social Differentials in Perceived
Service Needs

Persons who reported a need, whether they were having this need met or not, were grouped under perceived need (Tables 7.1 through 7.4*). The most often reported needs were assistance for home repairs and yard work (25.1%); information and referral services (19.8%); participation in planned and organized social, recreational, or group activities (15.2%); assistance with routine housework (13.3%); and someone to check on them five times a week (12.4%). The least reported need was for health care, where the responses were consistently low for all six needs, ranging from 5.1% down to 2.1%. It is likely that the low reporting of need for health care is due to the small proportion of respondents in the study who reported having functional limitations or chronic illnesses.

Comparing perceived need by service area (Table 7.1), the North appeared to be consistently below the sample average on reported needs while the Southeast was above the average. This sharp contrast between the North and Southeast areas has been noted throughout the study and is undoubtedly related to the difference in income and education levels found in these areas. The Southeast expressed greater than average need in the areas of counseling for personal or family problems, help with cost of medication, participation in planned activities, assistance in finding a job, and information and referral services. The Northeast showed the most need for assistance with home repairs or yard work (32.9%) compared to the other areas.

The tables portraying the responses by age (Table 7.3), retirement status, living arrangement (Table 7.4), and marital status (Table 7.5) generally show the same pattern found for the study population as a whole. There are, however, some interesting variations in these tables. The older group more often desires continuous care than their younger counterparts (Table 7.2). Older females(≥ 75 years), probably living alone, more often reported a need to have someone make frequent checks and assist with housework, while younger males (60–74 years) expressed greater needs for participation in planned activities than older men and women (≥ 75 years). Generally, it appears that the number of perceived needs increases with age.

---

*Tables appear in Appendix D.

When considering living arrangement (Table 7.3), there is very little variation except in the need to have someone check on them frequently and to help them with home repairs or yard work. As would be expected, persons living alone (24.6%) expressed a far greater need for someone to check on them five times a week than did those living with others (8.1%). Those living alone also expressed a greater need for assistance with yard work.

Whether a respondent was retired or working did not appear to have much effect on perceived need (Table 7.3). However, there were differences noted by marital status. More needs were expressed by those who were separated/divorced or widowed (Table 7.4). This was particularly true in the area of health care needs for the separated/divorced persons. This group expressed more need for help in paying for medication, having physical therapy, having status reviewed by doctor or social worker, and receiving help with basic personal skills than other marital groups. In addition, those separated and divorced also showed a disproportionately higher percentage expressing a need for information and referral services (I&R) and information about home security or crime preventive methods. Separated/divorced and widowed persons felt a need for someone to check on them frequently. Widowed persons expressed need for assistance with yard and routine housework. They also felt a need for participation in planned activities. A better understanding of the relationship between these perceived needs and socioeconomic and demographic variables is found by the statistical analysis that follows.

Relative Importance of Social Factors Affecting Perceived Service Needs

Multiple Classification Analysis (MCA) is an analytic technique that examines the effect of a predictor variable on a dependent variable when the predictor is taken by itself and also examines the predictor's effect after adjustments are made for intercorrelations with other predictors (Andrews, Morgan & Sonquist, 1967). First, we analyzed the five needs listed in the category *personal care needs* (Table 7.5) and found that poverty status was the most important variable in explaining four of the five personal care needs—need for counseling, constant care, regular visits, and legal assistance. Persons were categorized as "poor" if they reported that the amount of money they had was not adequate to take care of their basic needs. Poverty was the only significant variable in explaining the need for counseling and legal assistance. Persons most likely to need constant care were older males and females ($\geq$ 75 years), those living with others, and those classified as poor. On the other hand, those who need someone to make regular visits were living alone and poor. Service areas, age and sex, and marital status were significant in explaining perceived need for homemaker service. This need was more often reported by widowed persons, older males and females ($\geq$ 75 years), and persons living in the Northwest.

When examining *perceived health care needs* (Table 7.6), poverty status, again, was the most important predictor variable, and it was significant for all six of the needs listed. In all cases, being "poor" increased the percentage reporting a need. Older females, widowed persons, persons living with others, as well as poor respondents expressed the most need for ADL assistance, while younger females (60–74 years) and the widowed demonstrated greater need for help with basic skills. Along with "poor," older females ($\geq$ 75 years) and persons living in the Northwest and Southeast areas expressed greater frequencies of need for nursing care. Persons living in the Southeast had the most difficulty with the purchase of medication.

Under *perceived miscellaneous service needs*, an overall view of Table 7.7 shows that the poor and the widowed had higher percentage of needs in this category. Help in finding a job was significantly related to service area, age and sex, marital status, and living arrangement. Persons living in the Southeast, older males ($\geq$ 75 years), widowed persons, and persons living with others were more likely to need help in finding a job. Persons who expressed a need for participation in recreational activities were younger females (60–74 years), widowed persons, and those who regarded themselves as poor. Persons living in the Southeast area, separated/divorced, and "poor" persons had the highest proportion reporting a need for assistance in locating housing. Help with home repairs was a need most expressed by those living in the Northwest and by widowed persons. Marital status and poverty were significant in explaining perceived need for help with meal preparation and I&R services. The "poor," separated/divorced, and widowed had comparatively higher proportions reporting a need for these two services.

Social Differentials in Perceived Unmet Needs

The concept unmet needs implies differences between the amount of service needed and the amount of services actually received (Carr & Wolfe, 1979). Inconsistencies between service needed and service used may occur for different reasons. It may be that certain services are not provided in the community and are, therefore, not available to the client. Such barriers as cost or lack of transportation may exist, which prevent the client from using services that are available. It is also possible that the service is available, but if community members are unaware of the service they obviously will not use it.

The present study is limited by our inability to define specifically the cause of unmet need in our study population. In this study, unmet needs are operationally defined as service needs that the respondents perceive themselves to have but which they report are not presently being met. Our findings from the SNAP data indicate the highest rates of unmet need were reported for I&R services (18.3%) and participation in planned group activities (10.4%). In the case of need for I&R services, approximately the same level of perceived need (19.8%) and unmet need (18.3%) was reported. This indicates that very little of this need is being met by existing services.

Health care needs had the lowest reporting of perceived needs, but the lowest percentages of reported unmet needs were for assistance in finding a job and personal care. This would indicate that help in providing personal care and in finding jobs are being met largely by existing programs or through informal arrangements.

The Southeast (Table 7.8) consistently was above average in reporting unmet needs, particularly in such matters as health care, participation in planned group activities, and assistance in finding housing. The elderly in this service area should be a target for developing new initiatives or for providing appropriate information on the existing programs. The Northwest ranked second to the Southeast area in the reported unmet needs. This was especially true for assistance with home repairs or yard work and for someone to make regular checks. On the other hand, the North (Table 7.8) appeared to have the lowest reporting of unmet needs. This may be because the individuals in this area are able to meet their own needs through informal means or personal initiative, which is reasonable to expect in a relatively well-educated and affluent population.

Considering unmet needs by age and sex (Table 7.9), females appear to have higher unmet needs in planned group activities and assistance with home repairs or yard work. Older females ($\geq$ 75 years) had an above-average proportion reporting the unmet need for someone to check on them five times a week. Comparatively few younger men (60–74 years) reported unmet needs.

Persons who are separated/divorced or widowed (Table 7.10) have a higher proportion reporting unmet needs than other marital groups, which is consistent with our other findings. Those who are separated/divorced had a disproportionately larger proportion reporting the unmet needs for I&R services, help in finding a place to live, and information about home security or crime.

There was very little variation between the proportions reporting unmet needs by retirement status (Table 7.11). Persons living alone had a higher proportion reporting the unmet needs of assistance with routine housework and assistance with home repairs or yard work than persons living with others.

Relative Importance of Factors Affecting Perceived Unmet Needs

Table 7.12 shows the MCA of *perceived unmet personal care needs*. Poverty, again, was the most important predictor variable. It was significantly related to three of the five unmet personal care needs—counseling, constant care, and legal assistance. Being "poor" increased the proportion reporting perceived unmet needs. Persons who report that their "constant care" needs are unmet were likely to be older females (≥ 75 years). Age and sex differences produced little difference in reporting the unmet need for regular visits but this unmet need varied significantly by service area. Persons who reported this unmet need most often were more likely to live in the Northwest. Persons with the highest proportion reporting unmet homemaker needs were more likely to live in the Southwest and to live alone.

Poverty was significantly related to all six perceived *unmet health care needs* (Table 7.13). Being "poor" is associated with increased perceived unmet health care needs. The higher proportions of persons who reported the unmet need of learning basic skills also tended to be the young-old (60–74 years) and widowed persons. Elderly living in the Southeast had more reporting of unmet needs for assistance in paying for medicine and for nursing care than those living in other service areas.

Poverty was significantly related to five of the seven *miscellaneous perceived unmet needs* (Table 7.14) in the Multiple Classification Analysis. These were participation in activities, assistance locating housing, help with home repairs, help with meal preparation, and I&R services. Respondents who were "poor" more frequently reported perceived unmet needs in all five of these categories.

Elderly with unmet needs for participation in group activities were likely to be younger women (60–74 years) and the widowed. Persons with the highest proportion reporting unmet needs in locating housing tended to live in the Southeast and to be separated/divorced. Those who needed help with home repairs very often lived alone. Having high proportions of unmet needs for I&R service was related to living in the Southwest or Southeast and being separated/divorced. Levels of reported perceived unmet needs in help finding a job and crime prevention information were not significantly related to any of the sociodemographic variables.

Assessment of Transportation Use and Needs

In modern society, the ability to get around has become highly dependent on mechanized transportation. Few persons live within walking distance of their place of employment, doctor, church, or shopping centers. In this era of emphasis and interest on the problems of the aging, lack of adequate transportation has been identified as a significant barrier to the satisfaction of the needs of large segments of the elderly population (White House Conference on Aging, 1971).

Markovitz (1971) defines mobility as "access to opportunities." It is apparent that for the elderly to enjoy a life style that encompasses many and varied activities, availability of transportation and the ability to use this transportation are fundamental issues. Ability to get around has been shown to affect the life satisfaction of the elderly. In a study of noninstitutionalized older adults, Cutler (1976) found the highest proportions of older persons with low life-satisfaction were those who did not have personal transportation available to them and who lived greater distances from the centralized resources, facilities, and services of the community.

In assessing the transportation needs of Baltimore County's elderly population, respondents were questioned concerning their problems with transportation, their special needs, and their use of public and private transportation. When asked whether lack of transportation caused them problems in getting around, about 13% stated it did (Table 7.15). This is considerably lower than has been reported in other research. In studies of the elderly in Boston (Branch, 1978) and Philadelphia (Stirner, 1978), about 30% were found to have transportation problems. Possible reasons for the differences between these studies and ours will be discussed later in this section.

Social Differentials in Transportation Barriers: Service areas showed variation in the reporting of having transportation problems (Table 7.15). The Southeast had the largest proportion with transportation problems (16.7%) and the Northwest was an area with the least (8.6%). There were considerable differences by sex, with more females (≥ 75 years) having this difficulty (21.3%). When taking into account marital status, married persons had the smallest proportion (7.9%), followed by widowed (19.4%) (Table 7.16), and separated/divorced persons had the largest proportion (25.5%). There was very little variation between retired and working persons. Persons living alone, however, were more apt to report they had a problem with transportation (18.2%) than those living with others (11.1%) (Table 7.16).

When questioned concerning the availability of a car in the household, 80.4% (Table 7.17) gave a positive response and 70.6% stated they drove the car occasionally or frequently (Table 7.19). When compared to the previously mentioned studies, 47% of the Boston (Branch, 1978) population and only 24% of the Philadelphia sample (Stirner, 1978) named the car as a primary source of transportation. Also, only 27% of the Boston study and 11% of the people in the Philadelphia study drove themselves. The higher rate of car use by persons living in the suburbs when compared to city dwellers is understandable, because public transportation is less available in the suburbs than in the cities. The greater dependence on public transportation by the elderly in these large cities studied is probably the major source of the significant difference in reporting transportation problems when compared to the SNAP population. Also, it is estimated that only one-half of those 65 years and over own and operate automobiles (Crandall, 1980, p. 292). Therefore, the higher proportion of Baltimore County elderly who owned and operated automobiles, giving them flexible and convenient transportation, probably explains the lower reporting of transportation problems in our study.

Persons living in the North area were most likely to have a car in the household (92.9%), and persons living the the Southwest were the least likely (75.6%) (Table 7.17). Younger males (60–74 years), married persons, retired persons, and elderly living with others most often reported the availability of a car (Table 7.18). Older females (≥ 75 years), persons separated/divorced, retired persons, and elderly living alone were least likely to have a car available in the household. Although 80% of the study population had an automobile available, one-quarter stated they never drove the car (Table 7.19). The Northwest (54.5%) and North (58.3%) areas showed the highest reporting of frequently using a car. This is to be expected, since these service areas also had the highest proportion of households with cars (Table 7.17).

Younger males (60–74 years) were most likely to use their car frequently (68.9%), while older females (≥ 75 years) most often said they never drove a car (Table 7.20). Separated/divorced elderly most often said they frequently drove a car, while the widowed much more often said they never drove. Elderly living alone drove a car more often than persons living with others. There was no notable variation in car use between retired and nonretired persons.

When asked, "On the average, how many round trips do you make each week for shopping, visiting, work, or any other reason?", the range was from 0 to 52, the mean number of trips for the whole sample was 4.3, and the median was 3.4. The majority of the study population (86%) made between one and nine trips per week (Table 7.21). Only 6% were found to be housebound or making no trips outside the home. The Southeast area appeared to have the highest percentage with three or fewer trips per week (59%), while the North area had the lowest percentage (38%). It is significant that in the North only 1.8% reported that they made no trips out of the house (Table 7.17).

Persons who were more likely to be housebound are older females ($\geq$ 75 years), widowed, and persons living with others (Table 22). The fact that 8.3% of persons who have jobs make no trips outside of the home must logically be attributed to recording error on the part of the interviewer or some type of coding error that placed persons not answering the question into this category. Persons making the most frequent trips outside the home were most likely to be younger males (60–74 years), married persons, working persons, and persons living with others.

Tables 7.23 and 7.24 show the means of transportation used by the elderly to go shopping, to visit the doctor, and to visit friends, etc. It must be understood that the respondents probably use multiple means of transportation and were allowed to answer "yes" to any or all of the suggested modes. The largest proportions either drive themselves (58%) or are driven by others (56.9%) (Table 7.23). Smaller proportions walk (22.3%), ride the bus (22.8%), or take a taxi (14%). Only a very small percentage use Senioride or other public agency transportation (3.4%).

Persons in the Southwest area more often cited walking, taking a taxi, taking the bus, and being driven by others as means of transportation compared with the other areas (Table 7.23). They also more often cited using Senioride or other public agency transportation, while persons in the Northwest more often said they drove themselves. Bus use was lowest in the Southeast, Northeast, and Northwest areas. Again, it must be noted that respondents were able to answer "yes" to any or all of the means of transportation. Some persons may have answered "yes" to all means of transportation, even those they seldom used, while others may have answered "yes" to only those they used frequently.

Older females ($\geq$ 75 years) were more likely to be driven by others, to take a taxi, to use the bus or use Senioride than other females or males (Table 7.24). Females as a group used the bus more often than males. Younger males (60–74 years) were the group most likely to drive themselves. Married persons drove themselves more frequently than other marital groups, while widowed persons were the group most likely to be driven by others. Separated/divorced persons cited public transportation (taxi, Senioride, bus) more frequently as means of getting around.

Tables 7.25 through 7.29 deal with the use of bus service by the study population. Tables 7.25 and 7.26 include only those persons who answered "yes" to using the bus as a means of getting around. Of those persons who said they used the bus, 16.3% said they could get all the places they wanted to go on the bus, 21.2% most, 18.8% some, 26.6% a few, 14.9% none, and 2.2% did not know (Table 7.25). Only persons who had answered "yes" to using the bus were supposed to be asked this question, but by the large percentages under the "none" category it would appear that the interviewers may have also included some persons who answered "no" to this question. This is verified by the differences in numbers responding to the two questions—270 cited using the bus, while 368 answered the question on the numbers of places the bus would take them.

The elderly in the Southwest most often said they could get to all or most of the places they wanted to go by bus (Table 7.25). The Southwest population had also cited the bus as a means of getting around more frequently than other areas (Table 7.23). Bus users in the North and Northeast had the most difficulty in getting where they wanted to go. Table 7.26 gives a more detailed breakdown of this data by age, sex, marital status, retirement status, and living arrangement.

Table 7.27 gives a detailed breakdown of why persons do not use bus service. Some of these reasons for not using the bus were combined in later tables to facilitate analysis. The following reasons were combined to form a category called general dissatisfaction with the bus service: does not go where I want to go; costs too much; buses do not run often enough; seats are not available, seats are not comfortable; routes and schedules are difficult; bus stops are not safe; and there are no protected areas to wait for the bus.

Tables 7.28 and 7.29 consider only those persons who do not use bus service. The North area has disproportionately more persons who felt the bus was not convenient or the bus stops were too far away, 45.4% compared with 31.7% for the total sample (Table 7.28). Northeast area sample expressed the highest rate of dislike or lack of desire to ride the bus, 35.3% compared with 19.3% for the total sample. Those in the Southwest were most likely to give "other" reasons for not using bus service. The category "other" probably includes those persons who do not use bus service because of physical limitations or disability. Table 7.29 gives a more detailed breakdown of those data by age and sex, marital status, retirement status, and living arrangement.

When questioned about needs for additional transportation, only a small percentage of the total sample expressed a need for additional services for any given activity. Table 7.30 shows the most expressed need was for help in getting to the doctor, dentist, or clinic (10.2%). This was followed by the need of transportation to do shopping (8.1%). The least needs for additional transportation were for getting to work and going to educational programs. The Northwest and Southeast consistently expressed higher levels of need for multiple reasons, while the North and Northeast consistently expressed lower levels of need (Table 7.30).

Table 7.31 gives a more detailed breakdown of the transportation needs by age and sex, marital status, retirement status, and living arrangement. Females, especially older females ($\geq$ 75 years), consistently showed higher proportions reporting needs for multiple reasons as compared to males. This concurs with the fact that males more often drive themselves (Table 7.24), while females are more dependent on public transportation or being driven by others. Separated/divorced and widowed persons also expressed more transportation needs than married persons. These data agree with the data in Table 7.16, which gives a similar breakdown on the question "Do you have trouble getting around?"

Transportation and Functional Disabilities: A brief summary of Table 7.32 indicates the extent to which physical functional limitations (physical, mobility, and role limitations) influence perception of transportation options. As shown, persons with increasing numbers of limitations in functioning are more likely to report transportation difficulties and are less likely to drive a car frequently. The small number of respondents with eleven or more disabilities (N=3) precludes any valid assessment of response. Although it would appear that functional losses at this level may prohibit many activities requiring transportation, a larger number would be necessary to test this assumption. Persons with increasing levels of disability are also most likely to report that they need additional transportation for shopping, doctor and dental visits, and visiting friends. For example, 27.8% of those with five to seven disabilities said they needed additional transportation to the doctor or dentist as compared with 6.7% of those with no limitations and 10.8% of those with just one.

Difficulty with transportation, when considered independently, was found to be associated with fewer physician visits. However, when predisposing and need factors were controlled, difficulty in getting transportation was not significant.[1] Rate of hospitalization also was higher for respondents who had trouble getting transportation. This could be interpreted in several ways. First, because of transportation difficulties the individual may not have gone to the doctor in the early stages of the illness when treatment could be provided on an outpatient basis. It is also possible that physicians initiate hospitalization because the patient has difficulty getting to and from offices or clinics to receive services. Few doctors are willing to make housecalls. It is important to note that "transportation barriers," as an independent enabling variable, was not found to be significantly related to the variation in use of social service.[2]

In conclusion, the analysis of the relationship between transportation barriers and use of services reveals that difficulty in getting transportation

---

[1]Detailed presentation of these findings may be found in Tables 8.2, 8.5, 8.6, and 8.10 in Appendix D.
[2]Detailed presentation of these findings may be found in Table 9.1 in Appendix D.

may impede the use of health services, but that they have a negligible effect on the use of social service programs. A more detailed explanation of the effects of these and other factors affecting use of medical, health, and social services is presented in chapters 8 and 9.

SUMMARY

Considering eighteen specific needs grouped into personal needs, health-care needs and miscellaneous needs, the SNAP population was found to have the highest perceived needs and unmet needs for information and referral services, participation in planned group activities, and assistance with home repairs or yard work. Assistance with home repairs was the greatest perceived need, while need for information and referral services was the most frequently mentioned unmet need.

The following characteristics were found to be associated with unmet needs:

1. Persons living in the Southeast appeared to have the most unmet needs.
2. Being "poor" was significantly related to increased perceived unmet needs.
3. Persons who were separated/divorced or widowed appeared to have more unmet needs than other marital groups.

Compared to other large population studies, Baltimore County elderly did not appear to have too much trouble getting around. Only 13% cited lack of transportation as being a problem in getting around. This is probably due to the large proportion (80.4%) having an automobile available in the household. Most respondents were able to drive themselves, at least occasionally. Therefore, the above proportion of elderly owning and operating automobiles probably explains the low rate of reporting the existence of transportation problems.

Those with the greatest difficulty with transportation were characterized as follows:

1. persons living in the Southeast area;
2. older females (≥ 75 years);
3. persons separated or divorced;
4. persons living alone; and
5. persons with limitations in physical functioning.

REFERENCES

Andrews, F., J. Morgan, and J. Sonquist. 1967. *Multiple Classification Analysis.* Ann Arbor: University of Michigan Institute for Social Research.

Branch, L. G. 1978. *Boston Elders: A Survey of Needs.* 1978. City of Boston Commission on Affairs of the Elderly/Area Agency on Aging, Region VI. Boston: Center for Survey Research, a facility of the University of Massachusetts, The Joint Center for Urban Studies of M.I.T, Harvard University, and the Boston Urban Observatory of the University of Massachusetts.

Carr, W. and S. Wolfe. 1979. "Unmet Needs as Sociomedical Indicators." Pp. 33–46 in *Socio-medical Health Indicators*, edited by J. Elinson and A. Siegmann. Farmingdale, N.Y.: Baywood.

Crandall, Richard C. 1980. "The Environments of the Aged." Pp. 279–305 in *Gerontology: A Behaviorial Science Approach*, edited by R. C. Crandall. Reading, Mass.: Addison-Wesley.

Cutler, Stephen J. 1976. "The Availability of Personal Transportation, Residential Location, Life Satisfaction Among the Aged." Pp. 284–294 in *Contemporary Social Gerontology*, edited by B. C. Bell and E. Palmore. Springfield, Ill.: Thomas.

Keith, Pat. 1975. "Evaluation of Services for the Aged by Professionals and the Elderly." *Social Service Review* 49:271–278.

Markovitz, Joni K. 1971. "Transportation Needs of the Elderly." *Traffic Quarterly* 25(2):237–253.

Riesenfeld, M. J. et al. 1972. "Perceptions of Public Service Needs: The Urban Elderly and the Public Agency." *The Gerontologist* 12:185–190.

Stirner, F. W. 1978. "The Transportation Needs of the Elderly in a Large Urban Environment." *The Gerontologist* 18:207–211.

White House Conference on Aging. 1971. *Report of the Delegates from the Conference Sections and Special Concerns Sessions.* Washington, D.C.: White House Conference on Aging.

8

Use of Health Services by the Elderly: Social Differentials and Determinants

In the last chapter, we discussed the perceived service needs of the elderly and the characteristics of persons who expressed specific service needs. In the following two chapters on health and use of social services, we will tie the concept of *need* to the actual *use* of these services. In the medical context, need may be defined as "some disturbance in health or well-being" (Donabedian, 1973). As Donabedian (1973) notes, "The medical care system, like all other stable institutions, exists to meet some need." It can be assumed that need influences the use of medical services along many dimensions. Symptoms may cause a person to seek the care of a primary physician, referral to a specialist, hospitalization, or even institutionalization.

Examinations of health care use have focused upon the concept of need for service and have given rise to the related concept of unmet need, that is, needs for which services are unavailable. Perceptions of unmet need were discussed in the preceding chapter.

Although primary importance in promoting the use of health services has been attributed to such a need as a chronic illness, both the sociocultural characteristics of those in need and the organizational factors of the health care delivery system may also affect the use of services directly or indirectly through their effects on peoples' perception of needs and their willingness to take action based upon these needs. In this and the next chapter, we develop a model of service use based upon previous research. This model allows us to measure the relative influence of social and demographic variables on whether or not individuals are likely to use the services of physicians and dentists, seek hospitalization, and request institutionalization.

RELATED RESEARCH

In addition to reported health status, models for predicting the use of health services have incorporated both individual and social structural (contextual) variables. As Andersen and Aday (1978) note, utilization is influenced both by characteristics of the population and by such characteristics of the health care delivery system as its resources and organization. Individual variables include economic, sociodemographic, geographic, and social-psychological characteristics. The social-psychological variables encompass, primarily, peoples' motivation to seek care, their perception of needs, and their knowledge about available programs and services (McKinlay, 1972).

Analysis of the use of health care services implies not only use of services but also access to these services and the overall equity of service distribution. The term access implies (1) the availability of health facilities and personnel, (2) the costs of services, (3) the use of services, and (4) whether services are used to the extent they are needed (Andersen & Aday, 1978).

A multivariate approach has been widely applied in health care research on the use of services (Berki & Kobashigawa, 1976; Galvin & Fan, 1975; Andersen & Aday, 1978; Andersen & Newman, 1973; Wan & Soifer, 1974). Andersen & Newman (1973) classified determinants that influence the use of services into predisposing, enabling, and need variables. This analytical framework has been employed extensively for organizing sets of variables affecting utilization. In the Andersen and Newman model, predisposing variables include demographic, social-structural, and attitudinal factors concerning belief about health services. Enabling variables include family income, insurance benefits, access to care, and the availability of community services. Both perceived need, which is subjectively evaluated by the client, and needs as evaluated by professionals are considered as indicators of services required in this model.

Ward (1977) expanded upon the number of variables that may influence peoples' use of services within the framework set forth by Andersen and Newman (1973). To the enabling variables, Ward added the family variables of access to transportation and the distance people must travel to obtain services. To the community variables, he added urban/rural residence, means of financing health care in a community, and coordination of services.

The model of predisposing, enabling, and need variables has been applied to the study of the use of physician services, ambulatory care, and dental services to reveal the relative importance of different sets of variables that may influence health care (Wan & Soifer, 1974; Wan & Yates, 1975). In general, studies have found that perceived needs explain more variance

in the use of physician and ambulatory health services than do predisposing and enabling variables (Wan & Soifer, 1974; Berki & Kobashigawa,
1976; Andersen & Aday, 1978).

Looking at ambulatory services, Wan and Soifer (1974) found that
poor health and willingness to seek care for symptoms were the primary
determinants of family use of ambulatory services. Such social-structural
variables as the number of females in the household and the number of
persons over 65 years had less influence on the perception of needs. Similar
findings were reported by Andersen and Aday (1978) and Berki and
Kobashigawa (1976). Since the number of chronic conditions increases with
age, there is an apparent relationship between predisposing and need
variables. Berki and Kobashigawa (1976) have related number of chronic
conditions to use of services. The enabling variable of whether or not there
exists a regular source of care was also observed to contribute to the use
of ambulatory services (Andersen & Aday, 1978; German, Skinner &
Shapiro, 1976; Wan, 1982).

As with ambulatory services, research also demonstrates that illness
explains most of the variance in the number of visits made to physicians
(Wolinsky, 1978; Wan & Soifer, 1974), followed by the predisposing
variables of age and sex. Wan and Soifer noted, nonetheless, the importance of two enabling factors—cost per physician visit and possession of
insurance coverage. Research has, in fact, shown that people with any form
of health insurance, including Medicare and Medicaid, tend to consume
more services than those who have no such insurance (Wan & Soifer, 1974;
McKinley, 1972).

While need variables are highly associated with the use of nondiscre-
tionary health services (health services for which immediate care is required), some enabling and predisposing variables have also been shown
to be important in whether or not people decide to use dental services. The
people most likely to use dental services are females, whites, and persons
with higher incomes, higher levels of education, and urban residence
(Wolinsky, 1976; Andersen & Newman, 1973; Wan & Yates, 1975).

The application of theoretical models that incorporate the above
variables has been criticized to some extent because of the failure of enabling and predisposing variables to account for substantial variation in use
(Wolinsky, 1978). Considering health services in general, need variables
have the clearest direct effects on use, while the effects of predisposing and
enabling factors are indirect and therefore less readily assessed. It has been
suggested either that people are not always logical when they make decisions about whether or not to use services or that the relationship between
predisposing, enabling, and need variables may be interactive rather than
additive.

FINDINGS FROM THE SNAP DATA

In the analysis of the SNAP population, variables were grouped according to the basic framework of Andersen and Newman (1973) as predisposing, enabling, and need variables (see Figure 8.1). The predisposing variables include age, sex, educational level, marital status, retirement status, economic status, and living arrangement. We used perceived economic dependency as a way of defining economic status. Respondents were regarded as being economically dependent if they regarded themselves as being in need of additional financial resources. Enabling variables included social support, knowledge about service programs, insurance coverage, and access to transportation. The availability of social support was ascertained by asking people if they had someone to talk to , someone to trust and confide in, and someone who would give help if they were sick or disabled. Knowledge of programs relates to awareness of available social service programs that are health related, such as home nursing. Perception of access to transportation was presented as degrees of perceived difficulty in getting the transportation needed to use available health services. The several types of insurance coverage examined included Medicaid, Medicare "A" only, Medicare "A" and "B", Blue Cross/Blue Shield, and prepaid health plans.

DETERMINANTS

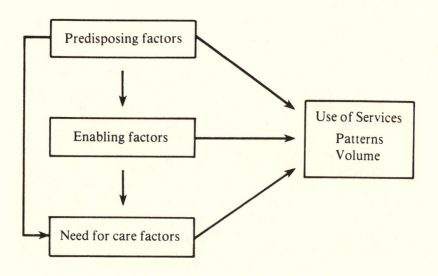

Figure 8.1. The Determinants of Use of Services

The distribution of those respondents having insurance coverage is shown in Table 8.1.* Seventy-three percent of all respondents had Blue Cross/Blue Shield insurance and 45% had Medicare "A" and "B" coverage. Respondents living in the North service area had substantially higher percentages of both Medicare "A" and "B" coverage and Blue Cross/Blue Shield than those in other areas. They were also more likely to belong to a prepaid health plan. While more residents of the Southeast received Medicaid coverage, they were somewhat less likely to belong to Blue Cross/Blue Shield plans.

Need for services was measured by the Activities of Daily Living scale (ADL) (Katz et al., 1963), the Instrumental Activities of Daily Living scale (IADL) (Lawton & Brody, 1969), depression score (Pfeiffer, 1975), and perceived service needs. Measurement of physical and psychological functioning has already been discussed (see chapters 4 and 5). Service needs were measured by subjective expressions of need for services.

Although the enabling and predisposing factors have been shown to be weak in explaining variation in the use of health services, we included these variables in our theoretical model because an understanding of the relationship between these sets of variables is critical to the health planner. In our model, we considered enabling variables to be mitigating factors that would either impede or facilitate decisions to use services. The ease with which such enabling factors as knowledge of programs and services can be changed makes them important targets for formal social intervention.

Our examination of the use of health services by the SNAP population proceeded in two stages. We used regression analysis to explore the relative importance of predisposing, enabling, and need factors in explaining variations in the use of physician and dental services and Multiple Classification Analysis (MCA) in order to further clarify the differences in patterns of use of health services when all but one of the population characteristics were controlled. MCA is an analytical technique that examines both the effect of a predictor variable on a dependent variable when taken by itself and also its effect on the dependent variable after adjustments are made for intercorrelations with other predictors (Andrews, Morgan & Sonquist, 1967).

Use of Physician Services

The results of regression analysis (See Table 8.2) clearly show that need factors are of primary importance in explaining variations in use of physician services. Such use was measured by the number of visits made to

---

*Tables appear in Appendix D.

physicians annually. All four of the need factors examined were statistically significant predictors of the use of physicians. Persons who had high levels of physical and psychological dysfunctioning, and perceived need for services, saw physicians more often. Having high levels of economic dependence, a predisposing factor, and low knowledge of available social services, an enabling factor, were also related to such use. It may be that people who have a knowledge of available social services use physicians more often as a sounding board for their health problems. They may consult physicians about discomforts experienced in coping with their condition at home. On the other hand,, those who are aware of and may be receiving assistance from social service programs in the form of home nursing care, physical therapy or help with activities such as meal preparation, bathing, dressing or feeding may have less need to consult a doctor as often because they are receiving support from other sources. Our study shows that the possession of insurance coverage, an enabling factor, was not associated with the use of physician's services although the literature stresses the importance of this determinant. Since most of the SNAP population are covered by Medicare, Medicaid or private insurance, the effect of health insurance variable on physician visits is negligible.

Multiple Classification Analysis further underscores the important influences need variables have in explaining the number of visits to a physician and the likelihood of using the services of a physician (See Table 8.3). Likelihood refers to having at least one visit to a physician during the year prior to this study. In our population the annual average number of visits to physicians was 5.61, somewhat lower than the national average of 6.7 (USDHEW, 1974). As was expected, having a disabling condition was the most significant predictor of the number of such visits (Table 8.3). Furthermore, it was also the only significant predictor of the likelihood to use the services of a physician (Table 8.4). Persons who reported thirty-one or more disability days had three times as many visits with a physician as those with no disabling condition. Marital status and living arrangements were less important but, nonetheless, signficant predictors of number of visits to a physician. Widowed ($\bar{x}=6.69$) or separated/divorced ($\bar{x}=6.26$) respondents had higher numbers of visits to a physician than persons who were married or never married. Similarly, persons living alone also had more visits to a physician per year ($\bar{x}=5.78$). This suggests that experiencing changes in marital status or living alone may have some adverse effect on health or on the perception of need for health services. It is possible that in some instances the physician may be consulted in his role as a counselor rather than as a healer. This assumption is explored in greater depth in chapter 11.

Hospitalization

Hospitalization is another indicator of the use of medical care services. Tables 8.5 and 8.6 show the effects of predisposing, enabling, and need factors on (1) the likelihood of being hospitalized and (2) the number of days hospitalized. Need factors account for 5% of the variation in rate of hospitalization and in the number of days hospitalized. Need was more important than either predisposing or enabling factors. Respondents who had high levels of instrumental disability and a perceived need for services were significantly more likely to be hospitalized and to spend more days in a hospital. When other factors were controlled, respondents who were significantly more likely to be hospitalized were those who had less education, higher levels of economic dependency, perceived greater transportation problems, and did not belong to a prepaid health insurance plan. Education and prepaid health insurance were similarly related to number of days hospitalized. While previous research suggests that insurance coverage is positively associated with hospitalization, our results, at least with respect to prepaid health insurance, imply that the emphasis on preventive or primary care may reduce both the incidence of the prepaid health practice (e.g., health maintenance organization) on hospitalization and the length of time spent in a hospital. The other possible interpretation of this finding is that other insurance plans are based on an acute care model and cover inpatient care better than outpatient care. Consequently, persons covered by such insurance plans often are hospitalized in order to have insurance cover the bill.

Multiple Classification Analysis showed that persons with a disabling condition were most likely to be hospitalized even when service area, age, sex, marital status, and living arrangement were controlled (Table 8.7).

When controlling for other characteristics of the population (Table 8.8), disability status was likewise the most significant predictor of the number of days respondents were hospitalized per year. Respondents experienced a mean of 3.16 days of hospitalization per year. This figure is far below the 1974 national average of 11.7 days for people over 65 years (USDHEW, 1976). Marital status and living arrangement were also significant predictors. Widowed persons were likely to be hospitalized a greater number of days per year $(x=4.80)$ than were persons not living alone $(x=3.30)$.

Institutionalization

Institutionalization is a third kind of use of health services that is indicative of a serious physical condition. Only 1% of the SNAP population had been institutionalized at some time during the year prior to our study (Table 8.9). This figure is lower than the national average of 4%. It should be noted, however, that the SNAP statistic represents persons who became well enough to leave an institutional setting, since the SNAP study interviewed only noninstitutionalized persons. As would be expected, we can conclude from MCA results that health status factors were the primary determinants of the likelihood of being "institutionalized." Disability status was the only significant predictor of institutionalization when area, age, sex, marital status, and living arrangement were controlled. An average of 6% of those who reported that they were disabled for thirty-one days or more were institutionalized.

Use of Dental Services

Turning to Table 8.10, it appears that while need variables were of prime importance in determining variation in the use of physician services and hospitalization, predisposing factors were most important in predicting the use of dental services. A total of 8% of the variance in dental visits was explained by these variables. The most significant predisposing factors affecting use were economic dependency, age, education level, and living arrangement. The selected enabling and need variables each accounted for only about 3% of dental service variance. Generally, higher levels of instrumental and mental health functioning, having insurance coverage, and perceiving no problems in obtaining transportation were related to having made a visit to a dentist. The results of MCA did not reveal any significant predictors of use of dental services (Table 8.11). However, younger males and younger females and persons who were not widowed appeared to be more likely to use dental services. Those who had never in their lives made any dental visits were more likely to be older males, residents of the Southeast, married or widowed persons, and the retired. The fact that the young-old used dental services more may be related, at least to some extent, to need. Persons over 75 years of age may already have dentures and, therefore, require less care. The lower use of dental services by the widowed may reflect financial constraints.

Looking at the percentages of respondents who had dental visits within a specified time period in Table 8.12, it appears that many of the SNAP population (41%) had made at least one dental visit in the past year. Only 1.8% had never visited a dentist. Profiling variations in dental services use by service area and sociodemographic characteristics, it is apparent that persons in the North service area were more likely to have seen a dentist within the past 12 months (60%) as compared with those in the Southwest (39.4%) and Southeast (27.1%) areas. The young-old (60-74 years) and persons who were not widowed were also more likely to have been to the dentist within the past year.

SUMMARY

In this chapter, we have analyzed the effects of *predisposing, enabling,* and *need* factors on use of health services. Our findings can be summarized as follows. *Need* factors were the principal determinants of variation in the use of physician services and hospitalization, while *predisposing* factors, particularly level of education and need for additional financial resources, were important predictors of dental visits. Persons who had poor physical and mental dysfunctioning saw physicians more frequently and were hospitalized for a greater number of days. Respondents who were better educated and who were less economically dependent used dental services more often than comparable groups. Persons who at some point experienced a loss of the marital role (widowed, separated/divorced) were most likely to see a physician, and widowed persons were more likely to be hospitalized.

Putting these findings in perspective, it is generally acknowledged that when access to or ability to obtain health services is evenly distributed, need is the primary determinant of use (Aday, Andersen & Fleming, 1980). In other words, predisposing and enabling factors such as personal characteristics and knowledge of services, availability of transportation, and the possession of insurance do not affect use of services as much as actual medical need. Our findings suggest that, at least with respect to use of physician and hospital services, access is equitable among the elderly population studied. Thus, planned interventions to facilitate access may not be required.

On the other hand, the finding that predisposing factors, particularly level of educational attainment and financial independence, were most influential in determining dental visits implies that access to these services is not as evenly distributed.

Instead, those who are better educated and who have more financial resources are more likely to obtain care. Less well educated elderly may not realize the importance of continuing dental care after they have lost their natural teeth and have dentures. The relevance of dental care to diet, appearance, and ultimately to physical and mental health makes planned interventions—subsidizing dental services through insurance coverage, increasing the availability of dental clinics and dental screening, and initiating programs to increase awareness of the need for dental care—an important consideration for the future in this community.

Comparing health service use of the SNAP population with what we know to be true of other elderly populations, we find that the SNAP population had a lower use of physician services and fewer days of hospitalization than the elderly population of the United States as a whole. The lower rates of use of health services in our sample, compared with the national population, may reflect the better health status of our sample.

The fact that a relatively high proportion of our sample had seen a dentist within the past year may be indicative of the population in the community studied. As you will recall (chapter 3), the SNAP population is "better off" economically than are the elderly nationwide. Thus, SNAP respondents have more resources for obtaining dental care when it is required.

Before closing this chapter, a word or two should be added about the model for examining health service use employed in this chapter. The overall model, which included predisposing, enabling, and need factors, explained only a modest proportion of the variation in physician and dental service use and in hospitalization. While use of this model did enable us to discern which sets of factors were more important than others, our findings confirm the conclusion of others (Wolinsky, 1978) that the model, as a whole, is not particularly helpful in predicting use of medical services among the elderly. In the future, planners who conduct studies of elderly's needs may wish to concentrate on physical and mental functioning of the elderly in their communities when attempting to understand use of physician and hospital services and on the personal characteristics of their populations when looking at use of dental services.

REFERENCES

Aday, L.A., R. Andersen, and G.V. Fleming. 1980. *Health Care in the U.S.— Equitable for Whom?* Beverly Hills: Sage Publication.

Andersen, R. and L.A. Aday. 1978. "Access to Medical Care in the U.S.: Realized and Potential." *Medical Care* 16:533–546.

Andersen, R. and J.F. Newman. 1973. "Societal and Individual Determinants of Medical Care Utilization in the United States." *The Milbank Memorial Fund Quarterly* 51:95–124.

Andrews, F., J. Morgan, and J. Sonquist. 1967. *Multiple Classification Analysis.* Ann Arbor: University of Michigan Institute for Social Research.

Berki, S.E. and B. Kobashigawa. 1976. "Socioeconomic and Need Determinants of Ambulatory Care Use: Path Analysis of the 1970 Health Interview Survey Data." *Medical Care* 14:405–421.

Donabedian, A. 1973. *Aspects of Medical Care Administration: Specifying Requirements for Health Care.* Cambridge: Harvard University Press.

Galvin, M.E. and M. Fan. 1975. "The Utilization of Physicians' Services in Los Angeles County, 1973." *Journal of Health and Social Behavior* 16:74–94.

German, P.S., E.A. Skinner, and S. Shapiro. 1976. "Ambulatory Care for Chronic Conditions in an Inner City Elderly Population." *American Journal of Public Health* 66:660–666.

Katz, S. et al. 1963. "Studies of Illness in the Aged: The Index of ADL—A Standardized Measure of Biological and Psychological Function." *Journal of the American Medical Association* 185:914–919.

Lawton, M.P. and E.M. Brody. 1969. "Assessment of Older People: Self-Maintenance and Instrumental Activities of Daily Living." *The Gerontologist* 9:179–186.

McKinlay, J.B. 1972. "Some Approaches and Problems in the Study of the Use of Services—An Overview." *Journal of Health and Social Behavior* 13:115–152.

Pfeiffer, E. 1975. "Short Portable Mental Status Questionnaire." *The Journal of the American Geriatric Society* 23:433–441.

U.S. Department of Health, Education, and Welfare. 1977. *Health: United States 1976–1977.* Washington, D.C.: Government Printing Office. DHEW Publication Number 77-1232.

Wan, T.T.H., 1982. "Use of Health Services by the Elderly in Low Income Communities." *Health and Society* (Milbank Memorial Fund Quarterly) 60:82–107.

Wan, T.T.H. and S.J. Soifer. 1974. "Determinants of Physician Utilization: A Causal Analysis." *Journal of Health and Social Behavior* 15:100–108.

Wan, T.T.H. and A.S. Yates. 1975. "Prediction of Dental Services Utilization: A Multivariate Approach." *Inquiry* 12:143–156.

Ward, R.A. 1977. "Services for Older People: An Integrated Framework for Research." *Journal of Health and Social Behavior* 18:61–70.

Wolinsky, F.D. 1976. "Health Service Utilization and Attitudes Toward Health Maintenance Organizations: A Theoretical and Methodological Discussion." *Journal of Health and Social Behavior* 17:221–236.

Wolinsky, F.D. 1978. "Assessing the Effects of Predisposing, Enabling, and Illness—Morbidity Characteristics on Health Services Utilization." *Journal of Health and Social Behavior* 10:384–396.

9

Use of Social Services by the Elderly: Social Differentials and Determinants

While numerous studies have examined what influences the use of medical services, little is known about the determinants of the use of social services. Although many social services, such as telephone reassurance, legal assistance, and community home care are currently being offered to the elderly, there has been limited opportunity to employ a sound analytical approach to the systematic examination of patterns in the use of social services. In this model, determinants of use are again grouped into a model composed of predisposing, enabling, and need variables using the same model described in relation to medical service use in chapter 8, with only minimal modifications. Since there has been no previous attempt to systematically examine social service use, it was felt that adopting this model would be a good beginning point for future multivariate studies in this area since many of the factors included have already been associated, at least to some extent, with use of services. The adoptation of the medical service use model also provides a basis for comparison of why types of factors (predisposing, enabling, or need) are most predictive of use of medical and social services and may give some clues as to whether use of these two distinct types of services are related. Because of the influence that educational level and general knowledge may have on the awareness of the myriad social services currently offered to the elderly, we postulated that either predisposing or enabling factors, rather than need, may be of prime importance in finding respondents who will avail themselves of existing social services. It should be noted that this assumption, which diminishes the importance of need, is different from our assumptions concerning the importance of need to use of medical services as described in chapter 8.

98

FINDINGS FROM THE SNAP DATA

Determinants of Social Services Use

In our model of the use of social services, predisposing factors include the following: sex, age, educational level, living arrangement, marital status, and retirement status. Enabling factors include knowledge of services, social support, insurance coverage, and access to transportation. Need factors include measures of physical functioning (ADL score and IADL score) and psychological functioning (depression score), economic dependency, and perceived need for services. All of the above factors were defined in the medical service model discussed in chapter 8. It is important to note that economic dependency is considered to be a need factor in the social service model rather than a predisposing factor as it was in the model of medical service use. Within the social service framework, having inadequate financial resources is indicative of a need that can be specifically addressed by such available financial subsidy services as rent supplements or Supplemental Security Income. While it is perhaps self-evident that such predisposing factors as age and sex and such need factors as level of physical and mental functioning could affect social service use, the possible influence of enabling factors may be less clear and, therefore, requires a word of explanation. Certainly, being aware of the social services offered to older adults and having access to transportation would be related to increased use of social services. Someone who knows about a recreational or nutritional program and has a way to get to the place where it is offered is more likely to use the service, assuming he or she has a need for it. We might also expect that persons who do not have relatives on whom they can call for help with meal preparation, household repairs, or other forms of assistance would be more apt to use formalized sources of help. The possible influence of insurance coverage on use of services is obvious. However, it may be that those who qualify as Medicaid recipients may also have already established ties with the social service network for other forms of income assistance. Persons who belong to a prepaid health plan may also be more aware of other forms of assistance available to them through educational programs offered by a comprehensive health program.

Table 9.1* shows that predisposing, enabling, and need factors accounted for almost fifteen percent of the total variance in the use of social services. As we anticipated, enabling factors were the most important determinants, accounting for 10% of the total variance in use as compared with less than 1% accounted for by predisposing factors and approximately 4% accounted for by need factors. It should be observed that this finding

---

*Tables appear in Appendix D.

is quite different from our analysis of medical service use in chapter 8, where need variables were the most important predictors of physician use and hospitalization.

When controlling for the influence of other factors, the variable "knowledge of available services" was the single most important predictor of the use of social services. As might be expected, persons who had higher levels of awareness of available services were more likely to use them. Other significant predictors included economic dependency, psychological functioning, perceived need for service, and living arrangement. Respondents who were frequent users of social services were characterized as those who lived alone, had higher levels of perceived need, were less financially dependent, and had fewer psychological problems.

Differentials in Social Services Use

To further tap the significance of the enabling factor we call "knowledge of services," patterns of use were examined in greater detail. We looked at the variation in the proportions of the respondents who had heard of or used a specific social service according to their selected demographic characteristics and service area. To simplify our examination, social service programs were classified into the three broad categories of health care services, personal services, and miscellaneous services. The latter included employment, educational, nutritional, transportation, and information and referral services.

Data in Table 9.2 show that our respondents had greater awareness of health-related services than of personal services. Over half of our sample had at least heard of Alcoholics Anonymous (78.1%), the Baltimore County Health Department (55.1%), and the Visiting Nurse Association (50.3%). Among the health care programs, the least well known were Community Home Care (18.9%), the Hospital Social Service Department Program (25.6%), and the Baltimore County Neighborhood Health Center (38.5%).

Considerably fewer respondents had heard of most of the personal service programs. The service which was by far the most widely known was the Senior Citizens Discount Program (71.9%). Many respondents (56.6%) had also heard of the Circuit Breaker tax program. Only 17% had heard of Telecare, and just 11% were familiar with the William Day Care Program.

Educational and employment services were somewhat better known than most personal services. Fifty-three percent of respondents were aware of the community college program, which offers discounts on tuition to seniors. Thirty-four percent had heard of the Over-60 Counseling and Employment Service.

The service area in which people live may be related to whether a person has knowledge of services available in the county as a whole. Respondents may be more familiar with services located in their own area than they are with services in other parts of the county. Respondents from the North area generally had less knowledge of health care services, while respondents in the Northeast and Northwest were among the best informed. Looking at personal services, the same pattern was found. It is noteworthy that substantially more of the respondents of the Southeast were aware of financial subsidiary programs, including Supplemental Security Income and rent supplements. Fewer respondents in this area, however, were aware of more indirect means of financial aid, such as senior citizen discount cards, even though these services are available in all areas.

Respondents in the North area were least informed about employment services, community college programs, and library services for seniors. Referring to our description of the population in chapter 2, it may be that the professional orientation of the majority of respondents in the North area obviates the need for awareness of employment services. Not facing mandatory retirement, these professionals may not need to consider future employment.

It might be noted that the Senior Digest, a forum that conveys information to seniors about services available, was least well known in the Southwest, although respondents living in this area revealed average knowledge of other services.

It should be observed that among the services grouped under the miscellaneous category, males who were age 75 or over had less awareness of nutritional, transportation services, and the senior center program than other groups (Table 9.3). Deficiencies of knowledge concerning these services may be particularly detrimental to older males, should they become widowed.

As could have been anticipated, the proportion of persons who actually have participated in a service is substantially less than those who have knowledge of programs (Table 9.4). Programs with the highest rates of reported participation included the senior discount card program (56.3%), Circuit Breaker tax program (40.7%), Senior Digest (37%), Library Services for Seniors (19.8%), and the Senior Center program (17.4%). All five of these programs could be characterized as addressing service needs that are not necessarily related to specific problems. Other programs, which addressed more specific health and social problems such as the need for a visiting nurse (10%) and community home care (3.5%), had lower rates of participation.

Residents of the North area tended to use health care services and personal services somewhat less than other areas. They particularly tended to participate less in such financial subsidy programs as rent supplements to seniors and Supplemental Security Income and did not report any participation in employment programs. It will be recalled that residents of the North have higher levels of economic well-being than those of the Southeast (chapters 2 and 3). The greater use of financial aids by Southeastern residents is clearly a reflection of their economic situation.

In addition to these variations, several other differentials in participation by service area are worth noting. Respondents of the Northwest area had the highest proportion of participation in the Lunch Plus program, information and referral services, and in the Senior Center program. This finding suggests that in the Northwest there may be an informal exchange of information concerning these services among participants or that directors of these programs in this area may be more aggressive in recruiting participants.

It is also interesting that more respondents used Senioride in the Southwest (8.6%) than in the Northeast (5.5%), Northwest (4.9%), Southeast (4%) and North (3.8%). It will be recalled that the residents of the Southwest were much more likely to say they used a bus as a means of transportation and were the least likely to report having a car in the household (see transportation section, chapter 6).

Finally, examining differentials in participation by age and sex, it is apparent that while a greater proportion of young-old respondents (60–74 years) were aware of social services (Table 9.5), a greater proportion of old-old persons (≥ 75 years) who have heard of such services actually participate in them. This may be due to the greater identification with aging programs among those seventy-five or over and to greater need for some services by this age group. For instance, looking at health care services, it is apparent that those 75 years and over participate in all health care services more than younger respondents, with the exception of those services in the Baltimore County Health Department. Older respondents also participated more than younger respondents in day care, senior citizen discount, tax relief, Supplementary Security Income, telephone reassurance, and nutritional, transportation, and senior center programs. Greater use of these services by those 75 and over is probably due to greater needs for these services to address such specific problems of this age group as failing health. Some differentials may also be the result of needing to be old enough to be eligible.

SUMMARY

In this chapter, the relative importance of selected determinants of social services use was identified, and the differentials in their use were explored. It was found that the enabling factor "knowledge of available services" was the single most important variable associated with the use of social services. Persons most likely to use social services were also those who lived alone, perceived a need for services, had relatively few psychological problems, and were less likely to be in need of financial assistance. These findings have several important implications. First, there apparently is a need to educate the elderly population concerning the availability of social services. People who do not know of available services obviously cannot be expected to use them. Second, the fact that persons who are less psychologically impaired and less financially dependent use more services raises the serious question as to whether existing services are reaching the segments of the elderly population with the greatest need for them. It seems that persons who have psychological problems and financial deficiencies would be the appropriate beneficiaries of many existing services. Clearly, those with psychological problems or with the need for financial aid should be made more aware of existing social services through an active program of community education.

Since "knowledge of services" proved to be of prime importance in whether or not services were used, differentials in knowledge and use of services were examined for the total study population and by geographical area, age, and sex. Social service programs were classified as health-related services, personal services, and miscellaneous services. The differences in awareness of services available and participation in these services can be summarized as follows:

1. More respondents were aware of health-care related services than of personal services.
2. Over half of the population sampled had at least heard of the Visiting Nurse Association, the Baltimore County Health Department, and Alcoholics Anonymous. The Community Home Care Program was the least well recognized.
3. With respect to personal services, programs that entail passive involvement of participants, such as the Senior Citizens Discount program and the Circuit Breaker tax program, were the best known. Programs that are more extensively and personally supportive, such as day care, Senior Aide, and Telecare were less well known.
4. Area variations in social service awareness and participation were also detected. Generally, residents of the Northeast and Northwest were better informed about available services, while residents of the North area were the least well informed. Residents of the North area also tended to participate less in social service programs. Respondents of the Southeast area were the most likely to participate in financial subsidy programs.
5. A relationship between age, knowledge, and participation was uncovered. Although persons between the ages of 60 and 74 years were

better informed about existing social services, persons 75 and over tended to be higher users of these services. This finding probably reflects a need for such services along with the fact that they more likely met the age requirements. Further, while older males showed the least awareness of services, those who were aware of services participated in more of them than older females.

The above differentials in awareness and participation suggest several planning directives. Generally, awareness concerning specialty services that offer support to persons with physical or psychological impairments need to be increased. The least well known services such as Telecare, home aid, day care, and community home care could prove critical in forestalling hospitalization and institutionalization. Secondly, the inequalities in use of services between different service areas need to be probed. Results showing that residents of the Southeast are the most likely participants in financial subsidy programs conform with previous findings that residents in this area tend to have greater need for financial help. Conversely, residents in the North area have higher reported economic well-being and, therefore, have less need to participate in these programs. These findings suggest equitable distribution of services according to need. However, such questions as why residents of the Southwest use Senioride more often and why residents of the Northwest more often participate in the Lunch Plus and Senior Center program require more attention. Lastly, findings that young-old are better informed about social services may indicate greater use of these services in the future as this group continues to age and their needs increase.

As noted in the beginning of this chapter, few systematic examinations of the use of social services among the elderly have been undertaken within the framework of a sound theoretical model. Our analysis has demonstrated the utility of this approach for planning of social services. The use of the model proposed in this chapter and in the previous chapter actually explained more variance in the use of social services than it did in the use of medical services (physician, dentist, and hospitalization) (see chapter 8). An enabling variable, "knowledge of services"—a factor relatively manipulable—is the most significant predictor of social service rather than less changeable factors such as mental or physical use status. This suggests that creating greater awareness of social service programs through media announcements, newsletters, and information and referral services could substantially enhance knowledge of and participation in these services. Increasing the use of social services may prove critical to elderly persons trying to live independent lives.

10

The Frail Elderly

In the preceding chapters, we have described the range of well-being of the SNAP population, their perceived and unmet service needs, and variations in their use of social and health services. In this chapter, we explore the ways in which the need for services and the actual use of services are interrelated. We chose to look at the ways in which need may affect use and vice versa among a specific population group, the frail elderly.

Because of the significance of the service delivery issues raised in connection with the frail elderly, this chapter explores their service needs and use of services in depth. The attention of government agencies that provide services to the aging and gerontological researchers are coming more and more to focus upon the frail elderly. In general, the frail elderly are thought to be 75 years of age and over. This age group is thought to describe those most in jeopardy of losing their ability to live independently due to failing health and limited economic and personal resources. Determining how to provide effective services for the frail elderly is an important concern of professionals in the health and social services fields because the services these aged people require (for example, day care) are among the most costly and difficult to deliver. Services are costly not only to the individual recipient but also to society. Yet this cost must be weighed by planners against the alternative cost of institutionalization. To further complicate matters, the frail elderly, without children or other relatives who can help them obtain services, usually have multiple service needs. For instance, an aged widower in poor health may need extensive medical services, help in maintaining his home, and advice on handling his limited income. There is growing recognition among professionals that the services the frail receive should be coordinated through a central caretaker. Channeling agencies have been suggested as one means of coordinating services.

In our study, we defined the frail elderly in terms of limitations in physical, mental, and social functioning. Functional limitations resulting from illness, either physical or mental, or social disability were considered as measures of frailty. We did not define frailty by age alone, as it has traditionally been conceived, since many old-old are not necessarily frail and many young-old, due to illness or isolation, are frail.

We regarded the elderly as having poor physical well-being if they rated their health as poor and had at least one area of dysfunctioning among those used in the Activities of Daily Living index (ADL) (see chapter 5 for an explanation of ADL). Poor psychological well-being was indicated by having at least one of the symptoms listed in the depression scale (for description see chapter 4) and a reported decline in mental health over the past five years. Poor social well-being was defined as having few sources of social support—that is, not having persons in whom they could confide and who could give help when required—and having at least one limitation that required human assistance in order to carry out such tasks as shopping or telephoning used in the Instrumental Activities of Daily Living (IADL) index (for a description of IADL see chapter 5).[1] In other words, we classified persons as having low social well-being when they require some human assistance but do not necessarily have others around to give them the help they need. The relevance of considering social well-being, particularly in assessing needs for services, was discussed in depth in chapter 3. To reiterate, variation in the availability of social support has been related to variations in levels of health (Gore, 1978; Myers, Lindenthal & Pepper, 1975; Nuckolls, Cassel & Kaplan, 1972) and in the use of health services (Langlie, 1977; de Araujo et al., 1973; Pratt, 1972). Research suggests that having persons to confide in and who can give help mitigates, to some extent, the negative consequences of illness. Investigators are beginning to suspect that the presence of social support may even reduce unnecessary use of health services. Our data indicates that those with impairments in several dimensions of well-being have the least informal social support. This implies that stronger formal social supports should be provided to enable more frail elderly to live independently in their community. For example, community-based organizations can target the most frail elderly as potential recipients of a coordinated array of social and health services.

In this analysis, the frail elderly were also thought of in relation to their vulnerability. Vulnerability refers to having perceived unmet service needs because of lack of knowledge of available services, the unavailability of needed services, or problems in receiving these services. Such "vulnerability" may contribute to or accelerate deterioration in well-being.

---

[1] Although the IADL is traditionally thought of as a measure of physical functioning, this scale can also be used as a measure of physical capacity to perform social roles. Thus, in this context, the IADL can be used as a measure of social well-being.

This definition of vulnerability, which employs unmet service needs as a qualifying criterion for determining frailty, is similar to the one employed by Branch (1978) in his needs assessment of the elderly population in Boston, Massachusetts.

As noted in the first chapter, an analysis of needs must address the whole person, as limitations in one area of functioning may affect capabilities in other areas. This is evident from the positive associations found among three well-being indicators:

Well-being Indicators	SWB	MWB	PWB
Social well-being (SWB)	1.0	0.103*	0.221*
Mental well-being (MWB)		1.0	0.263*
Physical well-being (PWB)			1.0

*Significant at 0.05 or lower level.

The fact that a greater proportion of persons with poor physical, psychological, and social functioning have problems in performing such tasks associated with independent living as securing transportation suggests that the frail elderly may need multiple supportive services and may have more difficulty in obtaining them. Table 10.1* shows the statistical relationship between levels of physical, psychological, and social well-being on the one hand, and "need and use variables" on the other. The correlation coefficients reveal that those with low levels of physical functioning were also likely to have low levels of psychological and social well-being and that these well-being indicators are also significantly correlated with perceived needs and unmet needs. A detailed analysis of the effects of frailty on need for and use of services follows.

Our analysis proceeds by (1) profiling the frail elderly in terms of social-demographic characteristics, (2) determining the effects of frailty on perceived needs and unmet needs, (3) examining the effects of frailty on the use of services, and (4) proposing program planning to tackle the problems of the frail elderly population.

PROFILE OF FRAILTY

Table 10.2 presents a profile of frailty by service area and social and demographic indicators. For the purpose of clarity, frailty was classified into low, medium, and high categories. These categories of frailty are based on a combination of degree of functional impairment and number of unmet

*Tables appear in Appendix D.

social service needs. Specifically, those with low frailty had no functional impairments in physical, psychological, or social well-being and less than one unmet service need. Those with medium impairment had an average of 1.28 unmet service needs and one or two areas of functional impairment. Those with high frailty had an average of three unmet service needs and impairments in both psychological and social well-being or impairment in all three areas of functioning.

As shown in Table 10.2, nearly 80% of the population studied had a low level of frailty, 18.6% had a medium level, and only 2.8% had a high level of frailty. All areas had very small proportions of respondents with high levels of frailty. The Southeast had considerably greater percentages of respondents with medium levels of frailty (25.7%) than other areas. This finding should be underlined in light of the poorer economic well-being of the Southeast.

Profiling the distribution of high frailty by age, living arrangement, employment status, and marital status did not reveal great variations. A slightly higher percentage of those 75 and over and the retired reported high frailty. More variation occurred among those reporting medium levels of frailty. Greater proportions of those 75 and over, living alone, not retired, and widowed reported medium levels of frailty than those in corresponding categories.

Persons with poor physical, psychological, or social functioning also appear to have more problems and to require more assistance in the form of financial aid or personal services. Table 10.3 shows that a greater proportion of persons with poor than with normal functioning were already receiving Medicaid, or Social Security income, or had someone to help with housework, shopping, and dressing. Further, those with poor well-being were also substantially more likely to have less knowledge of available social and health services and to report less social support available than the others with better levels of well-being. Differences in knowledge of services deserve a closer examination. Persons who are unfamiliar with available services are, of course, not able to get them when needed. While less than half of those with normal functioning had low knowledge of services, almost three-quarters of those with poor physical or social functioning and about 64% of those with poor psychological functioning recognized less than ten of the social and health services currently offered. Further, more persons with poor physical, psychological, or social functioning said they had problems getting medical treatment and transportation and were in need of health aids.

DIFFERENTIALS IN PERCEIVED NEEDS
AMONG THE FRAIL ELDERLY

Table 10.4 probes the relationship between frailty and perceived and unmet needs. Poor physical, psychological, or social well-being were all associated with higher levels of perceived and unmet needs. While only 6.4% of those with normal physical functioning expressed five or more needs, 37.3% of those with poor physical functioning expressed this level of need. Further, while only 6.6% of those with normal physical functioning had between three and eight unmet service needs, the same was true of 26% of those with poor functioning. This pattern was the same for psychological and social functioning.

Table 10.5 shows the percentages of the frail elderly who perceived specific service needs. Those with poor physical functioning, particularly, expressed the need for assistance to do routine housework (55.5%), information and referral services (53.7%), assistance in doing home repairs (38.9%), assistance in ADL functioning (35.2%), finding a job (35.2%), and the need for someone to check on them five times a week (31.5%).

Persons with poor psychological or social well-being expressed similar needs but to a lesser extent. Persons with poor psychological well-being most often perceived the need for assistance with home repairs (33.3%), information and referral services (33.3%), assistance for routine housework (26.4%), and someone to check on them five days a week (21.9%). The highest levels of perceived need among those with poor social functioning were for information and referral sevices (58.4%), assistance with housework (40.3%) and home repairs (39.0%), and someone to check on them (35.1%). This group had a much higher percentage of persons reporting the need for help in finding a place to live (28.0%) than the other two. Clearly, the predominant perceived needs in all three groups were for information and referral services and assistance with home repairs and routine housework.

Table 10.6 shows the percentages of specific unmet service needs reported by persons who have poor physical, mental, and social functioning. The percentages of persons reporting unmet needs are much lower than the comparable perceived needs, indicating that many needs of the frail elderly are being met by existing services. Nonetheless, high percentages of those with poor physical (46.3%), psychological (31.0%), and social (54.5%) functioning report the need for information and referral services. Unmet needs for assistance in doing routine housework and home repairs were also expressed. One-fifth of those with poor physical functioning said that their need for physical therapy was unmet.

FRAILTY AND USE OF HEALTH AND SOCIAL SERVICES

The effects of poor functioning on the number of physician visits per year and on the use of social services are displayed in Table 10.7. As stated previously, the total population had a mean of 5.61 physician visits per year and used an average of one social service. Results suggest that both the absence of problems in physical, psychological, and social functioning and the combined effects of problems in all three areas are related to low levels of use of physicians' services. While it would seem reasonable to expect that those with normal functioning would use physicians' services the least and that those with poor functioning in all the areas would use them the most, our findings did not confirm this hypothesis. Instead, those with poor functioning in all three areas appear to use physicians' services less than those with normal functioning in all areas. This may be because people with progressive deterioration in ability to function have less ability to get the services they need. Persons in this situation may mistakenly consider institutionalization to be their only recourse.

Having limitations in one or two areas of functioning does not reduce physician use. Differences in patterns of use of physician service on the basis of having one or two impairments were not distinguishable. It is, however, noteworthy that those who report normal physical but poor psychological and social functioning (NPP) have the greatest number of physician visits ($\bar{x}$ = 14.46). It would seem that this group may use physician services as a solution to nonmedical problems. Our data, however, did not allow us to conclude whether the respondents actually substitute physicians for more appropriate social services.

Somewhat similar findings were uncovered in our examination of the use of social services. Persons with problems in all three areas—physical, psychological, and social functioning (PPP)—used social services far less ($\bar{x}$ = .67) than persons who had nonpoort functioning in all areas (NNN). This finding further supports our previous conclusion that persons with poor social and psychological functioning are substituting medical services for social services.

Those with poor physical functioning and normal psychological and social function (PNN) use the most social services ($\bar{x}$ = 1.73). This raises the question of whether social services are at this time geared more toward aiding those with physical impairments at the expense of overlooking equally serious psychological and social deficiencies.

The findings presented in the table discussed above lead to a disturbing conclusion concerning the impact of multiple frailties. Persons with limitations in several areas of functioning appear unable to use physicians or social services to the extent required. They are thus increasingly susceptible to further deterioration. Clearly, this group should be the target of aggressive and comprehensive outreach programs.

A MODEL OF FRAILTY,
PERCEIVED NEED AND USE

As discussed above, the presence of frailty and multiple areas of frailty has a substantially different impact on percepted needs, unmet needs, and the use of health and social services than the absence of frailty. In this section, as a means of summarizing, four models were employed to analyze the effects of functioning, status, need, and knowledge of pertinent health and social services on the actual use of these services. In Model I, we looked at the effects of physical, psychological, and social functioning on the use of services. Model II added to the functional predictors the effects of perceived service needs. We suspected that frailty might affect perceived need which, in turn, might influence use. In Model III, we examined the effects of functional limitations and reported unmet service needs on use. While perceived needs might be met by increased use of services, we hypothesized that a high level of unmet needs coupled with frailty might create a situation of vulnerability that could have a distinct effect on use. Model IV looked at the effects of frailty, perception of needs, and knowledge of available services on the use of available services. Since knowledge may be the key to people getting the services they need, this variable could be crucial in explaining variations in use. Fortunately, knowledge is amenable to manipulation, and providing it should be an important part in the comprehensive planning for provision of services.

On analyzing the data, we were able to demonstrate that functioning status variables and perceived service needs are the most important predictors of use of physician services. Persons with higher levels of psychological dysfunctioning and a high level of perceived service need are most likely to visit physicians frequently.

Models II and IV, which included functioning status variables and the need factor, accounted for more variance in physician use than Models I and III, which included functioning status variables alone and functioning status and unmet needs respectively. Our findings reveal that a knowledge of health-related social services is not a significant factor in determining physician use.

While psychological functioning appears to be significantly related to the use of physicians, level of physical and social functioning are more relevant in explaining variations in hospitalization. Persons with low levels of physical and social well-being and persons with high levels of perceived need tended to be hospitalized for longer periods. Longer lengths of stay may be particularly related to the low levels of social well-being. The cost implications of longer hospital stay among this group should be considered in future planning, as it is possible that length of time spent in hospitals could be reduced by having necessary social supports outside of the institutional setting. As was found with the use of physician services, knowledge of health-related services was not a significant predictor of the length of time hospitalized.

While persons with poor physical, psychological, or social well-being tended to use physicians' services more often and to be hospitalized for longer periods of time than those of good well-being, recipients of social and health services appeared to have a distinctly different profile. Respondents with a high level of physical, psychological, and social well-being used more social and health services. Specifically, a high level of psychological well-being is a significant predictor of the use of social services.

In examining use of social services, Model IV—which includes the functioning level, perceived need, and knowledge variables—accounts for 11% of the variance in social service use as compared with less than 2% accounted for by other models. Clearly, knowledge of available health and social services is a critical factor in determining their use. Persons who had knowledge of the existing service programs, and ability to perceive their own needs, and were psychologically healthy were more likely to use social services than their counterparts.

SUMMARY

The relationships shown between functioning status, perceived need, knowledge of services, and the use of services allow us to draw several conclusions relevant to future planning.

- First, our findings indicate some inappropriate use of services. Persons with high levels of well-being more often use social services, while persons with low levels of well-being more often used physician and other medical services. It is possible that medically related services may be over-used by those with psychological and social impairments as a way of dealing with problems of aging that may be more efficiently taken care of by using social services. Our data reveal that this may be particularly true in relation to the use of physician services. Persons with low levels of psychological and social well-being are the most likely to use physician services. The counselor, adviser, or sympathetic listener role filled by the physician for these respondents may be more appropriately filled by social services. Our evidence indicates that, at present, physician services are perhaps being substituted for social services. More research needs to be undertaken to determine the extent and costs of this substitution pattern and the implications it has for the health care delivery system.

• Secondly, the demonstrated crucial importance of accurate perception of need and knowledge of available services suggests these may be the key factors in what appears to be a maldistribution of services. Our findings that persons with higher levels of well-being use social services more often implies that those with the greatest needs for these services may be underserved. Those with lower levels of well-being may be less able to identify their needs and less aware of sources of help available to them in the community.

REFERENCES

Branch, L.G. 1978. *Boston Elders: A Survey of Needs 1978*. City of Boston Commission on Affairs of the Elderly/Area Agency on Aging, Region VI. Boston: Center for Survey Research, a facility of the University of Massachusetts, the Joint Center for Urban Studies of M.I.T., Harvard University, and the Boston Urban Observatory of the University of Massachusetts.

de Araujo, G.P. et al. 1973. "Life Change, Coping Ability and Chronic Intrinsic Asthma." *Journal of Psychosomatic Research* 17:359-363.

Gore, S. 1978. "The Effect of Social Support in Moderating the Health Consequences of Unemployment." *Journal of Health and Social Behavior* 18:244-260.

Myers, J.K., J.J. Lindenthal, and M.P. Pepper. 1975. "Life Events, Social Integration and Psychiatric Symptomology." *Journal of Health and Social Behavior* 16:421-427.

Nuckolls, K.B., J.K. Cassel, and B.H. Kaplan. 1972. "Psychosocial Assets, Life Crisis and Prognosis of Pregnancy." *American Journal of Epidemiology* 95:431-441.

Pratt, L. 1972. "Conjugal Organization and Health." *Journal of Marriage and the Family* 2:85-95.

11

Comprehensive Planning
for the Elderly

In order to reduce costs, provide rational service delivery systems, and assure equal access to care, it is necessary to systematize the planning of human services. Planning for these services requires precise information on functional (well-being) status and perceived needs of the population and the factors that affect variations in the use of the human services available in each community.

It should be apparent that systematic planning requires a formal procedure for identifying service priorities. Kahn (1969, p. 16) states that "planning is policy choice and programming in the light of facts, projections, and application of values." Put another way, planning involves an attempt to reconcile means for providing services with ends or goals with respect to the quality of care the community decides should be provided.

In the case of the elderly, such planning is of vital importance. It is estimated that by the year 2000 the elderly (those 65 years and over) may constitute as much as 20% of the population nationally, with those 75 and over amounting to approximately 45% of this older population (Neugarten, 1970). The increase in the size of the latter group, the so-called old-old, is particularly relevant to service providers, since they are the most likely to be in need of health and social services. Those 75 years of age and over are more likely than those under 75 to see physicians, to be hospitalized, and to have some form of mental illness (Butler, 1977).

Previous chapters of this book have addressed the question, How should a target group be defined? This question was originally raised by the Federal Council on Aging (1979) in relation to the planning of social and health services for the elderly. This chapter also addresses such other questions raised by the Federal Council on Aging as, What should be the components of a comprehensive, coordinated social service program? and

What linkage, if any, should there be between health and social support services? In this chapter, the idea of creating information and referral systems and channeling mechanisms to increase linkage between social and health services is developed.

As observed in our opening chapter, there are several ways of approaching the task of comprehensive planning. Planning may be based upon (1) social indicators, which rely on census information or other nonspecifically collected data, (2) human services as demanded by elderly consumers, (3) professional assessment of the needs of the elderly, or (4) community-based assessment of elderly persons' specific needs for service and their patterns of use. It should be emphasized that each of these approaches should be supplemented by other approaches (see chapter 1). Moreover, data collected by all approaches will provide valuable information for designing comprehensive service programs for the elderly.

As noted earlier, needs assessment surveys may be used to (1) describe the demands for service, (2) set clearly defined goals for planning, (3) stimulate local coordination of services, (4) help to develop services in response to perceived community needs, (5) blend citizen preferences with professional viewpoints, (6) allow service agencies to set priorities, (7) identify target groups for effective actions, and (8) establish baseline data for program evaluation.

We have tried to outline the dimensions of needs assessment for communities, but the development of a national information system on the elderly is also being discussed (General Accounting Office, 1979). In its report to the Congress of the United States, the General Accounting Office (GAO) recommended that the Department of Health, Education and Welfare establish a "comprehensive national information system that determines the personal conditions of, problems of, and help available to older persons." Their finding were based upon a comprehensive needs assessment study of Cleveland's elderly, similar to this study, which considered several dimensions of personal well-being (health, security, loneliness, outlook on life) and unmet service needs. The GAO concluded that collecting data from national samples and making projections for the nation from this data would be cost-effective. In their report they state, ". . . the total cost would be relatively small compared to the benefits derived from better planning and resource allocation of billions of dollars of help for older people."

We hope the Baltimore County project will further the development of a survey instrument that could be used in the collection of data nationwide and contribute to the existing state of knowledge on the well-being of the elderly by identifying significant predictors of well-being and service needs.

Based upon a community survey of the elderly, our major findings can be summarized as follows:

1. On the whole, the elderly population of Baltimore County were relatively better off physically, psychologically, and socially than the elderly population of the nation. They had resources they could draw on in times of distress. Still, 8% of the study population reported functional disabilities that limited their ability to carry out such basic daily tasks as bathing, feeding, and grooming. Over one-quarter (27.1%) said they needed assistance in doing such things necessary to maintaining independent living as doing housework, preparing meals, and telephoning.

2. Persons who had never been married consistently showed a higher level of well-being than other marital groups of elderly. The never married seem to be tougher in tackling the problems associated with growing old. It may well be that the self-reliance learned in earlier years serves this group well in old age.

3. The frail elderly were identified as a group with high priority service needs. This group had poor physical, psychological, and social well-being, reported more service needs, and more often said their needs for service were not currently being met.

4. While the frail elderly constitute a relatively small proportion of the elderly population, the consequences resulting from lack of what we detect as services needed and inappropriate use of certain services may place an unnecessary cost on the county's population as a whole. Those with poor psychological and social functioning visited physicians more often than those with physical impairments. Those who were physically, psychologically, and socially healthy were more likely to use social services than those who had dysfunctioning in these areas. It was surmised that the expensive services of physicians, for example, may be being substituted for health and social services that might better meet the needs of older persons at a lower cost.

5. Variation in the knowledge of services available proved to be a key factor in the variation in the use of social services.

6. The need for information and referral services was expressed by many respondents. The frail elderly, in particular, expressed the need for this service.

7. The need for expansion of such supportive services as homemaker services, home repairs, maintenance programs, and telephone reassurance was also identified.

8. As compared to the other service areas, a disproportionately greater number of respondents from the Southeast area had at least one unmet service need and poor physical, psychological, and social functioning; respondents of this area also had lower levels of education, more blue-collar work experience, and received more formal financial assistance.

RECOMMENDATIONS:
A STRATEGY FOR PLANNING

The above findings suggest the need for immediate actions to increase the availability of social and health services to the underserved population and to identify inappropriate use of medical services. Several actions, which have been recognized in the literature as means of improving service delivery, can be taken. As observed in chapter 1, in developing an effective service delivery network three steps are necessary: (1) planning, (2) implementation, and (3) evaluation. Our recommendations presented within this framework include:

Planning

1. The frail elderly should be targeted as the group in greatest need of services and with the highest level of unmet needs. The *frail elderly*, as identified in this study, are those with poor physical, psychological, and social functioning.
2. The area in the greatest need of services has been identified as the Southeast service area, where a higher proportion of frail elderly were found. In addition, respondents in this area had relatively poor economic status, reported a higher level of unmet needs, and were less knowledgeable about the services available. Special attention needs to be directed toward alleviating the unmet needs of the elderly persons in this service area.
3. Planning sessions with community agencies should be established in which information obtained from needs assessment surveys can be properly disseminated to providers of services, planners, researchers, and consumers. These sessions can serve as forums for exchanging ideas, setting priorities for program intervention, and developing program goals for the elderly. An essential element in making the sessions work is the realistic examination of facts or findings made jointly by planners, policy makers, and community representatives so that a plan of action based on needs assessment results can be formulated.
4. In addition to the community survey of needs, planners need to systematically provide an inventory (analysis of services) both at the community-based and institution-based levels, so that information about area resources can be properly used in matching the service needs of the elderly.
5. Areas that have a disproportionately high number of frail elderly need to be continuously monitored in order to provide necessary services.

From our data, we concluded that services need to be decentralized and developed on a local basis to allow flexibility in addressing community needs. Local monitoring of well-being status in areas with proportionately higher numbers of frail elderly will also permit planners to determine accurately the effectiveness of social programs they implement. Changes in general well-being will indicate whether programs are helping to reduce problems.

6. In future research, the needs of minority and rural elderly should be identified. Oversampling of these groups, who proportionately are a small part of the county population, is necessary in future endeavors to assure that their needs are assessed. The present SNAP data, which did not include adequate samples of these groups, prevented us from generalizing our findings to minority or rural populations.

Implementation

1. *Assessment Instruments*
   A concise tool for identifying needs should be developed and employed as a routine means for assessing service needs in the community. The need for developing diagnostic tools to match services with needs in both community-based and institutional facilities has been cited by researchers across the country (Blanchard, 1964; Barry, 1959; Center for Study of Aging and Human Development, 1978; Plowman, 1967; Wasser, 1966; Naven, Weitzer & Nuller, 1968; Kaplan, Ford & Wain, 1967; Lawton, Newcomer & Byerts, 1977). Our data suggests that the evaluation of physical and social functioning level as measured by the ADL and IADL scores, and psychological functioning as tested by the depression score, provides a sound basis for the assessment of needs within a community. A simplified needs assessment tool could be used in a local setting to continuously identify the needs of the population within the area. Multipurpose senior centers would be ideal locations for making informal assessments of local needs. The determination of needs through a survey method should be a part of the routine activities of each local senior center.

2. *Service Priorities*
   Priorities for the provision of services should be outlined. Our data indicate that the development of a comprehensive information and referral service is of prime importance. Ideally, an information and referral service that employs a concise needs assessment instrument could ensure the appropriate matching of needs to existing services as well as

increase community awareness of available services. Other service priorities suggested by our data encourage the expansion of low-cost home repair and maintenance programs. The further development of telephone reassurance programs to be aimed primarily at the population over 75 years of age; the growth of recreational programs and organized, planned activities, particularly for the widowed young-old (60–74 years) who most frequently expressed the need for social outlets; and an increase in the provision of homemaker services for the frail elderly.

3. *Channeling Mechanisms*

The development of an efficient system of channeling clients to appropriate services is also a priority. Many mechanisms of case management have been developed in recent years including (1) the client-centered approach and (2) the agency-oriented approach, in which services provided within a particular governmental structure, such as the Department of Social Services, are coordinated. Since the present study did not address the question of case management per se, the extent of coordination among agencies providing services for the elderly needs to be studied in the near future. Our findings suggest that greater use could be made of services that are widely used, such as the Senior Citizen Discount Card, as intake points for more extensive evaluation of service needs. Also, physicians could be valuable sources of referral for persons in need of social services. In delivering comprehensive services to the frail elderly, a systems approach may be followed. This consists of (1) case assessment, (2) care-plan development, (3) case management, (4) case reassessment, and (5) discharge planning. It is essential that there should be a complete filing system developed in a central agency so that the services can be carefully monitored in order to ensure the continuity of care. The long-term support system proposed by Brody and Masciocchi appears to be a good way to achieve this goal. In their proposed system, as shown in Figure 11.1, available services are grouped according to whether they are offered in institutional, community, or home settings. It is important to observe that this system considers available social supports through identification of referral source and living arrangement. (Living arrangement was also found to be relevant in our study.) The system also takes into account the many dimensions of assuring linkages between services such as monitoring, information and referral, education, and transportation. Community education may not only increase knowledge of services, a crucial factor in social service use, but also may contribute to smoother delivery by enhancing the linkages.

Evaluation

1. Strategies for evaluating the effectiveness of service provision need to be developed. Issues to be evaluated include costs and benefits of substituting use of appropriate social services for medical services; cost-

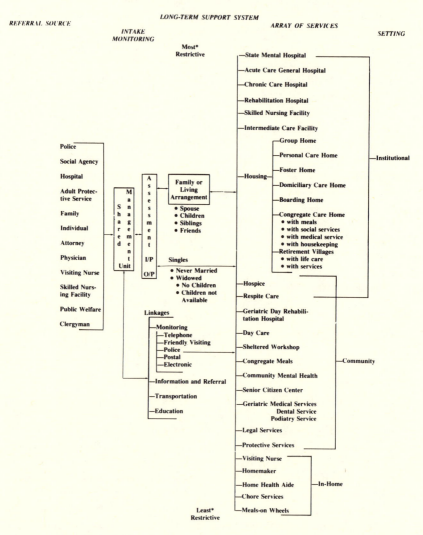

*The classification of most to least restrictive is a general view of services and may vary within each service.

Figure 11.1 Long-term Support System (Source: Brody and Masciocchi, 1980)

effective methods of channeling services to the frail elderly, particularly those with multiple frailties; and the effectiveness of information and referral services as a means of increasing awareness of service options.

2. The extent and effectiveness of coordination among such public and private agencies offering ambulatory care services to the elderly as the Department of Aging, Department of Social Services, and Department of Health needs to be determined. Agencies offering services to the elderly should be classified according to type of service provided, client population serviced, client capacity, geographical location, source of funding, and professional orientation. A clearer understanding of interorganizational linkages will facilitate the development of an efficient information and referral system.

3. A forum should be developed for reconciling consumer viewpoints with those of professionals. This report has presented the elderly consumers' viewpoint with respect to which services they believe are needed at the present time. Yet, the input of professionals is also necessary to assure that services are delivered appropriately. The development of a research institute at a local university could provide a basis for continued monitoring of the status of the community's elderly population and a forum for addressing the concerns of the elderly consumer and the professional provider in light of concrete information. Such an institute would have the potential of increasing the public's awareness of the problems of the elderly locally and nationally.

In conclusion, the development of systematic strategies which include stages of planning, implementation, and evaluation is essential for promoting the well-being of the elderly. Our study has contributed to the planning stage by providing detailed information on the well-being, status, perceived needs, and service use patterns of a sampling of Baltimore County's elderly residents. Although this study is limited by its cross-sectional focus, it provides a starting point for future planning. Follow-up studies of this population will lend a longitudinal perspective to our present findings, enabling us to identify not only the present status of the elderly but also future trends.

While the findings from the present study suggest that the senior population in this community, as a whole, was physically, psychologically, and socially relatively healthy, there was still 8% of the study population who reported that functional disabilities limited their performance of such activities of daily living as feeding, toileting, and grooming. In addition, 27.1% said they needed assistance in such activities necessary to maintain independent living as housework, preparing meals, and telephoning. Specifically, 18.3% reported needing help with homemaker services, 15.1% said they needed help with shopping, and 14.9% had difficulty traveling. There is clearly a pressing need for increasing the knowledge of available services among the elderly as well as a need to create effective channeling mechanisms to assure the receipt of services by the frail elderly. We hope this book will provide a basis for directing actions in many communities to meet these needs more effectively and efficiently in the future.

REFERENCES

Barry, M.C. 1959. "Community Organization." in *Proceedings of the Seminar on Aging, Aspen, Colorado.* New York: Council on Social Work Education.

Blanchard, B.M. 1964. "Geriatric Care in the Public Housing Area." *Geriatrics* 19:302.

Brody, S.J. and C. Masciocchi. 1980. "Data for Long-Term Care Planning by Health Systems Agencies." *American Journal of Public Health* 70:1194–1198.

Butler, R.N. 1977. "Questions on Health Care for the Aged." *Conditions for Change in the Health Care System.* Washington, D.C.: Health Resources Administration, DHEW Publication No. (HRA) 78-642, 98–106.

Duke University Center for the Study of Aging and Human Development. 1978. *Multidimensional Functional Assessment: The OARS Methodology,* Second Edition. Durham, N.C.: Duke University Center for the Study of Aging and Human Development.

Federal Council on Aging. 1979. *Annual Report to the President—1979.* Washington, D.C.: U.S. Dept. of Health and Human Services, DHEW Publication No. 79-20958.

General Accounting Office. 1979. *Report to the Congress of the United States.* Washington, D.C.: Government Printing Office.

Kahn, A. 1969. *Theory and Practice of Social Planning.* New York: Russell Sage Foundation.

Kaplan, J., C.S. Ford, and H. Wain. 1967. "Assessing the Impact of a Gerontological Counseling Service on Community Health Resources." *Geriatrics* 22:150–154.

Lawton, M.P., R.J. Newcomer, and T.O. Byerts, eds. 1977. *Community Planning for An Aging Society.* London: Dowden, Hutchinson, Ross.

Naven, R., N. Weitzer, and I.N.A. Nuller. 1968. "A Method for Planning for Care of Long-Term Patients." *American Journal of Public Health* 58:2111–2120.

Neugarten, B. 1970. "Age Groups in American Society and the Rise of the Young-Old." *Annals of the American Academy of Political and Social Science* 415:187–198.

Plowman, F.C. 1967. *Hospital-Nursing Home Demonstration Project, Final Report.* Detroit: United Community Services of Metropolitan Detroit.

Wasser, E. 1966. *Creative Approaches for Casework with the Aging.* New York: Family Service Association of America.

Appendixes

Appendix A

Number and Percentage of Respondents by Service Area and Census Tract in Baltimore County, Maryland

Service area and census tract	Number of respondents (N=1182)	Percent
Southwest		
(Total)	(406)	(34.3)
4001	52	4.4
4002	75	6.6
4012	1	0.1
4014	19	1.6
4039	1	0.1
4307	86	7.3
4309	171	14.5
5100.07	1	0.1
Northwest		
(Total)	(70)	(5.9)
4023.02	26	2.2
4026.01	6	0.5
4032.02	38	3.2
North		
(Total)	(163)	(13.8)
4080.15	1	0.1
4084	16	1.4
4087.01	44	3.7
4903.02	6	0.5
4904.02	1	0.1
4906.02	61	5.2
4907.01	15	1.3
4914	19	1.6
Northeast		
(Total)	(322)	(27.2)
4088	58	4.9
4405	106	9.0
4405.02	2	0.2
4407	12	1.0
4410	27	2.3
4505	1	0.1
4921	3	0.3
4921.01	113	9.6
Southeast		
(Total)	(221)	(18.7)
4502.02	1	0.1
4505.02	61	5.2
4510	67	5.7
4515	25	2.1
4515.07	1	0.1
4516	66	5.6

[*]Respondents who had complete information in the SNAP survey were included in the analysis

Appendix B

Survey Instrument

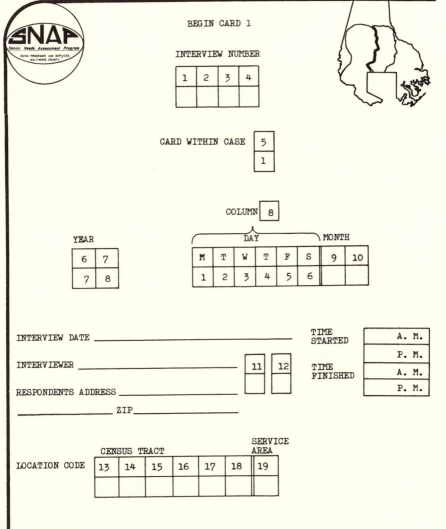

BEGIN CARD 1

INTERVIEW NUMBER

1	2	3	4

CARD WITHIN CASE

5
1

COLUMN | 8 |

YEAR

6	7
7	8

	DAY						MONTH	
	M	T	W	T	F	S	9	10
	1	2	3	4	5	6		

INTERVIEW DATE _____

INTERVIEWER _____ | 11 | 12 |

RESPONDENTS ADDRESS _____

_____ ZIP_____

TIME STARTED	A. M.
	P. M.
TIME FINISHED	A. M.
	P. M.

LOCATION CODE

	CENSUS TRACT						SERVICE AREA
	13	14	15	16	17	18	19

BALTIMORE COUNTY
Senior Needs Assessment Program
(SNAP) Survey

1. Sex of Respondent?

    MALE . . . .   20 - 1
    FEMALE . . . .   - 2

---

2. (ASK ONLY IF NOT OBVIOUS)
    What is your race or ethnic
    descent?

    WHITE (Caucasian) . . . . . .   21 - 1
    BLACK (Negro) . . . .   - 2
    ORIENTAL
    (Japanese,Chinese,Filipino) .   - 3
    ASIAN INDIAN . . . .   - 4
    AMERICAN INDIAN . . . .   - 5
    SPANISH AMERICAN(Spanish Surname)   - 6
    OTHER (Specify)_____   - 7
    NOT ANSWERED . . . .   - 0

---

3. Could you please tell me how
    old you were on your last
    birthday?
                                     22 -
                                     23 -
                    _____
                    (actual age)

---

4. How far have you gone in
    school?

    0-4 years . . . .   24 - 1
    5-8 years . . . .   - 2
    High School incomplete. . . .   - 3
    High School completed . . . .   - 4
    Post High School
    (Business or trade school). .   - 5
    1-3 years College . . . . . .   - 6
    4 years College completed . .   - 7
    Post graduate College . . . .   - 8
    Not answered or unknown . . .   - 0

NOW I'D LIKE TO ASK YOU SOME QUESTIONS ABOUT YOUR FAMILY AND FRIENDS.

5. What is your marital status
    now?

    Never married . . . .   25 - 1
    Married . . . .   - 2
    Separated . . . .   - 3
    Divorced . . . .   - 4
    Widowed . . . .   - 5
    Not answered. . . . .   - 0

---

6. Who lives with you? (Check YES (Code 1) or NO (Code 2) for each of the
    following.)

YES	NO

NO ONE   . . . .   26 - 1
                                     - 2
HUSBAND or WIFE. . . . .   27 - 1
                                     - 2
CHILDREN . . . .   28 - 1
                                     - 2
GRANDCHILDREN. . . . .   29 - 1
                                     - 2
PARENTS . . . .   30 - 1
                                     - 2
BROTHERS and/or SISTERS . . .   31 - 1
                                     - 2
OTHER RELATIVES . . . .   32 - 1
                                     - 2
FRIENDS . . . .   33 - 1
                                     - 2
ROOMING HOUSE;BOARDING HOUSE .   34 - 1
                                     - 2
OTHER (Specify)_____   35 - 1
                                     - 2

6a. (UNLESS RESPONDENT LIVES ALONE,ASK)
    How many people live in this house-   36 -
    hold?   (number of persons)   37 -

6b. (UNLESS RESPONDENT LIVES ALONE,ASK)
    How many people - including you -   38 -
    are 60 years of age or older?   (number of persons)   39 -

7.   Do you have any children?   Yes . . . . 40 - 1
                                No . . . .   - 2
                                Not answered . . . . - 0

7a. (IF R HAS CHILDREN,ASK)
    How many living children do you   41 -
    have?   (number of children) 42 -

7b. (IF R HAS CHILDREN,ASK)
    How many of your children live   None . . . . 43 - 1
    within an hour's driving time   Actual Number_____ 44-45 -
    from you?

7c. (IF R HAS CHILDREN,ASK)
    How often do you see any of   Daily. . . . . 46 - 1
    your children?   Several times a week . . . . - 2
                                Once or twice a week . . . . - 3
                                Once or twice a month. . . . - 4
                                Several times a year . . . . - 5
                                Once a year. . . . . - 6
                                Never. . . . . - 7
                                Not answered . . . . - 0

7d. (IF R HAS CHILDREN,ASK)
    Do you call on them for help   Yes . . . . 47 - 1
    with any problems?   No . . . . - 2
                                  Not answered . . . . - 0

7e. (IF R HAS CHILDREN,ASK)
    Would you like to see your   Yes . . . . 48 - 1
    children more often?   No . . . . - 2
                                  Not answered . . . . - 0

8.   How many people do you know   None . . . . 49 - 1
    well enough that you visit   One or Two . . . . - 2
    them in their homes?   Three to Five. . . . . - 3
                                Six or more. . . . . - 4
                                Not answered . . . . - 0

9.   About how many times did you   Not at all . . . . 50 - 1
    talk to someone---friends,   Once . . . . - 2
    relatives, or neighbors--on   2-6 times. . . . . - 3
    the telephone in the past week Once a day or more . . . . . - 4
    (either you called them or they Not answered . . . . - 0
    called you)?
    (IF R HAS NO PHONE,QUESTION
    STILL APPLIES.)

10. Do you have a telephone in this Yes . . . . 51 - 1
    place?   No . . . . - 2
                                  Not answered . . . . - 0

10a.	How many times during the past week did you spend some time with someone who does not live with you, that is you went to see them or they came to visit you, or you went out to do things together?	Not at all . . . . Once . . . . 2 - 6 times. . . . . Once a day or more	52 - 1 - 2 - 3 - 4
11.	Do you have someone you can trust and confide in?	Yes . . . . No . . . . Not answered	53 - 1 - 2 - 0
12.	Do you see your relatives and friends as often as you want to, or would you like to see them more often?	As often as wants. . . . . Like to see more . . . . . Not answered	54 - 1 - 2 - 0
13.	Is there someone who would give you any help at all if you were sick or disabled, for example your husband/wife, a member of your family, or a friend?	Yes . . . . No . . . . Don't know . . . . Not answered	55 - 1 - 2 - 3 - 0
13a.	(IF R ANSWERS "YES" TO Q.13,ASK) Who is this person?	Husband/Wife . . . . Children . . . . Other relative . . . . . . Friend/Neighbor. . . . . . Other (Specify)_____ Not answered	56 - 1 - 2 - 3 - 4 - 5 - 0
13b.	(IF R ANSWERED "YES"TO Q.13,ASK) Is there someone who would take care of you as long as you needed, or only for a short time, or only someone who would help you now and then (for example, taking you to the doctor, or fixing lunch occasionally, etc.)	Indefinitely . . . . Short time _ (few weeks to 6 months). . Now and then . . . . Not answered	57 - 1 - 2 - 3 - 0

NOW I'D LIKE TO ASK A FEW QUESTIONS ABOUT YOUR HOME AND THE NEIGHBORHOOD YOU LIVE IN.

14.	How long have you been living in this neighbor-hood? (DON'T READ CHOICES.)	Less than 1 year . . . . . 1 yr. to less than 3 yrs . 3 yrs. to less than 5 yrs. 5 yrs. to less than 10 yrs 10 yrs. to less than 15 yrs 15 yrs. to less than 20 yrs 20 yrs. or more. . . . . . Not answered	58 - 1 - 2 - 3 - 4 - 5 - 6 - 7 - 0
15.	Do you own your home, rent or is your rent provided free?	Own . . . . Rent . . . . Rent provided free . . . . Not answered	59 - 1 - 2 - 3 - 0
15a.	(IF R ANSWERED "OWN" TO Q.15,ASK) Are you making mortgage pay-ments or is your mortgage already paid?	Making payments. . . . . . Mortgage paid. . . . . . . Not answered	60 - 1 - 2 - 0

15b. (IF R ANSWERED "RENT" TO Q.15,ASK)
      Do you receive a rent supplement?   Yes . . . .   61 - 1
                                           No . . . .   - 2
                                           Not answered. . . . . . .   - 0

15c. (IF R ANSWERED "RENT FREE" TO
      Q. 15, ASK)
      Who owns this house or who pays   Relatives . . . .   62 - 1
      your rent?   Friends . . . .   - 2
                                           Church. . . . .   - 3
                                           Government. . . . .   - 4
                                           Other (Specify)_____   - 5
                                           Not answered. . . . . . .   - 0

16.   Would you say that this place is   Too large . . . .   63 - 1
      too large, too small, or just   Too small . . . .   - 2
      about right for your needs?   Just about right. . . . .   - 3
                                           Not answered. . . . . . .   - 0

17.   How many rooms do you have, not
      counting bathrooms, hallways and   _____   64 -
      out door areas?   (number of rooms)   65 -

18.   Do you (and your family) have a   Private . . . .   66 - 1
      private kitchen or do you share   Shared . . . .   - 2
      a kitchen with other households?   No kitchen . . . .   - 3
                                           Not answered . . . .   - 0

19.   Do you (and your family) have a   Private . . . . 67 - 1
      private bathroom, or do you share   Shared . . . .   - 2
      a bathroom with people in other   Outhouse . . . .   - 3
      families?   No facilities. . . . . . .   - 4
                                           Not answered . . . .   - 0

20.   Does your home have any safety   Fire alarm . . . . 68 - 1
      alarms such as fire or burglary?   Burglar alarm . . . . . .   - 2
                                           Fire and Burglar alarm . .   - 3
                                           No alarm . . . .   - 4
                                           Not answered . . . .   - 0

21.   Does this building need any   Yes . . . .   69 - 1
      repairs inside or outside?   No . . . .   - 2
                                           Not answered . . . .   - 0

                    READ APPROPRIATE
              LIST AND CHECK ALL THAT APPLY

21a. (IF R ANSWERED "YES" TO Q.21, ASK)   INSIDE REPAIRS   70-71 -
      What kinds of repairs does this   1. Walls, doors, floors,
      property need?   or ceilings(damaged) . . .   -10
                                           2. Basement leak . . . . .   -11
                                           3. Furnace or water heater   -12
                                           4. Electrical system . . .   -13
                                           5. Major appliances/stove,
                                           refrigerator,washer,dryer,
                                           air conditioner . . . . ..   -14
                                           6. Painting,wallpaper . ..   -15
                                           7. Plumbing . . . .   -16

```
                                    OFFICE CODING ONLY
                                    Two or Three, Inside . . . . .      -17
                                    Four or Five, Inside . . . . .      -18
                                    Six, Inside . . . . . . . .         -19
                                    OUTSIDE REPAIRS            72-73 -
                                    1. Roof, chimney or rainspout       -20
                                    2. Damaged porch, railings,
                                       patios, sidewalks. . . . . .     -21
                                    3. Rotted or missing shingle
                                       on sides of house . . . . .      -22
                                    4. Fence . . . . . . . . . . .      -23
                                    5. Doors, screens, or windows.      -24
                                    6. Painting. . . . . . . . .        -25
                                    OFFICE CODING ONLY
                                    Two or Three, Outside. . . . .      -26
                                    Four or Five Outside . . . . .      -27
                                    Six Outside . . . . . . . .         -28
```

22. Considering everything-amount   READ LIST
     of room, structure, condition,   Very satisfied . . . . 74 - 1
     and so forth - how satisfied   Somewhat satisfied . . . . . .   - 2
     are you with your present home?   (DON'T READ)
                                        Neither satisfied nor dis-
                                        satisfied . . . .   - 3
                                        Somewhat dissatisfied. . . . .   - 4
                                        Very dissatisfied. . . . . . .   - 5
                                        Not answered . . . .   - 0

23. How many of your friends live   All . . . . 75 - 1
     in this neighborhood?   Most . . . .   - 2
     Would you say (READ LIST).   Some . . . .   - 3
                                        Not many . . . .   - 4
                                        None . . . .   - 5
                                        Not answered . . . .   - 0

24. Do you belong to any organ-   Yes . . . . 76 - 1
     izations or clubs that are   No . . . .   - 2
     involved with neighborhood   Not answered . . . .   - 0
     activities? Please include
     any church clubs you belong
     to.

25. Are most of the places you   Inside . . . . 77 - 1
     go; such as doctors offices,   Outside. . . . .   - 2
     stores, religious meetings   Inside & Outside. . . . . . .   - 3
     and banks, inside or outside   Doesn't go anywhere. . . . . .   - 4
     this neighborhood?   Not answered . . . .   - 0

26. Do you feel that you are   Feel a part of . . . . 78 - 1
     really a part of this neigh-   Just a place to live . . . . .   - 2
     borhood, or do you see it as   Not answered . . . .   - 0
     just a place to live?
```

```
                        BEGIN CARD TWO
                       INTERVIEW NUMBER
                      | 1 | 2 | 3 | 4 |
                      | | | | |
                      | | | | |

                 CARD WITHIN CASE . . . .   5 - 2
```
```

27. Are you planning to remain
    here for the next two years?
    Yes . . . .   6 - 1
    No . . . .   - 2
    Not answered. . . . .   - 0

(IF R ANSWERED "NO" TO Q. 27,
ASK) DO NOT READ ANSWERS.
27a. Where are you planning to go?

    Different neighborhood in
    County. . . . .   7,8 -01
    Different County or State .   -02
    Baltimore City. . . . . . .   -03
    Senior housing. . . . . . .   -04
    With children/relatives,
    Baltimore County. . . . . .   -05
    With children/relatives, not
    Baltimore County. . . . . .   -06
    Smaller/less expensive place   -07
    Larger/more comfortable
    place . . . .   -08
    Away from family. . . . . .   -09
    Nursing or aged home. . . .   -10
    Other (specify)_____   -11
    Not sure. . . . .   -12
    Not answered. . . . .   -00

28. If you had a choice, would you
    like to move somewhere else?
    Yes . . . .   9 - 1
    No. . . . .   - 2
    Not answered. . . . .   - 0

(IF R ANSWERED "YES" TO Q. 28,
ASK) DO NOT READ ANSWERS.
28a. Where would you like to live?

    Different neighborhood in
    County. . . . . 10,11 -01
    Different County or State .   -02
    Baltimore City. . . . . . .   -03
    Senior Housing. . . . . . .   -04
    With children/relatives,
    Baltimore County. . . . . .   -05
    With children/relatives, not
    Baltimore County. . . . . .   -06
    Smaller/less expensive place   -07
    Larger/more comfortable
    place . . . .   -08
    Away from family. . . . . .   -09
    Nursing or aged home. . . .   -10
    Other (Specify)_____   -11
    Not sure. . . . .   -12
    Not answered. . . . .   -00

29. Generally speaking, how do you
    like living in this neighbor-
    hood? Would you say you like
    it -(READ LIST)
    Very much . . . .   12 - 1
    A little (it's o.k.). . . .   - 2
    Not at all. . . . .   - 3
    Have mixed feelings . . . .   - 4
    Don't know. . . . .   - 5
    Not answered. . . . .   - 0

PERSONAL WELL-BEING
LET'S TALK ABOUT SOME OTHER ASPECTS OF LIVING IN THIS NEIGHBORHOOD
FOR A MOMENT.

30. Have you been bothered by
    neighborhood children or
    teenagers?
    Yes . . . .   13 - 1
    No . . . .   - 2
    Not answered. . . . .   - 0

30a. (IF R ANSWERED "YES" TO Q.30,ASK)   (DO NOT READ LIST.)
      What is the one thing that has   Leaving toys, bikes or
      bothered you the most concerning   trash in yard. . . . . . .   14 - 1
      neighborhood youth?   Generally disrespectful:
                                          harass, curse, threaten. .   - 2
                                          Loiter on street at night.   - 3
                                          Noisy . . . .   - 4
                                          Drinking; drugs. . . . . .   - 5
                                          Not trustworthy; steal, lie,
                                          flaunt the law . . . . . .   - 6
                                          Other (specify)_____   - 7
                                          Not answered . . . .   - 0

31.   Would you feel safe walking   Yes . . . .   15 - 1
      alone in this neighborhood in   No . . . .   - 2
      the daytime?   Not answered . . . .   - 0

32.   Would you feel safe waiting   Yes . . . .   16 - 1
      alone for a bus in this neigh-   No . . . .   - 2
      borhood in the daytime?   Not answered . . . .   - 0

33.   Would you feel safe walking   Yes . . . .   17 - 1
      alone in this neighborhood at   No . . . .   - 2
      night?   Not answered . . . .   - 0

34.   Would you feel safe waiting   Yes . . . .   18 - 1
      alone for a bus in this neigh-   No . . . .   - 2
      borhood at night?   Not answered . . . .   - 0

35.   Are there any places in the   Yes . . . .   19 - 1
      neighborhood or anywhere else   No . . . .   - 2
      that you would like to go, but   Not answered . . . .   - 0
      that you do not go because you
      do not feel safe?

36.   In the past year have there been   Yes . . . .   20 - 1
      any crimes in the neighborhood?   No . . . .   - 2
                                          Don't know . . . .   - 3
                                          Not answered . . . . . .   - 0

37.   Have you ever been the victim of   Yes . . . .   21 - 1
      a crime?   No . . . .   - 2
                                          Not answered . . . .   - 0

37a. (IF R ANSWERED "YES" TO Q. 37,ASK) (READ LIST)   22,23 -
      Could you please tell me what   Home burglary. . . . . . .   -01
      type of crime this was?   Vandalism . . . .   -02
                                          Purse snatching. . . . . .   -03
                                          Mugging . . . .   -04
                                          Car theft. . . . .   -05
                                          Holdup at gunpoint . . . .   -06
                                          Arson . . . .   -07
                                          Sexual Assault . . . . . .   -08
                                          Con game . . . .   -09
                                          Other (specify)_____   -10
                                          Not answered . . . .   -00

38. If you have had any other difficulties in the neighborhood, please describe the one thing which has been the most problem for you?

(DO NOT READ LIST.)   24,25 -
Garbage collection . . . .   -01
Poor or no sidewalks . . .   -02
Poor street lighting . . .   -03
Poor drainage or no
stormdrains . . . .   -04
Pets run loose . . . . . .   -05
Traffic . . . .   -06
Slow police response . . .   -07
Poor cooperation by
neighbors (noisy,snoop,etc.)   -08
Lack of recreational
facilities . . . .   -09
Poor fire protection . . .   -10
Poor transportation
system . . . .   -11
Lack of convenient shopping
facilities . . . .   -12
Other (specify)_____   -13
I have no problems . . . .   -14
Not answered . . . .   -00

39. All things considered, do you think that this is a safe neighborhood in which to live?

Yes . . . .   26 - 1
No . . . .   - 2
Not answered . . . .   - 0

40. If you did feel safer around here, would you go out more often, less often, or about the same as you do now?

More often . . . .   27 - 1
Less often . . . .   - 2
About the same as now . .   - 3
Don't know . . . .   - 4
Not answered . . . .   - 0

41. What is the one thing that could be done to make you feel safer in this neighborhood?

(DO NOT READ LIST.)   28,29 -
Better police protection .   -01
Better neighbors or
community organizations.. .   -02
More streetlighting. . . .   -03
Sidewalks . . . .   -04
Better animal control. . .   -05
Better traffic control . .   -06
Personal escort. . . . . .   -07
Home security system . . .   -08
Better fire protection . .   -09
Programs for children and
teens (recreation, guidance,
etc.) . . . .   -10
Better transportation
system . . . .   -11
Other (specify)_____   -12
Nothing. . . . .   -13
Not answered . . . .   -00

42. Do you feel that you have ever been treated unfairly because of your age?

Yes . . . .   30 - 1
No . . . .   - 2
Don't know . . . .   - 3
Not answered . . . .   - 0

42a. (IF R ANSWERED "YES" TO Q.42,ASK) (DO NOT READ LIST.)
Would you please tell me how you

were treated unfairly?	Work related	31 - 1
	Financial-Loans,etc. . . .	- 2
	Service from government. .	- 3
	Health-Physician, Hospital, etc.	- 4
	Consumer-Repairs,Insurance, etc.	- 5
	Disrespect from younger people	- 6
	Other (Specify)_____	- 7
	Not answered	- 0

TRANSPORTATION

I'D LIKE TO ASK SOME QUESTIONS ABOUT HOW YOU GET AROUND WHEN YOU WANT
TO GO SOMEWHERE?

43. Does anyone in this household
have a car in working condition?

Yes	32 - 1
No	- 2
Not answered.	- 0

43a. (IF R ANSWERED "YES" TO Q.43,ASK)
Do you drive the car frequently,
occasionally, almost never, or
never?

Frequently	33 - 1
Occasionally	- 2
Almost never	- 3
Never	- 4
Not answered	- 0

44. When you go shopping, to the
doctor, visit friends, etc.,
how do you get there?
    (READ LIST, CHECK "YES" OR "NO" FOR EACH.)

DO YOU

	YES	NO		
(a)			Walk	34 - 1
				- 2
(b)			Drive yourself	35 - 1
				- 2
(c)			Family or friends drive. .	36 - 1
				- 2
(d)			Take taxi	37 - 1
				- 2
(e)			Use "Senioride", other . . public agency	38 - 1 - 2
F			Take MTA Bus	39 - 1
				- 2
(g)			Other (specify)_____	40 - 1 - 2

44a. (IF R ANSWERED "YES" TO Q.44F,ASK) (READ LIST.)
How many of the places that you
want to go can you get to, using
the MTA Bus system?

All	41 - 1
Most	- 2
Some	- 3
A few	- 4
None	- 5
(DON'T READ)	
Don't know	- 6
Not answered	- 0

44b. (IF R ANSWERED "NO" TO Q.44F, ASK)   42,43 -
     Why don't you use the bus?   Not convenient, too far
     (DO NOT READ LIST, CHECK ALL   from here . . . .   -01
          THAT APPLY.)   Bus does not go where I
                                     want to go. . . . .   -02
                                     Costs too much. . . . .   -03
                                     Buses don't run often
                                     enough. . . . .   -04
                                     Seats are not always avail-
                                     able . . . .   -05
                                     Seats are not comfortable . .   -06
                                     Drivers are not courteous . .   -07
                                     Drivers do not give change. .   -08
                                     Routes and schedules are
                                     difficult to understand . . .   -09
                                     Bus stops are not safe. . . .   -10
                                     No protected area to wait
                                     for bus . . . .   -11
                                     Don't like/want to ride
                                     the bus . . . .   -12
                                     Don't know. . . . .   -13
                                     Other (specify)_____   -14
                                     Not answered. . . . .   -00
                                     (OFFICE CODING ONLY)
                                     2-5 of above. . . . .   -15
                                     6-9 of above. . . . .   -16
                                     10-13 of above. . . . .   -17

---

45. On the average, how many round
     trips do you make each week for   44 -
     shopping, visiting, work, bus-   45 -
     iness or any other reason?   (number   of   trips)

---

46. In general, do you have any   Yes . . . . .46 - 1
     trouble getting around? That   No   . . . . - 2
     is, does lack of transporta-   Not answered. . . . .   - 0
     tion keep you from doing things
     you need or would like to do?

---

47. Do you need additional transportation for any of the following reasons?
          (READ LIST AND CHECK "YES" OR "NO" FOR EACH.)

	YES	NO
(a)		
(b)		
(c)		
(d)		
(e)		
(f)		
(g)		
(h)		
(i)		

To visit friends or relatives . . . .   47 - 1
                                                    - 2
To participate in recreational, social . . . . 48 - 1
activities   - 2
To go shopping . . . .   49 - 1
                                                    - 2
To go to a doctor, dentist, or medical. . . .   50 - 1
facility   - 2
To take a day trip or ride for enjoyment. . .   51 - 1
                                                    - 2
To get to Social Services Offices (Food . . .   52 - 1
stamps, Medicaid, Social Security, etc.)   - 2
To go to Post Office, Bank, Library, other. .   53 - 1
personal business   - 2
To participate in educational programs . . .   54 - 1
                                                    - 2
To go to work . . . .   55 - 1
                                                    - 2

ACTIVITY

NOW LET'S CHANGE THE SUBJECT AND TALK ABOUT THE KINDS OF THINGS
YOU ENJOY DOING IN YOUR SPARE TIME?

48.   I am going to read through a list of activities which a person might
       do in his/her spare time. I would like you to tell me if you do each
       of these things often, sometimes, or never.

ACTIVITY	OFTEN	SOMETIMES	NEVER
a. Read magazines or books	56 - 1	56 - 2	56 - 3
b. Go to movies, plays or concerts	57 - 1	57 - 2	57 - 3
c. Go to meetings, clubs	58 - 1	58 - 2	58 - 3
d. Go for walks	59 - 1	59 - 2	59 - 3
e. Play cards with others	60 - 1	60 - 2	60 - 3
f. Gardening indoors or out	61 - 1	61 - 2	61 - 3
g. Work on a hobby	62 - 1	62 - 2	62 - 3
h. Playing sports, golf, pool,swimming,tennis,etc.	63 - 1	63 - 2	63 - 3

49.   How many hours do you spend
       each day watching TV?   64 -
                                   (number of hours)   65 -

49a.   (IF R DOES WATCH TV, ASK)   (READ LIST, CHECK FAVORITE TYPE)
       What is your favorite kind   66,67 -
       of program?   Weekly comedies . . . .   -01
                                        Daytime Soap Operas . . . . .   -02
                                        Game Shows . . . .   -03
                                        Nature Programs . . . .   -04
                                        News Programs . . . .   -05
                                        Sports . . . .   -06
                                        Talk Shows. . . . .   -07
                                        Variety Specials. . . . . . .   -08
                                        Detective & Police Shows. . .   -09
                                        Informative Shows–like 60
                                        Minutes and Weekend . . . . .   -10
                                        (DO NOT READ–NO PREFERENCE) .   -11
                                        Not answered. . . . .   -00
                                        More than one . . . .   -12

49b.   (IF R DOES WATCH TV, ASK)
       Do you watch the public   Often . . . .   68 - 1
       educational TV channels   Sometimes . . . .   - 2
       67 or 22?   Hardly ever . . . .   - 3
                                        Never . . . .   - 4
                                        Not answered. . . . .   - 0

50. How often do you read news-   Daily . . . .   69 - 1
     papers? Would you say you   Sunday only . . . .   - 2
     read them daily, on Sunday,   Daily & Sunday. . . . .   - 3
     both daily & Sunday, or never?   Never . . . .   - 4
                                         Not answered. . . . .   - 0

50a. (IF R DOES READ NEWSPAPERS,ASK)
     Which newspapers do you read?   Sunpapers . . . .   70 - 1
                                          News American . . . .   - 2
                                          Sun & News American . . . .   - 3
                                          Out of town papers. . . . .   - 4
                                          Local & out of town papers.   - 5
                                          Not answered . . . . . .   - 0

51. Is there something in par-   Yes . . . .   71 - 1
     ticular that you are looking   No . . . .   - 2
     forward to doing next week?   Not answered. . . . .   - 0

52. Are you a member of any local   Yes . . . .   72 - 1
     or national organization for   No . . . .   - 2
     older Americans?   Not answered. . . . .   - 0

53. Are you registered to vote?   Yes . . . .   73 - 1
                                          No . . . .   - 2
                                          Not answered. . . . .   - 0

54. Do you attend religious   Yes . . . .   74 - 1
     services?   No . . . .   - 2
                                          Not answered. . . . .   - 0

55. In general do you feel you   Yes . . . .   75 - 1
     get to spend enough time do-   No . . . .   - 2
     ing the things you like to do?   Not sure. . . . .   - 3
                                          Not answered. . . . .   - 0

56. Would you say that you prefer   About your age. . . . . . .   76 - 1
     to spend time with people about   Younger people. . . . . . .   - 2
     your age, people younger than   Older people. . . . .   - 3
     you, people older than you, or   People of all ages. . . . .   - 4
     people of all ages?   Not answered. . . . .   - 0

MENTAL HEALTH

NEXT I'D LIKE TO ASK YOU SOME QUESTIONS ABOUT HOW YOU FEEL ABOUT LIFE:

57. How often would you say you   Very often . . . .   77 - 1
     worry about things---very   Fairly often. . . . .   - 2
     often, fairly often, or   Hardly ever . . . .   - 3
     hardly ever?   Not answered. . . . .   - 0

58. In general, do you find life   Exciting. . . . .   78 - 1
     exciting, pretty routine, or   Pretty routine. . . . . . .   - 2
     dull?   Dull. . . . .   - 3
                                         Not answered. . . . .   - 0

59. Taking everything into con-   Good. . . . .   79 - 1
     sideration, how would you de-   Fair. . . . .   - 2
     scribe your satisfaction with   Poor. . . . .   - 3
     life in general at the present   Not answered. . . . .   - 0
     time --good, fair, or poor?

<u>BEGIN CARD THREE</u>

INTERVIEW NUMBER

1	2	3	4

CARD WITHIN CASE . . . .   5 - 3

---

60. Please answer the following questions "<u>Yes</u>" or "No" as they apply to you now. There are no right or wrong answers, only what best applies to you. Occasionally a question may not seem to apply to you, but please answer either "Yes" or "No", whichever is more nearly correct for you.(*)

    <u>(CIRCLE "YES" OR "NO" FOR EACH.)</u>

(1) Do you wake up fresh and rested most mornings? . . . . . . YES   NO

(2) Is your daily life full of things that keep you interested? . . . . YES   NO

(3) Have you, at times, very much wanted to leave home?. . . . YES   NO

(4) Does it seem that no one understands you?. . . . . YES   NO

(5) Have you had periods of days, weeks, or months when you couldn't take care of things because you couldn't "get going"? . . . . YES   NO

(6) Is your sleep fitful and disturbed? . . . . YES   NO

(7) Are you happy most of the time? . . . . YES   NO

(8) Are you being plotted against? . . . . YES   NO

(9) Do you certainly feel useless at times?. . . . . YES   NO

(10) During the past few years, have you been well most of the time?. . . . . YES   NO

(11) Do you feel weak all over much of the time?. . . . . YES   NO

(12) Are you troubled by headaches? . . . . YES   NO

(13) Have you had difficulty in keeping your balance in walking?. . . . . YES   NO

(14) Are you troubled by your heart pounding and by a shortness of breath? . . . . YES   NO

(15) Even when you are with people, do you feel lonely much of the time? . . . . YES   NO

           <u>(OFFICE CODING ONLY)</u> . . . .   6 - 7

           Sum of Responses in Capital letters   _____

---

61. How would you rate your emotional health at the present time -- excellent, good, fair, or poor?

    Excellent . . . .   8 - 1
    Good . . . .   - 2
    Fair . . . .   - 3
    Poor . . . .   - 4
    Not answered. . . . .   - 0

---

62. Is your emotional health now better, about the same, or worse than it was five years ago?

    Better . . . .   9 - 1
    About the same. . . . .   - 2
    Worse . . . .   - 3
    Not answered. . . . .   - 0

PHYSICAL HEALTH

LET'S TALK ABOUT YOUR HEALTH NOW?

63. About how many times have you
     seen a doctor during the past
     six months?   (number of times)   10 -
                                                                   11 -

64. During the past six months,   None . . . .   12 - 1
     how many days were you so sick   A week or less . . . . . .   - 2
     that you had to give up most   More than a week but less
     of your regular activities --   than a month . . . . . .   - 3
     such as going to work or work-   1-3 months . . . .   - 4
     ing around the house?   4-6 months . . . .   - 5
     (READ LIST)   Not answered . . . .   - 0

65. How many days in the past six
     months were you in a hospital   13 -
     overnight or longer?   (number of days)   14 -

65a. (IF R WAS HOSPITALIZED, ASK)
     After you came home from the hospital did you need...
     (READ LIST. CHECK "YES" OR "NO" FOR EACH.)

	YES	NO	
1.			Nursing care or help with bathing and . . 15 - 1
			dressing - 2
2.			Help with cooking or housework . . . . . 16 - 1
			- 2
3.			Transportation for any reason . . . . . . 17 - 1
			- 2
4.			Someone to go shopping for you. . . . . . 18 - 1
			- 2
5.			Someone to stop by to see how you were. . 19 - 1
			feeling - 2

65b. (IF R ANSWERED "YES" TO ANY OF
     Q. 65a, ASK)
     Were you able to get all the   Yes . . . .   20 - 1
     help that you needed after you   No . . . .   - 2
     returned home from the hospital   Not answered . . . .   - 0

65c. (IF R WAS HOSPITALIZED, ASK)
     Did the hospital tell you about   Yes . . . .   21 - 1
     any services that you might   No . . . .   - 2
     qualify for after you returned   Not answered . . . .   - 0
     home?

65d. (IF R ANSWERED "YES" TO Q. 65c,
     ASK)
     Did you use any services that   Yes . . . .   22 - 1
     the hospital told you about?   No . . . .   - 2
                                       Not answered . . . .   - 0

66. How many days in the past six
     months were you in a Nursing   23 -
     Home, or rehabilitation center?   (number of days)   24 -

67. How satisfied are you with
the medical treatment that
you have received in the past
six months? Would you say
that you are very satisfied,
somewhat satisfied, some-
what dissatisfied, or very
dissatisfied?

Very satisfied . . . . . .   25 - 1
Somewhat satisfied . . . .   - 2
Somewhat dissatisfied. . .   - 3
Very dissatisfied. . . . .   - 4
Not answered . . . .   - 0

68. Do you have any problems
getting all the medical
care or treatment you feel
that you need?

Yes . . . .   26 - 1
No . . . .   - 2
Not answered . . . .   - 0

68a. (IF R ANSWERED "YES" TO Q.68, ASK)   27,28 -
What are those problems?
(DO NOT READ LIST. CHECK ALL   No doctor available in
     THAT APPLY.)   vicinity . . . .   -01
                                  Can't afford medical care.   -02
                                  Have difficulty getting
                                  transportation . . . . .   -03
                                  Don't know where to go . .   -04
                                  Can't get there because of
                                  physical condition . . . .   -05
                                  Can't get a doctor to treat
                                  me or my problem . . . . .   -06
                                  Can't get a doctor to come
                                  to the house . . . .   -07
                                  Other (specify)_____   -08
                                  Not answered . . . .   -00
                                  (OFFICE CODING ONLY)
                                  Two or three of above. . .   -10
                                  Four or five of above. . .   -11
                                  Six or seven of above. . .   -12
                                  Eight of above . . . . . .   -13

69. When was the last time you
went to a dentist?
(DO NOT READ LIST)

Never . . . .   29 - 1
Within last year . . . . .   - 2
More than one year but
less than 3 years ago. . .   - 3
3 or more years ago. . . .   - 4
Don't remember/don't know.   - 5
Not answered . . . .   - 0

70. Do you have any physical disabilities such as total or
partial paralysis, missing or
non-functional limbs, or broken
bones? (READ LIST. CHECK ALL
THAT APPLY.)

No . . . .   30 - 1
Total paralysis. . . . . .   - 2
Partial paralysis. . . . .   - 3
Missing or non-functional
limbs. . . . .   - 4
Broken bones . . . .   - 5
Not answered . . . .   - 0
(OFFICE CODING ONLY)
Two or three of above. . .   - 6
Four or five of above. . .   - 7

71. How is your eyesight (with
glasses or contacts)?

(DO NOT READ LIST)

Excellent . . . .   31 - 1
Good . . . .   - 2
Fair . . . .   - 3
Poor . . . .   - 4
Totally blind. . . . . . .   - 5
Not answered . . . .   - 0

72. How is your hearing?
    (DO NOT READ LIST)

    Excellent . . . .   32 – 1
    Good . . . .   – 2
    Fair . . . .   – 3
    Poor . . . .   – 4
    Totally deaf. . . . . . .   – 5
    Not answered. . . . . . .   – 0

---

73. Do you use any of the following aids all or most of the time?
    (READ LIST. CHECK "YES" OR "NO" FOR EACH.)

YES	NO	DO YOU USE A	
		Cane (including tripod-tip cane)	33 – 1 – 2
		Walker	34 – 1 – 2
		Wheelchair.	35 – 1 – 2
		Leg Brace	36 – 1 – 2
		Back Brace.	37 – 1 – 2
		Artificial Limb	38 – 1 – 2
		Mechanical Voice.	39 – 1 – 2
		Hearing Aid	40 – 1 – 2
		Kidney dialysis machine	41 – 1 – 2
		Other (specify)_____	42 – 1 – 2

---

74. Do you need any aids that you
    currently do not have?

    Yes . . . .   43 – 1
    No . . . .   – 2
    Not answered. . . . . . .   – 0

74a. (IF R ANSWERED "YES" TO Q. 75,ASK)
     What aids do you need? (Specify)

     _____

     _____   Q. 74a

     OFFICE CODING ONLY – SEE CODING MANUAL   44 –
                                                           45 –

---

75. Do you regularly participate in
    any vigorous activity such as
    jogging, tennis, swimming, bik-
    ing or hiking?

    Yes . . . .   46 – 1
    No . . . .   – 2
    Not answered. . . . . . .   – 0

76. Do you have any health or
medical coverage? Do you
have... (READ LIST, CHECK
"YES" OR "NO" FOR EACH.)

YES	NO	DO YOU HAVE		
		Medicaid	47	- 1
				- 2
		Medicare "A" only.	48	- 1
				- 2
		Medicare "A" & "B"	49	- 1
				- 2
		Blue Cross/Blue Shield	50	- 1
				- 2
		A prepaid health plan	51	- 1
				- 2
		Other (specify)_____	52	- 1
				- 2

77. Compared with other people   Excellent . . . .   53 - 1
    your age, would you say   Good . . . .   - 2
    your health is excellent,   Fair . . . .   - 3
    good, fair, poor, or very   Poor . . . .   - 4
    poor?   Not answered . . . .   - 0

78. Is your health now better,   Better . . . .   54 - 1
    about the same, or worse   About the same . . . .   - 2
    than it was five years ago?   Worse. . . . .   - 3
                                    Not answered . . . .   - 0

79. How much does your health   Not at all . . . .   55 - 1
    stand in the way of doing   A little (some). . . . . . .   - 2
    the things you want to do,   A great deal . . . .   - 3
    not at all, a little (some),   Not answered . . . .   - 0
    or a great deal?

ACTIVITIES OF DAILY LIVING

Now I'd like to ask you about some of the activities of daily
living, things that we all need to do as a part of our daily
lives. I would like to know if you can do these activities
without any help at all, or if you need some help to do them,
or if you can't do them at all.

(BE SURE TO READ ALL ANSWER CHOICES IF APPLICABLE IN QUESTIONS
80 THROUGH 91 TO RESPONDENT.)

Instrumental ADL

80. Can you use the telephone...
    (a) without help, including looking up numbers & dialing... 56 - 1
    (b) with some help (can answer phone or dial operator
        in an emergency, but need a special phone or help
        in getting the number or dialing)......................   - 2
    (c) or are you completely unable to use the telephone......   - 3
        Not answered...   - 0

81. Can you get to places out of walking distance...
    (a) without help (can travel alone on buses, taxis, or
        drive your own car)..................................... 57 - 1
    (b) with some help (need someone to help you or go with
        you when traveling) or................................   - 2
    (c) are you unable to travel unless emergency arrangements
        are made for a specialized vehicle like an ambulance?..   - 3
        Not answered...   - 0

82. Can you go shopping for groceries or clothes (ASSUMING R
    HAS TRANSPORTATION)...
    (a) without help (taking care of all shopping needs
        yourself, assuming you had transportation)............ 58 - 1
    (b) with some help (need someone to go with you on all
        shopping trips)....................................... - 2
    (c) or are you completely unable to do any shopping....... - 3
        Not answered... - 0

83. Can you prepare your own meals...
    (a) without help (plan and cook full meals yourself)...... 59 - 1
    (b) with some help (can prepare some things but unable to
        cook full meals yourself)............................ - 2
    (c) or are you completely unable to prepare any meals..... - 3
        Not answered... - 0

84. Can you do your housework...
    (a) without help (can scrub floors, etc.)................. 60 - 1
    (b) with some help (can do light housework but need help
        with heavy work)..................................... - 2
    (c) or are you completely unable to do any housework...... - 3
        Not answered... - 0

85. Can you take your own medicine...
    (a) without help (in the right doses at the right time)... 61 - 1
    (b) with some help (able to take medicine if someone
        prepares it for you and/or reminds you to take it).... - 2
    (c) or are you completely unable to take your medicine.... - 3
        Not answered... - 0

86. Can you eat...
    (a) without help (able to feed yourself completely)....... 62 - 1
    (b) with some help (need help with cutting, etc.)......... - 2
    (c) or are you completely unable to feel yourself......... - 3
        Not answered... - 0

87. Can you dress and undress yourself...
    (a) without help (able to pick out clothes, dress and
        undress yourself)...................... .... 63 - 1
    (b) with some help....................................... - 2
    (c) or are you completely unable to dress and undress
        yourself... - 3
        Not answered... - 0

88. Can you take care of your own appearance, for example combing
    your hair and (for men) shaving...
    (a) without help... 64 - 1
    (b) with some help....................................... - 2
    (c) or are you completely unable to maintain your
        appearance yourself.................................. - 3
        Not answered... - 0

89. Can you walk...
    (a) without help (except from a cane).................... 65 - 1
    (b) with some help from a person or with the use of a
        walker, or crutches, etc............................. - 2
    (c) or are you completely unable to walk................. - 3
        Not answered... - 0

90. Can you get in and out of bed...
    (a) without any help or aids............................. 66 - 1
    (b) with some help (either from a person or with the
        aid of some device).................................   - 2
    (c) or are you totally dependent on someone else to
        lift you..   - 3
        Not answered..   - 0

91. Can you take a bath or shower...
    (a) without help....................................... 67 - 1
    (b) with some help (need help getting in and out of
        the tub, or need special attachments on the tub)......   - 2
    (c) or are you completely unable to bathe yourself........   - 3
        Not answered..   - 0

92. Is there someone who helps you   Yes . . . . 68 - 1
    with such things as shopping,   No . . . .   - 2
    housework, bathing, dressing,   Not answered. . . . .   - 0
    and getting around?

92a. (IF R ANSWERED "YES" TO Q. 92, ASK)   69,70 -
     Who helps you?   Husband/Wife. . . . .   -01
     (READ LIST - CHECK ALL THAT   Other relative. . . . . . .   -02
     APPLY.)   Friend or neighbor. . . . .   -03
                                         Private nurse . . . .   -04
                                         Paid domestic -
                                         (maid or companion) . . . .   -05
                                         Health Dept. Visiting Nurse.   -06
                                         Home Health Aide from
                                         Social Service Agency . . .   -07
                                         Other (specify)_____   -08
                                         Not answered . . . .   -00
                                         (OFFICE CODING ONLY)
                                         Two or three of above . . .   -10
                                         Four or five of above . . .   -11
                                         Six or seven of above . . .   -12
                                         Eight of above . . . . . .   -13

NUTRITION

93. How many meals a day do you   More than three meals a
    normally eat?   day . . . . 71 - 1
                                      Three meals a day . . . . .   - 2
                                      Two meals a day . . . . . .   - 3
                                      One meal a day. . . . . . .   - 4
                                      Only snacks . . . .   - 5
                                      No usual routine. . . . . .   - 6
                                      Not answered. . . . .   - 0

94. Do you have a good diet?   Yes . . . . 72 - 1
                                      Sometimes yes; sometimes no   - 2
                                      No . . . .   - 3
                                      Don't know. . . . .   - 4
                                      Not answered. . . . .   - 0

95. Who usually prepares your   Self. . . . . 73 - 1
    main meal of the day?   Member of household . . . .   - 2
    (DO NOT READ LIST.)   Friend or relative. . . . .   - 3
                                      Paid domestic . . . .   - 4
                                      Nutrition Program (Lunch Plus) - 5
                                      Meals on Wheels . . . . . .   - 6
                                      Restaurant . . . .   - 7
                                      Other (specify)_____   - 8
                                      Not answered. . . . .   - 0

96.   Do you usually eat alone?

Yes . . . .   74 - 1
No . . . .   - 2
Not answered. . . . .   - 0

96a. (IF R ANSWERS "YES" TO Q.96,ASK)
      Do you think your diet might be   Yes . . . .   75 - 1
      better if you did not eat alone?   No . . . .   - 2
                                          Don't know. . . . .   - 3
                                          Not answered. . . . .   - 0

97.   Has your doctor prescribed a   Yes . . . .   76 - 1
      special diet for you?   No . . . .   - 2
                                          Not answered. . . . .   - 0

97a. (IF R ANSWERED "YES" TO Q. 97,ASK) (READ LIST, CHECK ALL THAT APPLY)
      What kind of diet did your   77,78 -
      doctor prescribe?   Low cholesterol . . . . . .   -01
                                          Low salt . . . .   -02
                                          Low triglyceride. . . . . .   -03
                                          Hypoglycemic. . . . .   -04
                                          Diabetic. . . . .   -05
                                          Weight loss . . . .   -06
                                          Other (specify)_____   -07
                                          Don't know. . . . .   -08
                                          Not answered. . . . .   -00
                                          (OFFICE CODING ONLY)
                                          Two or three of above . . .   -10
                                          Four or five of above . . .   -11
                                          Six or seven of above . . .   -12

97b. (IF R IS ON SPECIAL DIET,ASK)
      Do you follow your diet all the   All the time . . . .   79 - 1
      time, most of the time, almost   Most of the time. . . . . .   - 2
      never, or never?   Almost never . . . .   - 3
                                          Never . . . .   - 4
                                          Not answered. . . . .   - 0

97c. (IF R ANSWERED "ALMOST NEVER" OR "NEVER" FOLLOWS DIET,ASK)
      Would you please tell me why   Costs too much. . . . . . .   80 - 1
      you do not follow your diet?   Don't like it . . . .   - 2
      (DO NOT READ LIST)   Not necessary . . . .   - 3
                                          Too much bother . . . . . .   - 4
                                          Other (specify)_____   - 5
                                          Not answered. . . . .   - 0

BEGIN CARD FOUR

INTERVIEW NUMBER

1	2	3	4

CARD WITHIN CASE . . . .   5 - 4

98.   Do you take vitamin or   Yes . . . .   6 - 1
      mineral tablets?   No . . . .   - 2
                                          Not answered. . . . .   - 0

99.   Do you use Food Stamps?   Yes . . . .   7 - 1
                                          No . . . .   - 2
                                          Not answered. . . . .   - 0

99a. (IF R ANSWERED "NO" TO Q.99,ASK)   (READ LIST, CHECK ALL THAT APPLY)
     Could you tell me why you don't   Can't afford to purchase
     use Food Stamps?   Stamps . . . .   8 - 1
                                            Don't receive assistance .   - 2
                                            Don't want assistance. . .   - 3
                                            Not eligible . . . . . .   - 4
                                            Don't know about program .   - 5
                                            Don't like program . . . .   - 6
                                            Other (specify)_____   - 7
                                            Not answered . . . .   - 0
                                            (OFFICE CODING ONLY - SEE
                                            CODING MANUAL)
                                            Two or three of above. . .   - 8
                                            Four or five of above. . .   - 9

WORK AND FINANCES

NOW I'D LIKE TO ASK YOU SOME QUESTIONS ABOUT YOUR WORK SITUATION.

100. Are you presently...
     (READ LIST. CHECK "YES" OR " NO" FOR EACH.)

	YES	NO		
(1)			Employed full-time	9 - 1
				- 2
(2)			Employed part-time	10 - 1
				- 2
(3)			Retired	11 - 1
				- 2
(4)			Retired on disability	12 - 1
				- 2
(5)			Not employed and seeking work	13 - 1
				- 2
(6)			Not employed and not seeking work	14 - 1
				- 2
(7)			Full-time student	15 - 1
				- 2
(8)			Part-time student	16 - 1
				- 2

---

101. What kind of work have you done most of your life?
     (CHECK THE MOST APPROPRIATE.)   Never employed . . . . . .   17 - 1
                                          Housewife . . . .   - 2
                                          Other (See 101a) . . . . .   - 3
                                          Not answered . . . .   - 0

101a. (IF R ANSWERS "OTHER" TO Q. 101,ASK)
      What is/was your specific job?   (DO NOT READ)......
                                          (EXAMPLE: Teacher or office
                                          clerk, NOT "I worked in a
                                          school."
                                          Shop Foreman at a Tool Mfg.
                                          Plant, NOT "I was a super-
                                          visor at Black and Decker.")

      _____
      (SPECIFIC JOB)

                             (OFFICE CODING ONLY -
                             See Coding Manual for Occupation Code.)

      _____   18 -
                (OCCUPATION TYPE)   19 -

102. Does your husband/wife work or   Yes . . . .   20 - 1
      did he/she ever work?   No . . . .   - 2
      (Question applies to those who   Never married . . . .   - 3
      are widowed.)   Not answered . . . .   - 0

102a. (IF R ANSWERED "YES" TO Q.102,ASK)
      What is or was his/her specific
      job?
          (SPECIFIC JOB IN DETAIL)
                                          (OFFICE CODING ONLY -
                                    See Coding Manual for Occupation Code.)

                                    _____   21 -
                                        (OCCUPATION TYPE)   22 -

103. Are you doing any volunteer   Yes . . . .   23 - 1
      work?   No . . . .   - 2
                                          Not answered. . . . .   - 0

103a. (IF R IS DOING VOLUNTEER WORK,ASK)
      About how many hours a month do   _____   24 -
      you spend doing volunteer work?   (Hours per month)   25 -

103b. (IF R IS NOT DOING VOLUNTEER WORK,ASK)
      Would you like to do volunteer   Yes . . . .   26 - 1
      work?   No . . . .   - 2
                                          Don't know. . . . .   - 3
                                          Not answered. . . . .   - 0

104. I DO NOT WANT TO KNOW THE AMOUNT OF MONEY YOU RECEIVE, BUT I'D LIKE TO
      GET A CLEARER PICTURE OF THE FINANCIAL SITUATION OF OLDER PEOPLE. I
      WILL MENTION SOME SOURCES OF INCOME; PLEASE TELL ME IF YOU RECEIVED
      ANY MONEY FROM ANY OF THEM IN THE PAST YEAR.

      Did you receive any income from...? (CHECK "YES" OR "NO" FOR EACH
                                           SOURCE.)

YES	NO		
		Employment (wages, salary, business) . . .	27 - 1 - 2
		Social Security retirement benefits	28 - 1 - 2
		Other public or private pensions	29 - 1 - 2
		Veteran's benefits	30 - 1 - 2
		Savings	31 - 1 - 2
		Income from assets, like interest & dividends, rents, annuities, life insurance	32 - 1 - 2
		Disability payments (Social Security, Veteran's benefits, Workmen's compensation, private insurance)	33 - 1 - 2
		Contributions from relatives or others . . .	34 - 1 - 2
		Unemployment insurance or compensation . . .	35 - 1 - 2
		Supplementary Security Income - SSI . . . . (Old Age Assistance, Aid to the Blind, Aid to the Disabled, Public Assistance)	36 - 1 - 2
		Other (specify)_____	37 - 1 - 2

105. (IF LIVING ALONE, DO NOT ASK)
How many others in your house-
hold have an income?   _____   38-
                                        (number with income)

106. Including yourself, how many
dependents do you have? That
is, how many people do you pro-
vide at least half of their   _____   39 -
income?   (number of dependents)

107. Are your financial assets and   Yes . . . .   40 - 1
financial resources sufficient   No . . . .   - 2
to meet emergencies?   Don't know. . . . .   - 3
                                       Not answered. . . . .   - 0

108. Is your financial situation such Yes . . . .   41 - 1
that you feel you need financial   No . . . .   - 2
assistance or help beyond what   Not answered. . . . .   - 0
you are already getting?

109. Please tell me how well you   Better. . . . .   42 - 1
(and your family) are now   About the same. . . . . . .   - 2
doing financially as compared   Worse . . . .   - 3
to other people your age --   Not answered. . . . .   - 0
better, about the same or
worse?

110. How well does the amount of   Very well . . . .   43 - 1
money you have take care of   Fairly well . . . .   - 2
your needs -- very well, fairly   Poorly. . . . .   - 3
well, or poorly?   Not answered. . . . .   - 0

111. Do you usually have enough   Yes . . . .   44 - 1
to buy those little "extras";   No . . . .   - 2
that is those small luxuries?   Not answered. . . . .   - 0

112. Which of the following is the   (READ LIST THROUGH COMPLETELY
biggest problem to you finan-   BEFORE CHECKING ONLY ONE ANSWER.)
cially?   45,46 -
                                       Buying food . . . .   -01
                                       Housing (paying rent,
                                       mortgage, or taxes) . . . .   -02
                                       Getting adequate medical
                                       care . . . .   -03
                                       Transportation (including
                                       car payments. . . . .   -04
                                       Paying utility bills. . . .   -05
                                       Buying clothing . . . . . .   -06
                                       Paying for insurance. . . .   -07
                                       Paying for entertainment,
                                       recreation or a vacation. .   -08
                                       Home repairs. . . . .   -09
                                       Inflation . . . .   -10
                                       (DO NOT READ)
                                       I have no problem . . . . .   -11
                                       More than one or a
                                       combination . . . .   -12
                                       Not answered. . . . .   -00

113. Do you feel that you will have   Yes . . . .   47 - 1
enough money for your needs in   No . . . .   - 2
the future?   Don't know. . . . .   - 3
                                       Not answered. . . . .   - 0

114. How did/do you feel about retiring?
      (WRITE RESPONSE VERBATIM)

_____

_____

_____

                              (OFFICE CODING ONLY)
                              Positive about retirement. . 48 - 1
                              Ambivalent about retirement.   - 2
                              Negative about retirement. .   - 3
                              Not answered . . . .   - 0

---

115. Did you or are you attend-   Yes . . . . 49 - 1
      ing any organized classes or   No   . . . .   - 2
      meetings which concern re-   Not answered . . . .   - 0
      tirement planning?

---

116. I AM GOING TO READ A LIST OF PROGRAMS PROVIDED FOR THE ELDERLY IN
      BALTIMORE COUNTY. I WOULD LIKE TO KNOW - FOR EACH PROGRAM - IF YOU
      HAVE HEARD OF THAT PROGRAM. (CIRCLE ALL APPROPRIATE ANSWERS.)

PROGRAMS AVAILABLE	116a. Do you know of _(name)_		116b. (ASK FOR EACH PROGRAM R KNOWS OF) Do you participate in the _(name)_			116c. (ASK FOR EACH PROGRAM R PARTICIPATES IN) Are you satisfied with what you are getting out of the _(name)_		
	YES	NO	YES	NO	NOT APP.	YES	NO	NOT APP.
1.Mail Alert Program	50-1	-2	51-1	-2	-0	52-1	-2	-0
2.Visiting Nurse Assoc.	53-1	-2	54-1	-2	-0	55-1	-2	-0
3.Williams Day Care Center	56-1	-2	57-1	-2	-0	58-1	-2	-0
4.Lunch Program for Seniors (Lunch Plus)	59-1	-2	60-1	-2	-0	61-1	-2	-0
5.Hospital Social Service Dept. Programs	62-1	-2	63-1	-2	-0	64-1	-2	-0
6.Balto. County Health Dept.	65-1	-2	66-1	-2	-0	67-1	-2	-0
7.Meals on Wheels	68-1	-2	69-1	-2	-0	70-1	-2	-0
8.Senioride	71-1	-2	72-1	-2	-0	73-1	-2	-0
9.Information and Referral Services	74-1	-2	75-1	-2	-0	76-1	-2	-0
10.Senior Center Programs	77-1	-2	78-1	-2	-0	79-1	-2	-0

BEGIN CARD FIVE

INTERVIEW NUMBER

1	2	3	4

CARD WITHIN CASE . . . .   5 - 5

PROGRAMS AVAILABLE	116a. Do you know of (name)		116b. (ASK FOR EACH PROGRAM R KNOWS OF) Do you participate in the (name)			116c. (ASK FOR EACH PROGRAM R PARTICIPATES IN) Are you satisfied with what you are getting out of the (name)		
	YES	NO	YES	NO	NOT APP.	YES	NO	NOT APP.
11. Emergency Assistance	6-1	-2	7-1	-2	-0	8-1	-2	-0
12. Community College Programs for Seniors	9-1	-2	10-1	-2	-0	11-1	-2	-0
13. RSVP (Retired Senior Volunteer Program)	12-1	-2	13-1	-2	-0	14-1	-2	-0
14. Community Home Care	15-1	-2	16-1	-2	-0	17-1	-2	-0
15. Senior Citizens Discount Card Program	18-1	-2	19-1	-2	-0	20-1	-2	-0
16. Library Services for Seniors	21-1	-2	22-1	-2	-0	23-1	-2	-0
17. Senior Digest	24-1	-2	25-1	-2	-0	26-1	-2	-0
18. Over 60 Counseling & Employment Services	27-1	-2	28-1	-2	-0	29-1	-2	-0
19. Senior Aide Program	30-1	-2	31-1	-2	-0	32-1	-2	-0
20. Circuit Breaker Tax Program	33-1	-2	34-1	-2	-0	35-1	-2	-0
21. Rent Supplements to Senior Renters	36-1	-2	37-1	-2	-0	38-1	-2	-0
22. SSI (Supplemental Security Income)	39-1	-2	40-1	-2	-0	41-1	-2	-0
23. Alcoholics Anonymous	42-1	-2	43-1	-2	-0	44-1	-2	-0

	116a. Do you know of _____(name)_____		116b. (ASK FOR EACH PROGRAM R KNOWS OF) Do you par- ticipate in the _____(name)_____			116c. (ASK FOR EACH PROGRAM R PAR- TICIPATES IN) Are you satis- fied with what you are gett- ing out of the _____(name)_____		
PROGRAMS AVAILABLE	YES	NO	YES	NO	NOT APP.	YES	NO	NOT APP.
24. Telecare	45-1	-2	46-1	-2	-0	47-1	-2	-0
25. Balto. County Neighborhood Health Center	48-1	-2	49-1	-2	-0	50-1	-2	-0

SELF-PERCEIVED NEEDS

NOW I WANT TO ASK YOU SOME QUESTIONS ABOUT THE ACTIVITIES YOU
PARTICIPATE IN AND THE KINDS OF HELP YOU ARE GETTING OR FEEL YOU
NEED. WE WOULD LIKE TO KNOW NOT ONLY ABOUT THE HELP YOU RECEIVE
FROM AGENCIES OR ORGANIZATIONS BUT ALSO WHAT HELP YOU HAVE BEEN
GETTING FROM YOUR FAMILY AND FRIENDS.

117.   Do you feel you need to
       participate in any planned
       and organized social or
       recreational programs or in
       any group activities or
       classes such as arts and
       crafts, or exercise classes?

       Yes . . . .   51 - 1
       No . . . .   - 2
       Not answered. . . . .   - 0

117a. Are you participating in any
       of these activities?

       As often as necessary . . .   52 - 1
       Would like to participate .   - 2
       None . . . .   - 3
       Not at all. . . . .   - 4
       Not answered. . . . .   - 0

118.   Do you feel you need someone
       to help you find a job?

       Yes . . . .   53 - 1
       No . . . .   - 2
       Not answered. . . . .   - 0

119.   Do you think you need any
       special training or instruc-
       tion in learning basic person-
       al skills, for example:
       cooking, driving lessons,
       handling your finances, speech
       therapy, or training for the
       blind or physically handicapped?

       Yes . . . .   54 - 1
       No . . . .   - 2
       Not answered. . . . .   - 0

119a. Are you receiving any in-
      struction in these special
      areas?

As much as necessary . . . .   55 - 1
Need more training . . . . .   - 2
Not at all . . . .   - 3
Not answered . . . .   - 0

---

120. Do you feel that you need
      counseling for personal or
      family problems?

Yes . . . .   56 - 1
No . . . .   - 2
Not answered. . . . .   - 0

120a. Are you receiving profession-
      al counseling?

As often as necessary . . .   57 - 1
Need more often . . . . . .   - 2
Not at all. . . . .   - 3
Not answered. . . . .   - 0

---

121. Do you feel that you need any
      medicine that you are not
      able to get because you can-
      not afford it?

Yes . . . .   58 - 1
No . . . .   - 2
Not answered. . . . .   - 0

---

122. Do you feel you need any nurs-
      ing care, in other words some-
      one to give you treatment or
      medications prescribed by a
      doctor?

Yes . . . .   59 - 1
No . . . .   - 2
Not answered. . . . .   - 0

122a. Are you receiving nursing
      care?

As often as necessary . . .   60 - 1
Need more often . . . . . .   - 2
Not at all. . . . .   - 3
Not answered. . . . .   - 0

---

123. Do you think you need physical
      therapy?

Yes . . . .   61 - 1
No . . . .   - 2
Not answered. . . . .   - 0

123a. Are you receiving physical
      therapy?

As often as necessary . . .   62 - 1
Need more often . . . . . .   - 2
Not at all. . . . .   - 3
Not answered. . . . .   - 0

---

124. Do you feel you need help with
      bathing, dressing, eating, or
      using the bathroom, etc.?

Yes . . . .   63 - 1
No . . . .   - 2
Not answered. . . . .   - 0

124a. Are you getting assistance
      with these activities?

As often as necessary . . .   64 - 1
Need more often . . . . . .   - 2
Not at all. . . . .   - 3
Not answered. . . . .   - 0

---

125. Do you think that you need to
      have someone regularly pre-
      pare meals for you?

Yes . . . .   65 - 1
No . . . .   - 2
Not answered. . . . .   - 0

125a. Does someone prepare your
      meals?

As often as necessary . . .   66 - 1
Not as often as necessary .   - 2
Not at all. . . . .   - 3
Not answered. . . . .   - 0

126.   Do you think you need to   Yes . . . .   67 - 1
        have someone with you all   No . . . .   - 2
        the time to look after you?   Not answered. . . . .   - 0

126a.   Is someone presently looking   Yes . . . .   68 - 1
        after you all the time?   No . . . .   - 2
                                          Not answered. . . . .   - 0

127.   Do you feel you need to have   Yes . . . .   69 - 1
        someone check on you (at   No . . . .   - 2
        least five times a week) by   Not answered. . . . .   - 0
        phone or in person to make
        sure you are all right?
        (CHECK "NO" IF R ANSWERED "YES"
        TO Q. 126.)

127a.   Is someone checking with you?   At least 5 days/week . . .   70 - 1
                                          Less than 5 days/week . . .   - 2
                                          Not at all. . . . .   - 3
                                          Not answered. . . . .   - 0

128.   Do you feel you need help in   Yes . . . .   71 - 1
        finding a (another) place   No . . . .   - 2
        to live?   Not answered. . . . .   - 0

128a.   Is someone helping you find   Yes . . . .   72 - 1
        another place to live?   No . . . .   - 2
                                          Not answered. . . . .   - 0

129.   Do you feel you need help   Yes . . . .   73 - 1
        with routine housework such   No . . . .   - 2
        as cleaning, washing clothes,   Not answered. . . . .   - 0
        etc., because you are not able
        to do it yourself?

129a.   Is someone helping you with   As often as necessary . . .   74 - 1
        the housework?   Need more help . . . . . .   - 2
                                          Not at all. . . . .   - 3
                                          Not answered. . . . .   - 0

130.   Do you think you need someone   Yes . . . .   75 - 1
        to help with inside or out-   No . . . .   - 2
        side home repair or yardwork?   Not answered. . . . .   - 0

130a.   Does someone help you with   As often as necessary . . .   76 - 1
        home repair?   Need more help. . . . . . .   - 2
                                          Not at all. . . . .   - 3
                                          Not answered. . . . .   - 0

131.   Do you think you need help   Yes . . . .   77 - 1
        with any legal matters or   No . . . .   - 2
        with managing your personal   Not answered. . . . .   - 0
        business affairs?

131a.   Is someone helping you with   As often as necessary . . .   78 - 1
        these matters?   Need more help. . . . . . .   - 2
                                          Not at all. . . . .   - 3
                                          Not answered. . . . .   - 0

132. Do you think that you need
someone to inform you about
home security or other crime
prevention methods?

Yes	79 - 1
No	- 2
Not answered.	- 0

BEGIN CARD SIX

INTERVIEW NUMBER

1	2	3	4

CARD WITHIN CASE. . . . .   5 - 6

133. Do you think you need to
have someone review and
evaluate your overall condition including your health
and your social and financial
situation?

Yes	6 - 1
No	- 2
Not answered.	- 0

133a. In the past 6 months has a
doctor or a social worker reviewed your situation?

Yes	7 - 1
No	- 2
Not answered.	- 0

134. Do you feel that you need to
have someone to give you information about the kind of
services that are available
to help you or put you in touch
with those who could help you?

Yes	8 - 1
No	- 2
Not answered.	- 0

134a. During the past six months did
someone give you the information about available services
or put you in touch with those
who can help you?

As often as necessary	9 - 1
Not as often as necessary . .	- 2
Not at all.	- 3
Not answered.	- 0

135. We have talked about many
things concerning the needs
of senior citizens. Who do
you think should take the responsibility for providing for
these needs?
(DO NOT READ LIST)

Senior's children	10-01
Other relatives	-02
Friends or neighbors.	-03
Clergy or church.	-04
Government -Federal	-05
State or local.	-06
Individual senior (me/us) . .	-07
Private agencies.	-08
Other (specify)_____	-09
Not sure/don't know	-10
Not answered.	-00

136. Is there anything that we have
not talked about that might help
older Americans in their daily lives?

(WRITE R'S COMMENTS BELOW. QUESTION WILL NOT BE CODED, BUT MAY BE
INCLUDED IN THE ANALYSIS.)

_____

_____

_____

_____

137. Some persons we have talked   Yes . . . .   11 - 1
     to have said that persons like   No . . . .   - 2
     myself, representing Balto.
     County could ask them these
     kinds of questions again.
     Would you be willing to be
     contacted again?

INTERVIEWER:
        THANK YOU VERY MUCH FOR YOUR PATIENCE AND COOPERATION.
     YOU'VE BEEN VERY HELPFUL. GOOD-BYE.

THIS SECTION IS TO BE COMPLETED BY THE INTERVIEWER ONLY AFTER
LEAVING THE RESPONDENT.

1. What kind of structure does R   Single family, detached . . .   12 - 1
   live in?   Single family townhouse . . .   - 2
                                       Apartment in private home or
                                       business structure . . . . .   - 3
                                       Apartment in commercial
                                       complex . . . .   - 4
                                       Trailer . . . .   - 5
                                       Rooming house or hotel. . . .   - 6
                                       Other (specify)_____   - 7

---

2. How would you describe the   Very clean and well-kept. . .   13 - 1
   home interior?   Fairly clean and well-kept. .   - 2
                                       Dirty and disorderly. . . . .   - 3
                                       Interview conducted outside .   - 4

---

3. How would you describe the   Generally good condition. . .   14 - 1
   condition of the home's   Fair condition but needs
   structure: walls, ceiling,   some work . . . .   - 2
   doors, windows, siding, roof,   Deteriorating condition,
   porches, etc.   needs extensive work. . . . .   - 3

---

4. Did R have any of the following conditions?
   (CHECK "YES" OR "NO" FOR EACH.)

YES	NO

Difficulty seeing . . . .   15 - 1
                                                - 2
Blindness . . . .   16 - 1
                                                - 2
Difficulty hearing . . . .   17 - 1
                                                - 2
Deafness . . . .   18 - 1
                                                - 2
Missing limbs. . . . .   19 - 1
                                                - 2
Obesity. . . . .   20 - 1
                                                - 2
Palsy, shakes, tremors . . . .   21 - 1
                                                - 2
Speech impediments . . . .   22 - 1
                                                - 2
Major lack of personal grooming . . . .   23 - 1
                                                - 2
Other (specify)_____   24 - 1
                                                - 2

5. How did R understand the
   questions?

   Good understanding and
   answered readily . . . . . . 25 - 1
   Fair understanding and
   answered satisfactorily . . .   - 2
   Slow understanding and
   difficulty answering . . . .   - 3

---

6. Was R very interested and
   concerned, fairly interested
   and concerned, generally not
   interested or concerned, with
   the questions?

   Very interested and concerned . 26 - 1
   Fairly interested and
   concerned . . . . - 2
   Not interested or concerned . . - 3

---

7. Were the respondent's answers
   influenced by any other person
   present during the interview?

   Yes . . . . 27 - 1
   No . . . . - 2

7a. (IF YOU ANSWERED "YES" TO Q. 7,)
    What was the person's (the one
    who had the biggest influence)
    relationship to R?

    Spouse. . . . . 28 - 1
    Child . . . . - 2
    Brother or sister . . . . - 3
    Grandchild. . . . . - 4
    Other relative. , ... - 5
    Friend. . . . . - 6
    Other (specify)_____ - 7
    Not answered. . . . . - 0

7b. (IF R WAS INFLUENCED BY SOME-
    ONE), How did that person
    influence the respondent's
    answer?

    Inhibiting. . . . . 29 - 1
    Expanding on answers. . . . . . - 2
    Not answered. . . . . - 0

Appendix C

An Explanation of Multiple Classification Analysis

Multiple Classification Analysis (MCA) is a technique for examining the relationship between categorical (nominal or ordinal) predictor variables and a dependent variable. The dependent variable must be at the interval level of measurement or dichotomous and not extremely skewed. MCA results show how each predictor variable relates to the dependent variable before and after adjusting for the effects of other predictors (Andrews et al., 1973:1). MCA summary statistics include eta, beta and R^2. The eta is the correlation ratio that indicates the proportion of the total sum of squares explained by each predictor individually without controlling for the effect of other predictors in the model. The beta refers to the net effect of a predictor on the dependent variable after adjusting for the effects of other predictors in the model. The beta coefficients indicate the relative importance of the various predictors.

Appendix D

Tables

Table 2-1. Age and sex distribution by service area (in percents)

Age and Sex	Total (N= 1,182)	Service area				
		South-west (N= 406)	North-west (N= 70)	North (N= 163)	North-east (N= 322)	South-east (N= 221)
Total	100.0	34.3	5.9	13.8	27.2	18.7
Age						
Young-old (60-74)	77.9	72.9	78.5	72.4	81.0	86.0
Old-old (≥75)	22.1	27.1	21.4	27.6	18.9	14.1
Sex						
Male	36.8	33.5	42.8	37.4	36.6	40.8
Female	63.2	66.5	57.1	62.6	64.3	59.3
Age and sex						
Young-old						
Male	29.4	26.1	37.1	27.6	27.6	36.7
Female	48.5	46.8	41.4	44.8	53.4	49.3
Old-old						
Male	7.4	7.4	5.7	9.8	9.0	4.1
Female	14.7	19.7	15.7	17.8	9.9	10.0

Source: 1978 SNAP Survey of the Elderly, Baltimore County, Maryland.

2.1

Table 2-2. Marital status by service area (in percents)

Marital Status	Total (N= 1,182)	Service area				
		South-west (N= 406)	North-west (N= 70)	North (N= 163)	North-east (N= 322)	South-east (N= 221)
Total	100.0	100.0	100.0	100.0	100.0	100.0
Never married	5.2	5.2	1.4	6.7	5.0	5.4
Married	53.8	51.2	65.7	56.4	50.3	57.9
Separated/divorced	4.0	4.4	2.9	5.5	2.2	5.0
Widowed	37.1	39.2	30.0	31.3	42.5	31.7

Source: 1978 SNAP Survey of the Elderly, Baltimore County, Maryland

2.2

Table 2-3. Educational level by service area (in percents)

| Educational Level | Total (N= 1,182) | Service area | | | | |
		South- west (N= 406)	North- west (N= 70)	North (N= 163)	North- east (N= 322)	South- east (N= 221)
Total	100.0	100.0	100.0	100.0	100.0	100.0
Less than 9 years	31.1	28.8	17.1	13.5	32.9	50.2
High school incomplete	18.4	18.7	17.1	8.6	20.8	21.7
High school completed	24.5	28.1	28.6	25.2	24.8	15.8
Some college	16.3	17.0	22.9	23.9	14.9	9.5
Four years of college completed or post-graduate	9.6	7.4	14.3	28.8	6.5	2.7

Source: 1978 SNAP Survey of the Elderly, Baltimore County, Maryland

Table 2-4. Longest occupation by service area (in percents)

| Longest Occupation | Total (N= 1,182) | Service area | | | | |
		South- west (N= 406)	North- west (N= 70)	North (N= 163)	North- east (N= 322)	South- east (N= 221)
Total	100.0	100.0	100.0	100.0	100.0	100.0
Professional	18.2	17.2	25.7	33.1	16.1	9.5
Managerial	13.5	14.8	12.9	15.3	12.4	11.3
Sales workers	8.5	10.6	7.1	5.5	9.9	5.4
Clerical	20.7	22.4	28.6	23.3	20.8	13.1
Craftsmen	9.3	10.1	5.7	5.5	7.8	14.0
Mechanic	5.3	5.7	1.4	3.7	5.9	6.3
Transport equipment operators	2.7	3.2	1.4	.6	3.1	3.2
Laborer/except farmers	11.7	9.6	7.1	3.7	13.4	20.4
Farmers, farm managers	.7	.7	0.0	1.2	.3	.9
Farm laborers	.7	.2	0.0	.6	.9	1.4
Service workers	5.9	3.9	7.1	6.1	5.9	9.0
Private household workers	1.3	.7	2.9	.6	1.9	1.4
Unknown	1.5	.7	0.0	.6	1.6	4.1

Source: 1978 SNAP Survey of the Elderly, Baltimore County, Maryland

Table 2-6. Employment status by service area (in percents)

| Employment Status | Total (N= 1,182) | Service area | | | | |
		South- west (N= 406)	North- west (N= 70)	North (N= 163)	North- east (N= 322)	South- east (N= 221)
Total	100.0	100.0	100.0	100.0	100.0	100.0
Retired	71.3	78.1	72.9	70.6	67.7	64.3
Not retired						
Employed (full-time)	5.8	3.4	2.9	9.2	5.0	9.5
Employed (part-time)	2.8	2.2	7.1	1.8	4.3	.9
Unemployed	1.4	.4	2.8	.6	1.8	2.3
Unknown	18.8	15.8	14.3	17.8	21.1	23.1

Source: 1978 SNAP Survey of the Elderly, Baltimore County, Maryland

Table 2-5. Sources of income by service area (in percents)

Sources of income	Total	Service area				
		South-west	North-west	North	North-east	South-east
Employment						
Yes	16.0	14.5	15.7	19.0	15.8	16.7
No	84.0	85.5	84.3	81.0	84.2	83.3
Social security retirement benefits						
Yes	78.6	81.8	70.0	76.1	78.9	76.9
No	21.4	18.2	30.0	23.9	21.1	23.1
Other public or private pension						
Yes	42.3	49.0	42.9	49.1	36.3	33.5
No	57.7	51.0	57.1	50.9	63.7	66.5
Veterans benefits						
Yes	8.5	10.8	4.3	8.6	5.3	10.0
No	91.5	89.2	95.7	91.4	94.7	90.0
Savings						
Yes	53.8	53.9	54.3	69.3	52.5	43.9
No	46.2	46.1	45.7	30.7	47.5	56.1
Income from assets						
Yes	40.2	39.9	42.9	57.7	40.4	26.7
No	59.8	60.1	57.1	42.3	59.6	73.3
Disability payments						
Yes	8.1	6.9	4.3	7.4	7.8	12.7
No	91.9	93.1	95.7	92.6	92.2	87.3
Contributions from relatives or others						
Yes	4.3	4.4	5.7	6.1	3.4	3.6
No	95.7	95.6	94.3	93.9	96.6	96.4
Unemployment compensation						
Yes	1.6	.7	1.4	.6	3.4	1.4
No	98.4	99.3	98.6	99.4	96.6	98.6
Supplemental security income						
Yes	2.5	1.0	2.9	1.2	2.8	5.4
No	97.5	99.0	97.1	98.8	97.2	94.6

Source: 1978 SNAP Survey of the Elderly, Baltimore County, Maryland

Table 2-7. Home ownership and rental status by service area (in percents)

Home ownership and rental status	Total (N= 1,182)	Service area				
		South-west (N= 406)	North-west (N= 70)	North (N= 163)	North-east (N= 322)	South-east (N= 221)
Total	100.0	100.0	100.0	100.0	100.0	100.0
Home Owner						
Making payments	7.7	5.7	14.3	12.3	6.2	8.1
Mortgage paid	59.9	61.8	64.3	46.6	64.6	57.9
Rental						
Rent	25.4	28.3	12.9	30.7	20.2	27.6
Rent paid by others	5.6	3.9	8.6	9.2	6.5	3.6
Unknown	1.4	.2	0.0	1.2	2.5	2.7

Source: 1978 SNAP Survey of the Elderly, Baltimore County, Maryland

2.8

Table 2-8. Residence duration by service area (in percents)

Residence duration	Total	Service area				
	(N= 1,182)	South- west (N= 406)	North- west (N= 70)	North (N= 163)	North- east (N= 322)	South- east (N= 221)
Total	100.0	100.0	100.0	100.0	100.0	100.0
Less than 1 year	4.7	4.2	2.9	1.8	4.0	9.0
1-2 years	5.5	4.4	1.4	7.4	5.9	6.8
3-5 years	4.4	3.9	2.9	6.7	2.8	6.3
6-9 years	11.8	8.9	12.9	18.4	10.6	14.0
10-14 years	14.0	11.3	21.4	22.7	14.0	10.0
15-19 years	9.1	5.9	11.4	16.6	9.0	9.0
20 or more years	50.4	61.1	47.1	26.4	53.7	44.8
Unknown	.1	.2	0.0	0.0	0.0	0.0

Source: 1978 SNAP Survey of the Elderly, Baltimore County, Maryland

3.1

Table 3-1. Living arrangement (in percents)

Characteristics	Living arrangement		
	Total	Alone	Not alone
Total	100.0	26.6	73.4
Area			
Southwest	100.0	28.1	71.9
Northwest	100.0	11.4	88.6
North	100.0	25.2	74.8
Northeast	100.0	29.8	70.2
Southeast	100.0	24.9	75.1
Sex and age			
Male (60-74)	100.0	12.7	87.3
Female (60-74)	100.0	29.8	70.2
Male ($\geq$ 75)	100.0	26.1	73.9
Female ($\geq$ 75)	100.0	43.7	56.3
Marital status			
Never married	100.0	47.5	52.5
Married	100.0	1.6	98.4
Separated/divorced	100.0	55.3	44.7
Widowed	100.0	56.8	43.2
Work status			
Retired	100.0	26.6	73.4
Not retired	100.0	26.5	73.5

Source: 1978 SNAP Survey of the Elderly, Baltimore County, Maryland

Table 3-2. "Do you have children?" (in percents)

| Characteristics | Children | | | |
	Total	Yes	No	Not answered
Total	100.0	80.4	19.2	0.4
Area				
Southwest	100.0	80.0	19.2	0.7
Northwest	100.0	82.9	17.1	0.0
North	100.0	73.0	27.0	0.0
Northeast	100.0	84.8	15.2	0.0
Southeast	100.0	79.2	19.9	0.9
Sex and age				
Male (60-74)	100.0	85.3	14.7	0.0
Female (60-74)	100.0	75.5	20.6	0.9
Male ($\geq$ 75)	100.0	73.9	26.1	0.0
Female ($\geq$ 75)	100.0	79.9	20.0	0.0
Marital status				
Never married	100.0	8.2	90.2	1.6
Married	100.0	85.5	14.2	0.3
Separated/divorced	100.0	76.6	23.4	0.0
Widowed	100.0	83.3	16.2	0.5
Retirement status				
Retired	100.0	77.8	21.8	0.4
Not retired	100.0	86.7	12.7	0.6
Living arrangement				
Living alone	100.0	70.1	29.6	0.3
Not living alone	100.0	84.1	15.4	0.5

Source: 1978 SNAP Survey of the Elderly, Baltimore County, Maryland

Table 3-3. Respondent has child living within an hour's driving time
           (in percents)

| Characteristics | Proximity of children | | |
	Total.	Children near	Children not near
Total	100.0	83.2	16.8
Area			
Southwest	100.0	85.7	14.3
Northwest	100.0	80.0	20.0
North	100.0	77.9	22.1
Northeast	100.0	84.5	15.5
Southeast	100.0	81.4	18.6
Sex and age			
Male (60-74)	100.0	85.9	14.1
Female (60-74)	100.0	83.1	16.9
Male ($\geq$ 75)	100.0	75.0	25.0
Female ($\geq$ 75)	100.0	82.2	17.8
Marital status			
Never married	100.0	68.9	31.1
Married	100.0	85.2	14.8
Separated/divorced	100.0	72.3	27.7
Widowed	100.0	83.3	16.7
Retirement status			
Retired	100.0	85.3	14.7
Not retired	100.0	82.3	17.7
Living arrangement			
Living alone	100.0	86.2	13.8
Not living alone	100.0	74.8	25.2

Source: 1978 SNAP Survey of the Elderly, Baltimore County, Maryland

3.4

Table 3-4. "How many people do you know well enough that you visit them in their homes?" (in percents)

Characteristics	Friends					
	Total	None	One-two	Three-five	Six or more	NA[a]
Total	100.0	9.6	15.7	18.0	55.0	1.7
Area						
Southwest	100.0	8.9	13.5	16.3	59.9	1.5
Northwest	100.0	4.3	17.1	17.1	60.0	1.4
North	100.0	5.5	11.0	22.7	60.7	0.0
Northeast	100.0	11.8	16.5	16.8	52.2	2.8
Southeast	100.0	12.7	21.3	19.9	44.3	1.8
Sex and age						
Male (60-74)	100.0	6.3	11.8	17.0	63.7	1.2
Female (60-74)	100.0	10.6	14.7	18.7	54.6	1.4
Male (≥ 75)	100.0	11.4	15.9	15.9	53.4	3.4
Female (≥ 75)	100.0	12.1	26.4	19.0	39.7	2.9
Marital status						
Never married	100.0	11.5	6.6	26.2	49.2	6.6
Married	100.0	7.4	12.4	16.2	62.9	1.1
Separated/divorced	100.0	12.8	17.0	27.7	40.4	2.1
Widowed	100.0	12.3	21.5	18.5	45.9	1.8
Retirement status						
Retired	100.0	9.3	15.5	19.1	54.3	1.8
Not retired	100.0	10.6	15.9	15.3	56.6	1.5
Living arrangement						
Living alone	100.0	9.6	15.7	18.0	51.9	1.6
Not living alone	100.0	9.7	14.7	17.7	56.1	1.7

[a]Not answered

Source: 1978 SNAP Survey of the Elderly, Baltimore County, Maryland

3.5

Table 3-5. "Do you have someone you can trust and confide in?" (in percents)

Characteristics	Someone to trust/confide in			
	Total	Yes	No	NA[a]
Total	100.0	95.9	3.8	0.3
Area				
Southwest	100.0	96.3	3.2	0.5
Northwest	100.0	98.6	1.4	0.0
North	100.0	95.1	4.9	0.0
Northeast	100.0	95.7	4.3	0.0
Southeast	100.0	95.5	4.1	0.5
Sex and age				
Male (60-74)	100.0	96.5	3.2	0.3
Female (60-74)	100.0	95.8	4.0	0.2
Male (≥ 75)	100.0	96.6	2.3	1.1
Female (≥ 75)	100.0	94.8	5.2	0.0
Marital status				
Never married	100.0	91.8	8.2	0.0
Married	100.0	97.3	2.5	0.2
Separated/divorced	100.0	95.7	4.3	0.0
Widowed	100.0	94.5	5.0	0.5
Retirement status				
Retired	100.0	96.7	3.1	.2
Not retired	100.0	94.1	5.6	.3
Living arrangement				
Living alone	100.0	94.9	4.5	.6
Not living alone	100.0	96.3	3.6	.1

[a]Not answered

Source: 1978 SNAP Survey of the Elderly, Baltimore County, Maryland

Table 3-6. "Is there someone who would give you any help at all if you were sick or disabled?" (in percents)

Characteristics	Social Support Resources			
	Total	Yes	No	NA[a]
Total	100.0	92.0	4.7	3.3
Area				
Southwest	100.0	90.9	5.2	3.9
Northwest	100.0	90.0	7.1	2.9
North	100.0	96.3	2.5	1.2
Northeast	100.0	93.5	3.1	3.4
Southeast	100.0	89.6	6.8	3.7
Sex and age				
Male (60–74)	100.0	93.7	4.3	2.0
Female (60–74)	100.0	91.6	5.1	3.3
Male (≥ 75)	100.0	90.9	6.8	2.3
Female (≥ 75)	100.0	90.8	2.9	6.3
Marital status				
Never married	100.0	96.7	1.6	1.6
Married	100.0	93.2	5.0	1.8
Separated/divorced	100.0	93.6	4.3	2.1
Widowed	100.0	89.5	4.6	5.9
Retirement status				
Retired	100.0	93.0	3.9	3.1
Not retired	100.0	89.7	6.5	3.8
Living arrangement				
Living alone	100.0	89.2	3.5	7.3
Not living alone	100.0	93.1	5.1	1.8

[a]Not answered

Source: 1978 SNAP Survey of the Elderly, Baltimore County, Maryland

Table 3-7. "Is there someone who would take care of you as long as you needed help, or only for a short time, or only someone who would help you now and then?" (in percents)

Characteristics	Help				
	Total	Indefinitely	Short time	Now and then	NA[a]
Total	100.0	71.2	10.2	9.0	9.7
Area					
Southwest	100.0	66.7	11.1	8.6	13.5
Northwest	100.0	68.6	12.9	8.6	10.0
North	100.0	79.8	9.2	6.7	4.3
Northeast	100.0	72.4	9.3	9.3	9.0
Southeast	100.0	7.19	9.5	10.9	7.7
Sex and age					
Male (60–74)	100.0	74.6	9.8	7.8	7.8
Female (60–74)	100.0	69.6	11.5	8.6	10.3
Male (≥ 75)	100.0	71.6	4.5	10.2	13.6
Female (≥ 75)	100.0	69.0	9.2	12.1	9.8
Marital status					
Never married	100.0	65.6	16.4	11.5	6.6
Married	100.0	73.7	9.0	8.5	8.8
Separated/divorced	100.0	61.7	14.9	12.8	10.6
Widowed	100.0	69.2	10.5	8.9	11.4
Retirement status					
Retired	100.0	71.9	10.2	8.8	9.1
Not retired	100.0	69.3	10.0	9.4	11.2
Living arrangement					
Living alone	100.0	63.4	13.1	11.5	12.1
Not living alone	100.0	74.0	9.1	8.1	8.9

[a]Not answered

Source: 1978 SNAP Survey of the Elderly, Baltimore County, Maryland

Table 3-8. Self-assessed economic status by service area (in percents)

Economic status	Service area					
	Total (N=1,182)	Southwest (N=406)	Northwest (N=70)	North (N=163)	Northeast (N=322)	Southeast (N=221)
Total	100.0	100.0	100.0	100.0	100.0	100.0
Have insufficient financial resources to meet emergencies	15.1	15.8	14.3	8.6	10.9	25.3
Need financial assistance	18.4	16.0	14.3	19.0	18.3	24.0
Have a worse financial status as compared to others their age	4.8	7.1	1.4	3.1	3.7	4.5
Cannot take care of one's needs	7.5	7.9	8.6	2.5	5.6	13.1
Don't have enough to buy those little extra luxuries	23.9	25.4	21.4	8.6	23.0	34.8
Don't have financial problems	23.6	21.2	22.9	31.3	25.5	19.9
Have enough money for future problems	55.4	56.9	60.0	44.2	60.9	51.6

Source: 1978 SNAP Survey of the Elderly, Baltimore County, Maryland

Table 3-9. "Are your financial assets and financial resources sufficient to meet emergencies? (in percents)

Characteristics	Sufficient			
	Total	Yes	No	NA[a]
Total	100.0	7.4	15.1	10.1
Sex-age				
Male (60-74)	100.0	79.3	12.7	8.1
Female (60-74)	100.0	71.9	17.5	10.6
Male ($\geq$ 75)	100.0	78.4	14.8	6.8
Female ($\geq$ 75)	100.0	73.0	12.6	14.4
Marital status				
Never married	100.0	80.3	8.2	11.5
Married	100.0	78.9	13.2	6.9
Separated/divorced	100.0	51.1	36.2	12.8
Widowed	100.0	70.3	16.7	11.9
Retirement status				
Retired	100.0	75.9	14.4	8.9
Not retired	100.0	71.7	17.1	11.2
Living arrangement				
Living alone	100.0	71.7	15.9	12.4
Not living alone	100.0	75.8	14.9	9.3

[a]Not answered
Source: 1978 SNAP Survey of the Elderly, Baltimore County, Maryland

Table 3-10. "Is your financial situation such that you feel you need financial assistance or help beyond what you are already getting?" (in percents)

3.10

Characteristics	Financial dependency			
	Total	Yes	No	NA[a]
Total	100.0	18.4	80.6	0.9
Sex-age				
Male (60-74)	100.0	26.1	30.1	27.3
Female (60-74)	100.0	21.6	77.7	0.7
Male (≥ 75)	100.0	12.5	86.4	1.1
Female (≥ 75)	100.0	14.9	83.3	1.7
Marital status				
Never married	100.0	11.5	88.5	0.0
Married	100.0	16.2	83.3	0.5
Separated/divorced	100.0	38.3	57.4	4.3
Widowed	100.0	20.5	78.1	1.4
Retirement status				
Retired	100.0	17.1	82.1	0.8
Not retired	100.0	21.8	77.0	1.2
Living arrangement				
Living alone	100.0	23.2	75.2	1.6
Not living alone	100.0	16.7	82.6	0.7

[a]Not answered
Source: 1978 SNAP Survey of the Elderly, Baltimore County, Maryland

Table 3-11. "How well are you doing financially compared with other people your age?" (in percents)

3.11

Characteristics	Comparative economic status				
	Total	Better	About the same	Worse	NA[a]
Total	100.0	18.9	67.3	4.8	9.0
Sex-age					
Male (60-74)	100.0	19.9	64.6	5.5	10.1
Female (60-74)	100.0	18.8	67.2	5.8	8.2
Male (≥ 75)	100.0	22.7	65.9	2.3	9.1
Female (≥ 75)	100.0	14.9	74.1	1.7	9.2
Marital status					
Never married	100.0	27.9	59.0	3.3	9.8
Married	100.0	19.7	68.1	4.9	7.4
Separated/divorced	100.0	17.0	68.1	8.5	6.4
Widowed	100.0	16.7	67.4	4.6	11.4
Retirement status					
Retired	100.0	18.3	68.0	4.4	9.4
Not retired	100.0	20.4	66.1	5.9	8.0
Living arrangement					
Living alone	100.0	19.1	64.3	6.1	10.5
Not living alone	100.0	18.8	68.4	4.4	8.4

[a]Not answered
Source: 1978 SNAP Survey of the Elderly, Baltimore County, Maryland

3.12

Table 3-12. "How well does the amount of money you have
take care of your needs?" (in percents)

Characteristics	Financial needs met				
	Total	Very well	Fairly well	Poorly	NA[a]
Total	100.0	34.8	56.9	7.5	0.8
Sex-age					
Male (60-74)	100.0	36.3	55.3	7.8	0.6
Female (60-74)	100.0	34.6	56.9	8.0	0.5
Male (≥ 75)	100.0	36.4	54.5	8.0	1.1
Female (≥ 75)	100.0	31.6	61.5	5.2	1.7
Marital status					
Never married	100.0	34.4	59.0	6.6	0.0
Married	100.0	36.3	56.6	6.4	0.6
Separated/divorced	100.0	14.9	63.8	19.1	2.1
Widowed	100.0	34.7	56.4	8.0	0.9
Retirement status					
Retired	100.0	34.0	58.6	6.5	0.8
Not retired	100.0	36.6	52.8	10.0	0.6
Living arrangement					
Living alone	100.0	36.3	54.8	8.0	1.0
Not living alone	100.0	34.2	57.7	7.4	0.7

[a]Not answered
Source: 1978 SNAP Survey of the Elderly, Baltimore County, Maryland

3.13

Table 3-13. Do you usually have enough to buy those little "extras"

Characteristics	Buy extra luxuries			
	Total	Yes	No	NA[a]
Total Percent	100.0	74.8	23.9	1.3
Sex-age:				
Male (60-74)	100.0	79.5	19.0	1.4
Female (60-74)	100.0	72.3	26.4	1.4
Male (>75)	100.0	78.4	20.5	1.1
Female (>75)	100.0	71.8	27.6	0.6
Marital status:				
Never married	100.0	80.3	19.7	0.0
Married	100.0	79.1	19.8	1.1
Separated/divorced	100.0	55.3	42.6	2.1
Widowed	100.0	69.9	28.5	1.6
Living Arrangements:				
Living alone	100.0	72.3	26.4	1.3
Not living alone	100.0	75.7	23.0	1.3

[a]Not answered

Source: 1978 SNAP Survey of the Elderly, Baltimore County, Maryland

Table 3-14. "Do you feel that you will have enough money
            for your needs in the future?" (in percents)

| Characteristics | Total | Money for future needs | | |
		Yes	No	NA[a]
Total	100.0	55.4	13.6	30.9
Sex-age				
Male (60-74)	100.0	57.1	14.4	28.6
Female (60-74)	100.0	53.6	15.0	31.4
Male ($\geq$ 75)	100.0	56.8	13.6	29.5
Female ($\geq$ 75)	100.0	57.5	7.5	35.0
Marital status				
Never married	100.0	52.5	13.1	34.4
Married	100.0	56.9	13.2	29.9
Separated/divorced	100.0	31.9	21.3	46.8
Widowed	100.0	56.2	13.5	30.4
Retirement status				
Retired	100.0	57.1	12.2	30.7
Not retired	100.0	51.3	17.1	31.6
Living arrangement				
Living alone	100.0	52.9	13.7	33.4
Not living alone	100.0	56.3	13.6	30.0

[a]Not answered
Source: 1978 SNAP Survey of the Elderly, Baltimore County, Maryland

Table 3-16. Feelings about retirement by work status, sex and age (in percents)

| Work Status | Total | Feelings about retirement | | | |
		Positive	Ambivalent	Negative	NA[a]
Total	100.0 (1,182)	52.4	11.9	21.9	13.8
Work status					
Retired	100.0 (843)	60.4	11.6	21.8	6.2
Not Retired	100.0 (33)	32.4	12.7	22.1	32.7
Sex and age					
Male (60-74)	100.0 (347)	63.4	9.5	30.1	4.6
Female (60-74)	100.0 (573)	46.8	11.3	22.3	19.5
Male ($\geq$ 75)	100.0 (88)	61.4	9.1	20.5	9.1
Female ($\geq$ 75)	100.0 (74)	44.3	20.1	20.1	15.5

[a]Not answered

Source: 1978 SNAP Survey of the Elderly, Baltimore County, Maryland

Table 3.15 appears on page 172.

Table 3-15. "Which of the following is the biggest problem to you financially?" (in percents)

Characteristic	Total	Food	Housing	Medical care	Transportation	Utilities	Clothing	Insurance	Entertainment	Home repair	Inflation	No problems	Many problems	NA[a]
General Population	100.0	9.4	7.7	3.7	1.0	4.1	.5	.7	.6	2.3	19.4	23.6	25.4	2.3
Area:														
Southwest	100.0	11.1	7.1	2.0	1.2	4.9	.5	.2	1.0	1.7	17.7	21.2	30.5	.7
Northwest	100.0	15.7	7.1	2.9	0.0	1.4	0.0	0.0	0.0	2.9	27.1	22.9	20.0	0.0
North	100.0	3.7	4.3	2.5	.6	1.2	0.0	.6	0.0	0.0	25.2	31.3	29.4	0.0
Northeast	100.0	7.8	8.1	2.8	1.2	4.3	0.0	.9	.9	2.2	19.6	25.5	22.0	4.7
Southeast	100.0	10.9	6.3	.9	5.0	1.8	1.4	0.0	0.0	5.0	15.4	19.9	19.5	3.2
Sex and age														
Male (60-74)	100.0	10.7	7.8	2.3	.9	2.3	0.0	.3	.6	2.3	25.6	18.2	25.9	3.2
Female (60-74)	100.0	8.9	7.5	3.5	1.0	5.8	.9	1.2	.7	2.4	19.7	20.8	25.3	2.3
Male (≥ 75)	100.0	8.0	8.0	0.0	0.0	1.1	0.0	0.0	0.0	0.0	14.8	40.9	26.1	1.1
Female (≥ 75)	100.0	9.2	8.0	5.2	1.7	3.4	.6	0.0	.6	2.9	8.0	35.1	24.1	1.1
Marital status														
Never married	100.0	4.9	8.2	1.6	1.6	3.3	0.0	0.0	0.0	3.3	14.8	34.4	26.2	1.6
Married	100.0	9.6	7.4	2.0	.6	3.5	.2	.6	.3	2.0	25.0	20.3	25.9	2.5
Separated/Divorced	100.0	6.4	10.6	4.3	2.1	2.1	2.1	0.0	0.0	0.0	12.8	31.9	27.7	0.0
Widowed	100.0	10.0	7.8	4.8	1.4	5.3	.9	.9	1.1	2.7	12.6	26.0	24.2	2.3
Work Status														
Retired	100.0	10.1	7.8	3.2	1.2	3.7	.5	.6	.7	2.4	19.5	23.8	24.4	2.1
Not Retired	100.0	7.7	7.4	2.9	.6	5.0	.6	.9	.3	2.1	19.2	23.0	27.7	2.7
Living Arrangement														
Living alone	100.0	8.3	10.2	2.5	1.3	4.1	1.0	.3	.3	3.5	12.1	27.1	27.4	1.9
Not living alone	100.0	9.8	6.8	3.3	.9	4.0	.3	.8	.7	1.8	22.0	22.4	24.4	2.4

[a]Not answered

Source: 1978 SNAP Survey of the Elderly, Baltimore County, Maryland

Table 3-17. Assessment of environmental well-being in terms of personal feelings toward the neighborhood by service area

3.17

Environmental well-being	Total	Service area				
		Southwest	Northwest	North	Northeast	Southeast
Feel a part of this neighborhood	75.8	76.1	60.0	79.8	80.1	71.0
Like living in this neighborhood	93.0	91.6	88.6	95.7	96.6	89.6
Think this is a safe neighborhood to live in	96.3	95.6	95.7	97.5	98.8	93.3
Feel safe waiting alone for a bus in this neighborhood in the day time	88.3	91.4	92.9	88.3	89.8	79.2
Feel safe waiting alone for a bus in this neighborhood at night	43.5	36.0	30.0	43.6	51.2	50.2
Feel safe walking alone in this neighborhood in the day time	95.2	95.6	92.1	96.3	94.7	93.7
Feel safe walking alone in this neighborhood at night	48.8	41.4	32.9	48.5	56.2	57.0
Have ever been the victim of a crime	19.5	24.4	14.3	16.0	20.8	12.7
Have been bothered by children/ teenagers	17.3	15.5	18.6	13.5	15.2	25.8

Source: 1978 SNAP Survey of the Elderly, Baltimore County, Maryland

Table 3-18. "Do you feel that you are really a part of this neighbor-hood?" (in percents)

3.18

Characteristics		Integration into neighborhood		
	Total	Feel a part of	Just a place to live	NA[a]
Total	100.0	75.8	23.1	1.1
Sex and age				
Male (60-74)	100.0	79.8	19.3	0.9
Female (60-74)	100.0	74.5	24.3	1.2
Male (≥ 75)	100.0	76.1	22.7	1.1
Female (≥ 75)	100.0	71.8	27.0	1.1
Marital status				
Never married	100.0	67.2	31.1	1.6
Married	100.0	78.9	20.0	1.1
Separated/divorced	100.0	61.7	36.2	2.1
Widowed	100.0	74.0	25.1	0.9
Retirement status				
Retired	100.0	75.3	23.6	0.0
Not retired	100.0	77.0	21.8	1.2
Living arrangement				
Living alone	100.0	73.9	24.5	1.6
Not living alone	100.0	76.5	22.6	0.7

[a]Not answered

Source: 1978 SNAP Survey of the Elderly, Baltimore County, Maryland

3.19

Table 3-19. "How do you like living in this neighborhood?" (in percents)

Characteristics	Feelings about neighborhood				
	Total	Like	Dislike	Mixed Feelings	NA[a]
Total	100.0	92.8	1.2	5.5	0.4
Sex and age					
Male (60-74)	100.0	92.5	0.9	6.1	0.3
Female (60-74)	100.0	91.9	1.6	6.3	0.0
Male ($\geq$ 75)	100.0	96.6	1.1	1.1	1.1
Female ($\geq$ 75)	100.0	95.4	0.6	4.0	0.0
Marital status					
Never married	100.0	88.5	0.0	8.2	3.3
Married	100.0	93.2	1.3	5.3	0.0
Separated/divorced	100.0	87.2	4.3	8.5	0.0
Widowed	100.0	93.8	0.9	5.0	0.0
Retirement status					
Retired	100.0	93.2	1.1	5.3	0.2
Not retired	100.0	92.3	1.5	5.9	0.0
Living arrangement					
Living alone	100.0	93.2	1.1	5.3	0.2
Not living alone	100.0	92.3	1.5	5.9	0.0

[a]Not answered

Source: 1978 SNAP Survey of the Elderly, Baltimore County, Maryland

3.20

Table 3-20. "Do you think that this is a safe neighborhood in which to live?" (in percents)

Characteristics	A safe place to live			
	Total	Yes	No	NA[a]
Total	100.0	96.3	2.5	1.2
Sex-age				
Male (60-74)	100.0	95.4	2.9	1.7
Female (60-74)	100.0	96.2	2.6	1.2
Male ($\geq$ 75)	100.0	95.5	3.4	1.1
Female ($\geq$ 75)	100.0	98.9	1.1	0.0
Marital status				
Never married	100.0	100.0	0.0	0.0
Married	100.0	95.3	3.5	1.2
Separated/divorced	100.0	91.5	6.4	2.1
Widowed	100.0	97.7	1.1	1.2
Retirement status				
Retired	100.0	96.4	2.7	0.8
Not retired	100.0	95.9	2.1	2.2
Living arrangement				
Living alone	100.0	97.1	1.0	1.9
Not living alone	100.0	96.0	3.1	0.9

[a]Not answered

Source: 1978 SNAP Survey of the Elderly, Baltimore County, Maryland

Table 3-21. "Have you ever been the victim of a crime?" (in percents)

| Characteristics | Victim of a crime | | | |
	Total	Yes	No	NA[a]
Total	100.0	19.5	79.2	1.4
Sex-age				
Male (60-74)	100.0	22.5	75.2	2.3
Female (60-74)	100.0	19.4	79.8	0.9
Male (≃ 75)	100.0	19.3	79.5	1.1
Female (≳ 75)	100.0	13.8	85.1	1.1
Marital status				
Never married	100.0	29.5	70.5	0.0
Married	100.0	20.0	78.5	1.6
Separated/divorced	100.0	12.8	85.1	2.1
Widowed	100.0	18.0	80.8	1.1
Retirement status				
Retired	100.0	19.3	79.5	1.2
Not retired	100.0	19.8	78.5	1.8
Living arrangement				
Living alone	100.0	18.8	79.6	1.6
Not living alone	100.0	19.7	79.0	1.3

[a]Not answered
Source: 1978 SNAP Survey of the Elderly, Baltimore County, Maryland

Table 3-22. "Do you feel that you have been unfairly treated because of your age?" (in percents)

| Characteristics | Feel unfairly treated | | | |
	Total	Yes	No	NA[a]
Total	100.0	6.2	92.5	1.4
Area				
Southwest	100.0	6.7	92.4	.9
Northwest	100.0	7.1	92.9	0.0
North	100.0	3.7	95.1	1.2
Northeast	100.0	5.6	92.9	1.5
Southeast	100.0	7.7	90.0	2.3
Sex and age				
Male (60-74)	100.0	6.6	91.6	1.7
Female (60-74)	100.0	7.0	91.6	1.4
Male (≳ 75)	100.0	5.7	94.3	0.0
Female (≳ 75)	100.0	2.9	96.0	1.1
Marital status				
Never married	100.0	6.6	91.8	1.6
Married	100.0	6.0	92.8	1.2
Separated/divorced	100.0	10.6	85.1	4.3
Widowed	100.0	5.9	92.9	1.2
Retirement status				
Retired	100.0	5.9	92.9	1.2
Not retired	100.0	6.3	92.3	1.4
Living arrangement				
Living alone	100.0	5.9	93.0	1.2
Not living alone	100.0	7.0	91.1	1.9

[a]Not answered

Source: 1978 SNAP Survey of the Elderly, Baltimore County, Maryland

3.23

Table 3-23. Interviewer's observation of the kind of structure in which the respondent lives (in percents)

Characteristics	Total	Type of housing structure						
		Single family detached	Single family townhouse	Apt. in private home	Apt. in commercial complex	Trailer	Other	Unspecified
Total	100.0	66.5	11.6	4.7	14.3	1.8	0.7	0.4
Area								
Southwest	100.0	58.9	19.0	5.4	15.3	0.0	1.2	0.2
Northwest	100.0	91.4	0.0	4.3	4.3	0.0	0.0	0.0
North	100.0	64.4	6.7	2.5	25.8	0.0	0.6	0.8
Northeast	100.0	74.5	5.9	5.3	13.0	0.3	0.3	0.6
Southeast	100.0	62.4	13.6	4.5	9.0	9.0	0.5	0.9
Sex and age								
Male (60-74)	100.0	76.7	9.8	3.5	6.9	2.0	0.3	0.9
Female (60-74)	100.0	62.7	12.9	6.1	15.4	2.1	0.7	0.2
Male ($\geq$ 75)	100.0	69.3	10.2	2.3	18.2	0.0	0.0	0.0
Female ($\geq$ 75)	100.0	57.5	11.5	4.0	23.6	1.1	1.7	0.6
Marital status								
Never married	100.0	41.0	18.0	13.1	23.0	1.6	3.3	0.0
Married	100.0	75.6	8.6	3.5	9.4	1.9	0.5	0.5
Separated/divorced	100.0	25.5	29.8	4.3	38.3	2.1	0.0	0.0
Widowed	100.0	61.2	13.0	5.5	17.6	1.6	0.7	0.5
Retirement status								
Retired	100.0	64.7	12.6	5.1	15.3	1.2	0.7	0.5
Not retired	100.0	71.1	9.1	3.8	11.8	3.2	0.6	0.3
Living arrangement								
Alone	100.0	48.7	11.8	7.6	27.7	2.9	1.0	0.3
Not living alone	100.0	72.9	11.5	3.7	9.4	1.4	0.6	0.5

Source: 1978 SNAP Survey of the Elderly, Baltimore County, Maryland

Table 3-24. "Do you (and your family) have a private kitchen or do you share a kitchen with other households?" (in percents)

3.24

Characteristics	Kitchen facilities				
	Total	Private	Share	No kitchen	NA[a]
Total	100.0	97.8	1.4	0.1	0.7
Area					
Southwest	100.0	99.0	1.0	0.0	0.0
Northwest	100.0	94.3	4.3	0.0	1.4
North	100.0	100.0	0.0	0.0	0.0
Northeast	100.0	96.4	0.6	0.3	2.2
Southeast	100.0	96.4	3.6	0.0	0.0
Sex and age					
Male (60-74)	100.0	99.1	0.3	0.3	0.3
Female (60-74)	100.0	97.2	1.7	0.0	1.0
Male (≥ 75)	100.0	98.9	1.1	0.0	0.0
Female (≥ 75)	100.0	96.6	2.9	0.0	0.6
Marital status					
Never married	100.0	98.4	1.6	0.0	0.0
Married	100.0	98.4	0.8	0.2	0.6
Separated/divorced	100.0	97.9	2.1	0.0	0.0
Widowed	100.0	96.8	2.3	0.0	0.9
Retirement status					
Retired	100.0	98.3	1.2	0.1	0.4
Not retired	100.0	96.5	2.1	0.0	1.5
Living arrangement					
Living alone	100.0	99.0	0.0	0.0	1.0
Not living alone	100.0	97.4	2.0	0.1	0.6

[a]Not answered

Source: 1978 SNAP Survey of the Elderly, Baltimore County, Maryland

Table 3-25. "Do you (and your family) have a private bathroom, or do you share a bathroom with people in other families?" (in percents)

3.25

Characteristics	Bathroom facilities					
	Total	Private	Shared	Outhouse	No facilities	NA[a]
Total	100.0	97.9	1.4	0.1	0.1	0.6
Area						
Southwest	100.0	99.3	0.7	0.0	0.0	0.0
Northwest	100.0	95.7	2.9	0.0	0.0	1.4
North	100.0	99.4	0.0	0.6	0.0	0.0
Northeast	100.0	97.2	0.9	0.0	0.0	1.9
Southeast	100.0	95.9	3.6	0.0	0.5	0.0
Sex and age						
Male (60-74)	100.0	98.6	1.2	0.0	0.0	0.3
Female (60-74)	100.0	97.4	1.6	0.2	0.0	0.9
Male (≥ 75)	100.0	98.9	1.1	0.0	0.0	0.9
Female (≥ 75)	100.0	97.7	1.1	0.0	0.6	0.6
Marital status						
Never married	100.0	95.1	3.3	1.6	0.0	0.0
Married	100.0	98.6	0.8	0.0	0.0	0.6
Separated/divorced	100.0	95.7	4.3	0.0	0.0	0.0
Widowed	100.0	97.5	1.6	0.0	0.2	0.7
Retirement status						
Retired	100.0	98.1	1.3	0.1	0.1	0.4
Not retired	100.0	97.3	1.5	0.0	0.0	1.2
Living arrangement						
Living alone	100.0	98.7	0.0	0.0	0.3	1.0
Not living alone	100.0	97.6	1.8	0.1	0.0	0.5

[a]Not answered

Source: 1978 SNAP Survey of the Elderly, Baltimore County, Maryland

3.26

Table 3-26. "Does this building need repairs inside or outside?" (in percents)

Characteristics	Total	Needs repairs		
		Yes	No	NA[a]
Total	100.0	27.9	71.6	0.5
Area				
Southwest	100.0	31.8	68.0	0.2
Northwest	100.0	30.0	68.6	1.4
North	100.0	16.0	83.4	0.6
Northeast	100.0	26.7	73.0	0.3
Southeast	100.0	30.8	68.3	0.9
Sex and age				
Male (60-74)	100.0	27.1	72.0	0.9
Female (60-74)	100.0	28.6	71.0	0.3
Male (≥ 75)	100.0	30.7	69.3	0.0
Female (≥ 75)	100.0	25.9	73.6	0.6
Marital status				
Never married	100.0	34.4	65.6	0.0
Married	100.0	26.6	73.0	0.5
Separated/divorced	100.0	21.3	78.7	0.0
Widowed	100.0	29.7	69.6	0.7
Retirement status				
Retired	100.0	28.0	71.6	0.4
Not retired	100.0	27.7	71.4	0.9
Living arrangement				
Living alone	100.0	31.5	67.5	1.0
Not living alone	100.0	26.6	73.0	0.3

[a]Not answered

Source: 1978 SNAP Survey of the Elderly, Baltimore County, Maryland

3.27

Table 3-27. Interviewer's observations of the condition of the home structure (in percents)

Characteristics	Total	Condition			
		Generally good	Fair	Deteriorating	Unspecified
Total	100.0	84.9	12.5	.9	1.6
Area					
Southwest	100.0	81.3	16.3	1.2	1.2
Northwest	100.0	88.6	8.6	0.0	2.9
North	100.0	89.0	9.2	1.8	0.0
Northeast	100.0	90.1	7.8	0.0	2.2
Southeast	100.0	80.1	16.3	1.4	2.3
Sex and age					
Male (60-74)	100.0	86.7	10.1	0.9	2.3
Female (60-74)	100.0	85.7	12.4	0.7	1.2
Male (≥ 75)	100.0	77.3	19.3	3.4	0.0
Female (≥ 75)	100.0	82.8	14.4	0.6	2.3
Marital status					
Never married	100.0	83.6	13.1	3.3	0.0
Married	100.0	87.1	10.7	0.6	1.6
Separated/divorced	100.0	74.5	23.4	0.0	2.1
Widowed	100.0	83.1	13.9	1.1	1.8
Retirement status					
Retired	100.0	85.2	12.2	1.2	1.4
Not retired	100.0	84.4	13.3	0.3	2.1
Living arrangement					
Living alone	100.0	80.9	15.9	1.6	1.6
Not living alone	100.0	86.4	11.3	0.7	1.6

Source: 1978 SNAP Survey of the Elderly, Baltimore County, Maryland

Table 3-28. "Considering everything – amount of room, structure, condition and so forth – how satisfied are you with your home?" (in percents)

3.28

| Characteristics | Total | Satisfaction with recent home | | | | | |
| | | Satisfied | | Neither | Dissatisfied | | |
		Very	Somewhat	Satisfied nor Dissatisfied	Somewhat	Very	NA[a]
Total	100.0	83.8	12.7	0.6	1.4	1.3	0.3
Area							
Southwest	100.0	81.5	13.5	0.5	2.2	1.7	0.5
Northwest	100.0	78.6	20.0	0.0	0.0	0.0	1.4
North	100.0	86.5	11.7	0.6	0.6	0.0	0.6
Notheast	100.0	90.1	9.0	0.3	0.6	0.0	0.0
Southeast	100.0	78.3	14.9	1.4	1.8	3.6	0.0
Sex and age							
Male (60-74)	100.0	85.6	11.8	0.6	0.6	1.2	0.3
Female (60-74)	100.0	80.5	15.2	0.7	1.7	1.4	0.5
Male (≥ 75)	100.0	86.4	10.2	0.0	1.1	2.3	0.0
Female (≥ 75)	100.0	89.7	7.5	0.6	1.7	0.6	0.0
Marital status							
Never married	100.0	83.6	9.8	1.6	1.6	0.0	3.3
Married	100.0	84.7	12.3	0.5	0.9	1.4	0.2
Separated/divorced	100.0	68.1	23.4	2.1	2.1	4.3	0.0
Widowed	100.0	84.0	12.6	0.5	1.8	0.9	0.2
Retirement status							
Retired	100.0	84.7	11.5	0.6	1.3	1.4	0.5
Not retired	100.0	81.4	15.6	0.6	1.5	0.9	0.0
Living arrangement							
Alone	100.0	81.8	13.1	1.0	1.9	1.3	1.0
Not living alone	100.0	84.4	12.6	0.5	1.2	1.3	0.1

[a]Not answered

Source: 1978 SNAP Survey of the Elderly, Baltimore, Maryland

Table 3-29. "Would you say that the place is too large, too small or just about right for your needs?" (in percents)

3.29

| Characteristics | Size | | | | |
	Total	Too large	Too small	Just about right	NA[a]
Total	100.0	14.5	2.5	81.7	1.3
Area					
Southwest	100.0	14.3	3.0	81.8	1.0
Northwest	100.0	20.0	1.4	75.7	2.9
North	100.0	14.1	1.2	84.0	0.6
Northeast	100.0	14.9	2.2	81.4	1.6
Southeast	100.0	12.7	3.6	82.4	1.4
Sex and age					
Male (60-74)	100.0	17.0	1.7	80.1	1.2
Female (60-74)	100.0	12.7	3.1	82.7	1.4
Male (≥ 75)	100.0	13.6	2.3	81.8	2.3
Female (≥ 75)	100.0	15.5	2.3	81.6	0.6
Marital status					
Never married	100.0	11.5	0.0	86.9	1.6
Married	100.0	13.7	2.7	82.5	1.1
Separated/divorced	100.0	8.5	6.4	85.1	0.0
Widowed	100.0	16.7	2.3	79.5	1.6
Retirement status					
Retired	100.0	13.6	2.4	82.8	1.2
Not retired	100.0	16.5	2.9	79.1	1.5
Living arrangement					
Living alone	100.0	19.1	0.6	78.0	2.2
Not living alone	100.0	12.8	3.2	83.1	0.9

[a]Not answered

Source: 1978 SNAP Survey of the Elderly, Baltimore County, Maryland

4.1

Table 4-1. "Taking everything into consideration, how would you describe your satisfaction with life in general?" (in percents)

Characteristics	Satisfaction with life				
	Total	Good	Fair	Poor	NA[a]
Total	100.0	71.2	24.5	3.5	.9
Area					
Southwest	100.0	69.2	27.1	3.2	.5
Northwest	100.0	70.0	25.7	2.9	1.4
North	100.0	73.0	24.5	2.5	0.0
Northeast	100.0	74.8	21.1	3.4	.6
Southeast	100.0	68.3	24.0	5.0	2.7
Sex and age					
Male (60-74)	100.0	73.8	22.2	2.6	1.4
Female (60-74)	100.0	69.8	25.5	3.8	0.9
Male (≥ 75)	100.0	76.1	19.3	4.5	0.0
Female (≥ 75)	100.0	67.8	28.2	3.4	0.6
Marital status					
Never married	100.0	68.9	26.2	4.9	0.0
Married	100.0	75.5	21.2	2.2	1.1
Separated/divorced	100.0	61.7	29.8	6.4	2.1
Widowed	100.0	66.2	28.3	4.8	0.7
Retirement status					
Retired	100.0	72.7	23.8	2.8	0.6
Not retired	100.0	67.3	26.0	5.0	1.8
Living arrangement					
Living alone	100.0	72.0	23.7	3.0	1.3
Not living alone	100.0	68.8	26.4	4.8	0.0

[a]Not answered

Source: 1978 SNAP Survey of the Elderly, Baltimore County, Maryland

4.2

Table 4-2. "In general, do you find life exciting, pretty routine or dull?" (in percents)

Characteristics	Opinion of life				
	Total	Exciting	Pretty routine	Dull	NA[a]
Total	100.0	32.3	59.1	7.9	.8
Area					
Southwest	100.0	32.0	58.4	8.9	.7
Northwest	100.0	37.1	50.0	11.4	1.4
North	100.0	30.1	65.0	4.3	.6
Northeast	100.0	34.5	58.1	7.1	.3
Southeast	100.0	29.9	60.2	8.6	1.4
Sex and age					
Male (60-74)	100.0	35.9	56.2	6.9	.9
Female (60-74)	100.0	33.2	58.3	7.7	.9
Male (≥ 75)	100.0	25.0	67.0	8.0	0.0
Female (≥ 75)	100.0	25.9	63.2	10.3	0.6
Marital status					
Never married	100.0	37.7	59.0	3.3	0.0
Married	100.0	33.8	59.7	5.7	0.8
Separated/divorced	100.0	31.9	55.3	12.8	0.0
Widowed	100.0	29.5	58.4	11.2	0.9
Retirement status					
Retired	100.0	32.0	59.1	8.5	0.4
Not retired	100.0	33.0	59.0	6.2	1.8
Living arrangement					
Living alone	100.0	30.3	58.6	10.5	0.6
Not living alone	100.0	33.1	59.2	6.9	0.8

[a]Not answered

Source: 1978 SNAP Survey of the Elderly, Baltimore County, Maryland

Table 4-3. The relationship between the average number of psychological symptoms reported and selected characteristics

Characteristics	Mean	Standard deviation	F-value
Total	2.5	2.6	
Area			9.5*
Southwest	2.7	2.7	
Northwest	2.9	3.0	
North	1.6	1.9	
Northeast	2.1	2.4	
Southeast	3.0	2.8	
Sex and age			4.0*
Male (60-74)	2.2	2.3	
Female (60-74)	2.5	2.8	
Male ($\geq$ 75)	2.0	2.1	
Female ($\geq$ 75)	2.9	2.7	
Marital status			8.0*
Never married	2.1	2.0	
Married	2.2	2.5	
Separated/divorced	3.0	3.0	
Widowed	2.9	2.8	
Work status			0.1
Retired	2.4	2.5	
Not retired	2.5	2.8	
Living arrangement			1.4
Living alone	2.6	2.6	
Not living alone	2.4	2.5	

*Indicates a statistically significant effect at 0.05 or lower level.

Source: 1978 SNAP Survey of the Elderly, Baltimore County, Maryland

Table 4-4. "How often would you say you worry about things?" (in percents)

Characteristics	Worry				
	Total	Very Often	Fairly often	Hardly ever	NA[a]
Total	100.0	27.1	30.1	42.0	.8
Area					
Southwest	100.0	32.5	30.0	37.2	.2
Northwest	100.0	22.9	30.0	47.1	0.0
North	100.0	19.6	44.2	36.2	0.0
Northeast	100.0	23.0	25.2	50.6	1.2
Southeast	100.0	29.9	27.1	41.2	1.8
Sex and age					
Male (60-74)	100.0	19.9	27.1	52.9	.6
Female (60-74)	100.0	31.4	35.1	32.5	1.0
Male ($\geq$ 75)	100.0	10.2	27.3	61.4	1.1
Female ($\geq$ 75)	100.0	35.6	21.3	43.1	0.0
Marital status					
Never married	100.0	24.6	27.9	45.9	1.6
Married	100.0	25.2	31.4	42.5	.9
Separated/divorced	100.0	25.5	46.8	25.5	2.1
Widowed	100.0	30.4	26.7	42.7	.2
Retirement status					
Retired	100.0	24.6	32.1	42.6	.7
Not retired	100.0	33.3	25.1	40.7	.9
Living arrangement					
Living alone	100.0	28.3	28.3	42.7	.6
Not living alone	100.0	26.6	30.8	41.8	.8

[a]Not answered

Source: 1978 SNAP Survey of the Elderly, Baltimore County, Maryland

4.5

Table 4-5. "Is your emotional health now better, about the same, or worse than it was five years ago?" (in percents)

| Characteristics | Total | Emotional health | | | |
		Better	About the same	Worse	NA[a]
Total	100.0	20.1	63.9	15.3	.7
Area					
Southwest	100.0	20.4	61.6	17.5	.5
Northwest	100.0	24.3	61.4	14.3	0.0
North	100.0	13.5	73.0	12.3	1.2
Northeast	100.0	17.7	68.9	12.7	0.6
Southeast	100.0	26.7	54.8	17.6	0.9
Sex and age					
Male (60-74)	100.0	21.3	65.1	12.4	1.2
Female (60-74)	100.0	21.5	62.3	15.7	0.5
Male (≥ 75)	100.0	15.9	69.3	14.8	0.0
Female (≥ 75)	100.0	15.5	63.8	20.1	0.6
Marital status					
Never married	100.0	21.3	67.2	11.5	0.0
Married	100.0	19.3	67.3	12.7	0.6
Separated/divorced	100.0	19.1	68.1	12.8	0.0
Widowed	100.0	21.2	58.0	19.9	0.9
Retirement status					
Retired	100.0	19.3	64.7	15.3	0.7
Not retired	100.0	22.1	61.9	15.3	0.6
Living arrangement					
Living alone	100.0	22.6	58.9	17.8	0.6
Not living alone	100.0	19.2	65.7	14.4	0.7

[a]Not answered

Source: 1978 SNAP Survey of the Elderly, Baltimore County, Maryland

4.6

Table 4-6. "How would you rate your emotional health at the present time as compared to others of the same age?" (in percents)

| Characteristics | Total | Emotional health | | | | |
		Excellent	Good	Fair	Poor	NA[a]
Total	100.0	25.5	51.7	19.9	2.7	.3
Area						
Southwest	100.0	25.6	49.0	21.9	3.0	.5
Northwest	100.0	30.0	52.9	15.7	1.4	0.0
North	100.0	25.2	61.3	11.7	1.8	0.0
Northeast	100.0	24.8	53.4	18.9	2.8	0.0
Southeast	100.0	24.9	46.6	24.9	3.2	0.5
Sex and age						
Male (60-74)	100.0	29.7	48.4	18.7	2.6	0.6
Female (60-74)	100.0	25.0	53.1	19.2	2.8	0.0
Male (≥ 75)	100.0	27.3	44.3	25.0	3.4	0.0
Female (≥ 75)	100.0	17.8	57.5	21.8	2.3	0.6
Marital status						
Never married	100.0	27.9	49.2	21.3	1.6	0.0
Married	100.0	28.6	52.0	16.5	2.5	0.3
Separated/divorced	100.0	14.9	55.3	25.5	4.3	0.0
Widowed	100.0	21.7	51.1	24.0	3.0	0.2
Retirement status						
Retired	100.0	25.1	52.0	20.3	2.4	0.2
Not retired	100.0	26.3	51.0	18.9	3.5	0.3
Living arrangement						
Living alone	100.0	24.2	51.3	22.0	2.5	0.0
Not living alone	100.0	25.9	51.8	19.1	2.8	0.3

[a]Not answered

Source: 1978 SNAP Survey of the Elderly, Baltimore County, Maryland

Table 5-1. Nature and type of physical disability and impairment by service
area   (in percents)

Physical disability and impairment	Total	Service area				
		South-west	North-west	North	North-east	South-east
Physical disability	8.8	8.4	5.7	5.5	9.0	12.7
Missing limbs	1.2	0.5	0.0	1.2	1.6	2.3
Poor vision even with glasses	7.4	8.9	7.1	3.7	5.9	9.5
Difficulty in seeing	9.2	10.1	8.6	6.1	9.0	10.4
Blind	1.5	2.2	0.0	0.6	0.3	3.2
Poor hearing	8.5	9.1	11.4	8.6	6.2	10.0
Deaf	1.6	1.5	1.4	0.6	0.9	3.6
Use cane	9.9	10.6	10.0	9.2	8.1	11.8
Use walker	2.0	2.5	1.4	1.8	1.2	2.7
Use wheelchair	1.4	1.5	0.0	0.6	1.2	2.7
Use hearing aid	4.9	5.7	1.4	9.2	2.8	4.5

Source: 1978 SNAP Survey of the Elderly, Baltimore County, Maryland

Table 5-2. "Do you have any physical disabilities such as total or partial
paralysis, missing or non-functional limbs, or broken bones?"
(in percents)

Characteristics	Physical disabilities			
	Total	Yes	No	NA[a]
Total	100.0	8.8	89.8	1.4
Sex and age				
Male (60-74)	100.0	12.4	85.9	1.7
Female (60-74)	100.0	7.5	91.3	1.2
Male (≥ 75)	100.0	9.5	88.6	2.3
Female (≥ 75)	100.0	5.7	93.7	0.6
Marital status				
Never married	100.0	6.6	93.4	0.0
Married	100.0	9.1	89.0	1.9
Separated/divorced	100.0	8.5	91.5	0.0
Widowed	100.0	8.7	90.4	0.9
Retirement status				
Retired	100.0	8.8	89.9	1.3
Not retired	100.0	8.8	89.7	1.5
Living arrangement				
Living alone	100.0	8.6	90.1	1.3
Not living alone	100.0	8.9	89.7	1.4

[a]Not answered

Source: 1978 SNAP Survey of the Elderly, Baltimore County, Maryland

5.3

Table 5-3. "How much does your health stand in the way of doing the things you want to do?" (in percents)

Characteristics	Total	Not at all	Moderate	Severe	NA[a]
			Health a hindrance		
Total	100.0	52.0	32.1	15.4	0.4
Area					
Southwest	100.0	46.3	34.5	18.7	0.5
Northwest	100.0	54.3	35.7	8.6	1.4
North	100.0	61.3	30.1	8.6	0.0
Northeast	100.0	55.3	31.4	13.0	0.3
Southeast	100.0	50.2	29.4	19.9	0.5
Sex and age					
Male (60-74)	100.0	51.9	29.1	18.4	0.6
Female (60-74)	100.0	56.0	30.7	12.9	0.3
Male (≥ 75)	100.0	47.4	36.4	5.9	0.0
Female (≥ 75)	100.0	41.4	40.8	17.2	0.6
Marital status					
Never married	100.0	50.8	31.1	14.8	3.3
Married	100.0	55.5	28.8	15.6	0.2
Separated/divorced	100.0	61.7	25.5	12.8	0.0
Widowed	100.0	46.1	37.9	15.5	0.5
Retirement status					
Retired	100.0	52.1	32.3	15.3	0.4
Not retired	100.0	51.9	31.9	15.6	0.6
Living arrangement					
Living alone	100.0	49.4	35.4	14.3	1.0
Not living alone	100.0	53.0	31.0	15.8	0.2

[a]Not answered

Source: 1978 SNAP Survey of the Elderly, Baltimore County, Maryland

5.4

Table 5-4. The relationship of functional dependency to selected social and demographic factors

Factors	Activities of daily living (ADL) score[a]	Instrumental activities of daily living (IADL) score[b]
Total percent (with one or more limitations)	8.0	27.1
Correlates		
Age	0.12*	0.32*
Sex (1=male; 0=female)	-0.03*	-0.05*
Educational level	-0.06*	-0.17*
Living alone (1=alone; 0=not alone)	-0.05*	-0.03
Married (1=married; 0=not married)	-0.01	-0.04
Retirement (1=retired; 0= not retired)	0.01	0.03

*Significant at 0.05 or lower level

[a]ADL items include human assistance needed for bathing, dressing, grooming, walking, transferring and feeding

[b]IADL items include human assistance needed for carrying out such activities as to telephoning, traveling, shopping, preparing meals, doing housework and taking medication

Source: 1978 SNAP Survey of the Elderly, Baltimore County, Maryland

Table 5-5. Human assistance needed in performing selected activities of daily living (ADL)   (in percents)

Activities	Total	Service area				
		South-west	North-west	North	North-east	South-east
Instrumental ADL						
Telephoning	3.3	3.0	0.0	1.8	2.8	6.8
Traveling	14.9	15.5	10.0	9.2	15.2	19.0
Shopping	15.1	15.2	14.3	11.6	14.6	18.6
Preparing meals	7.5	7.4	2.8	6.6	7.2	10.4
Do housework	18.3	20.0	15.7	14.8	16.5	21.3
Take medicine	2.2	2.0	1.4	1.8	2.8	2.3
ADL						
Grooming	1.9	1.7	0.0	1.2	2.5	2.3
Walking	4.5	5.6	4.3	1.8	3.1	6.8
Transferring	1.7	1.7	1.4	1.8	0.6	3.2
Bathing	5.1	4.7	7.1	4.3	5.3	5.4
Dressing	2.2	2.0	0.0	1.2	2.5	3.6
Feeding	0.5	0.5	1.4	0.6	0.6	0.0

Source: 1978 SNAP Survey of the Elderly, Baltimore County, Maryland

Table 5-7. Self-assessed physical health by service area (in percents)

Self-assessed physical health	Total (N=1182)	Service area				
		South-west (N=406)	North-west (N=70)	North (N=163)	North-east (N=322)	South-east (N=221)
Total	100.0	100.0	100.0	100.0	100.0	100.0
"Compared with other people your age would you say your health is"						
Excellent	29.4	31.8	32.9	31.3	26.7	26.7
Good	48.0	41.9	48.6	55.2	51.2	48.9
Fair	17.4	20.9	17.1	10.4	16.1	18.1
Poor	4.7	5.4	1.4	3.1	5.9	6.3
"Is your health now better, about the same or worse than it was 5 yrs. ago?"						
Better	13.5	13.1	11.4	9.8	12.1	19.5
About the same	63.6	59.4	71.4	74.8	67.1	55.7
Worse	22.9	27.6	17.1	15.3	20.8	24.9

Source: 1978 SNAP Survey of the Elderly, Baltimore County, Maryland

Table 5.6 appears on page 186.

5.6

Table 5-6. Human assistance needed in performing instrumental activities of daily living (IADL) by social and demographic factors

Human assistance needed	Telephon-ing	Travel-ing	Shop-ping	Meals	Housework	Medicine	Feeding	Dress-ing	Groom-ing	Walk-ing	Transfer-ring	Bath-ing
Total:	3.3	14.9	15.1	7.5	18.3	2.2	0.5	2.2	1.9	4.5	1.7	5.1
Sex and age												
Male (60-74)	3.2	5.2	6.3	8.1	10.1	1.2	0.3	2.3	0.9	2.6	1.2	3.2
Female (60-74)	2.3	12.9	12.0	3.3	15.3	5.7	0.3	1.7	1.7	3.9	1.8	3.7
Male (≥ 75)	8.0	21.5	25.0	25.0	37.5	3.4	2.3	5.6	4.5	4.5	1.1	8.0
Female (≥ 75)	4.5	37.3	27.9	12.1	34.4		0.6	1.7	2.9	10.9	2.9	12.0
Marital status												
Never married	1.6	8.2	8.2	8.2	9.8	1.6	0.0	1.6	1.6	1.6	3.3	4.9
Married	4.1	7.9	8.3	6.6	13.8	2.1	0.6	2.1	1.3	3.3	1.6	4.1
Separated/divorced	2.1	19.1	19.1	6.4	14.9	2.1	0.0	4.3	2.1	4.3	0.0	6.4
Widowed	2.6	25.6	25.5	8.9	26.3	2.5	0.5	2.3	2.7	6.8	1.8	6.4
Retirement status												
Retired	3.7	15.1	15.4	8.6	19.1	2.0	0.6	2.2	1.9	4.9	1.6	5.2
Not retired	2.4	14.2	14.4	5.0	16.3	2.7	0.3	2.1	1.8	3.8	1.8	4.7
Living arrangement												
Living alone	1.3	16.9	18.2	3.8	15.6	0.3	0.0	0.6	0.6	4.1	1.3	3.5
Not living alone	4.1	14.2	14.0	8.9	19.3	2.8	0.7	2.8	2.3	4.8	1.8	5.6

Source: 1978 SNAP Survey of the Elderly, Baltimore County, Maryland

Table 5-8. "Compared with other people your age, would you say your health is excellent, good, fair or poor?" (in percents)

Characteristics	Total	Health compared with others				
		Excellent	Good	Fair	Poor	NA[a]
Total	100.0	29.4	48.0	17.4	4.7	0.4
Sex and age						
Male (60-74)	100.0	30.3	49.3	15.3	4.9	0.3
Female (60-74)	100.0	28.3	49.4	17.5	4.5	0.3
Male (≥ 75)	100.0	37.5	36.4	18.2	6.8	1.1
Female (≥ 75)	100.0	27.6	46.6	21.3	4.0	0.6
Marital status						
Never married	100.0	37.7	45.9	13.1	1.6	1.6
Married	100.0	29.2	49.8	16.2	4.6	0.2
Separated/divorced	100.0	27.7	53.2	10.6	8.5	0.0
Widowed	100.0	28.8	45.0	20.5	5.0	0.7
Retirement status						
Retired	100.0	30.5	47.7	16.6	4.9	0.4
Not retired	100.0	26.8	48.7	19.5	4.4	0.6
Living arrangement						
Living alone	100.0	30.6	47.1	16.9	5.1	0.3
Not living alone	100.0	29.0	48.3	17.6	4.6	0.5

[a]Not answered

Source: 1978 SNAP Survey of the Elderly, Baltimore County, Maryland

Table 5-9. "Is your health now better, about the same, or worse than it was five years ago?" (in percents)

Characteristics	Total	Health now vs. five years ago			
		Better	About the same	Worse	NA[a]
Total	100.0	13.5	63.6	22.6	0.3
Sex and age					
Male (60-74)	100.0	14.4	62.2	23.1	0.3
Female (60-74)	100.0	14.3	64.0	21.5	0.2
Male (≥ 75)	100.0	6.8	69.3	22.7	1.1
Female (≥ 75)	100.0	12.1	62.1	25.3	0.6
Marital status					
Never married	100.0	11.5	67.2	21.3	0.0
Married	100.0	14.3	65.1	20.3	0.3
Separated/divorced	100.0	17.0	66.0	17.0	0.0
Widowed	100.0	12.1	60.7	26.7	0.5
Retirement status					
Retired	100.0	13.5	64.1	22.2	0.2
Not retired	100.0	13.3	62.5	23.6	0.6
Living arrangement					
Living alone	100.0	13.4	60.5	25.8	0.3
Not living alone	100.0	13.5	64.7	21.4	0.3

[a]Not answered

Source: 1978 SNAP Survey of the Elderly, Baltimore County, Maryland

Table 5-10. Nutritional status by service area (in percents)

Nutritional Status	Total	South-west	North-west	North	North-east	South-east
						Service area
Have a good diet	89.2	90.4	87.1	91.4	88.5	86.9
Have three or more meals a day	70.0	71.6	78.6	79.1	69.2	58.3
Have a special diet prescribed by a doctor	25.5	28.6	24.3	17.8	22.4	30.3
Take vitamin or mineral tablets	38.3	36.2	40.0	40.5	42.9	33.5
Prepare own main meal of the day	60.6	65.0	51.4	55.8	60.9	58.4

Source: 1978 SNAP Survey of the Elderly, Baltimore County, Maryland

Table 5-11. "Do you have a good diet?" (in percents)

Characteristics	Total	Yes	Sometimes	No	NA [a]
			Have a good diet		
Total	100.0	89.2	5.7	4.3	0.9
Sex and age					
Male (60-74)	100.0	89.9	3.7	5.8	0.6
Female (60-74)	100.0	89.0	6.1	4.0	0.9
Male (≥ 75)	100.0	90.9	2.3	5.7	1.1
Female (≥ 75)	100.0	87.4	9.8	1.7	1.2
Marital status					
Never married	100.0	95.1	3.3	1.6	0.0
Married	100.0	91.0	3.3	4.9	0.8
Separated/divorced	100.0	89.4	4.3	6.4	0.0
Widowed	100.0	85.6	9.6	3.7	1.2
Retirement status					
Retired	100.0	90.3	6.8	5.6	1.2
Not retired	100.0	86.4	5.2	3.8	0.8
Living arrangement					
Living alone	100.0	83.1	11.5	3.8	1.0
Not living alone	100.0	91.4	3.6	4.5	0.0

[a] Not answered

Source: 1978 SNAP Survey of the Elderly, Baltimore County, Maryland

Table 5-12. "Has your doctor prescribed a special diet for you?" (in percents)

Characteristics		Special diet		
	Total	Yes	No	NA[a]
Total	100.0	25.5	73.7	0.8
Sex and age				
Male (60-74)	100.0	29.1	70.0	0.9
Female (60-74)	100.0	24.8	74.5	0.7
Male (≥ 75)	100.0	22.7	77.3	0.0
Female (≥ 75)	100.0	21.8	76.4	1.7
Marital status				
Never married	100.0	26.2	72.1	1.6
Married	100.0	26.4	72.6	0.9
Separated/divorced	100.0	29.8	70.2	0.0
Widowed	100.0	23.5	75.8	0.7
Retirement status				
Retired	100.0	26.2	73.0	0.8
Not retired	100.0	23.6	75.5	0.9
Living arrangement				
Living alone	100.0	22.6	76.4	1.0
Not living alone	100.0	26.5	72.7	0.8

[a]Not answered

Source: 1978 SNAP Survey of the Elderly, Baltimore County, Maryland

Table 6-1. "Are you registered to vote?" (in percents)

Characteristics		Registered to vote		
	Total	Yes	No	NA[a]
Total	100.0	78.3	21.2	0.5
Area				
Southwest	100.0	75.6	23.9	0.5
Northwest	100.0	85.7	11.4	2.9
North	100.0	87.7	12.3	0.0
Northeast	100.0	81.1	18.6	0.3
Southeast	100.0	69.7	29.9	0.5
Sex and age				
Male (60-74)	100.0	86.2	13.5	0.3
Female (60-74)	100.0	77.0	22.2	0.9
Male (≥ 75)	100.0	87.5	12.5	0.0
Female (≥ 75)	100.0	62.1	37.9	0.0
Marital status				
Never married	100.0	77.0	23.0	0.0
Married	100.0	83.6	15.9	0.5
Separated/divorced	100.0	72.3	27.7	0.0
Widowed	100.0	71.2	28.1	0.7
Retirement status				
Retired	100.0	80.2	19.5	0.4
Not retired	100.0	73.5	25.7	0.9
Living arrangement				
Living alone	100.0	78.0	21.1	0.3
Not living alone	100.0	78.3	21.7	0.6

[a]Not answered

Source: 1978 SNAP Survey of the Elderly, Baltimore County, Maryland

6.2

Table 6-2. "Are you doing any volunteer work?" (in percents)

Characteristics	Total	Volunteer work		
		Yes	No	NA[a]
Total	100.0	15.7	82.9	1.4
Area				
Southwest	100.0	16.3	82.8	1.0
Northwest	100.0	17.1	80.0	2.9
North	100.0	19.6	79.8	.6
Northeast	100.0	15.8	82.0	2.2
Southeast	100.0	10.9	87.8	1.4
Sex and age				
Male (60-74)	100.0	17.3	79.8	2.9
Female (60-74)	100.0	16.9	82.2	.9
Male (≥ 75)	100.0	11.4	88.6	0.0
Female (≥ 75)	100.0	10.3	88.5	1.1
Marital status				
Never married	100.0	16.4	83.6	0.0
Married	100.0	17.6	80.5	1.9
Separated/divorced	100.0	6.4	93.6	0.0
Widowed	100.0	13.7	85.2	1.1
Retirement status				
Retired	100.0	16.4	82.1	1.3
Not retired	100.0	13.3	85.0	1.8
Living arrangement				
Living alone	100.0	16.6	82.8	.6
Not living alone	100.0	15.3	82.9	1.7

[a]Not answered

Source: 1978 SNAP Survey of the Elderly, Baltimore County, Maryland

6.3

Table 6-3. "Would you like to do volunteer work?" (in percents)

Characteristics	Total	Like to do volunteer work		
		Yes	No	NA[a]
Total	100.0	15.8	60.4	23.7
Area				
Southwest	100.0	16.7	63.5	19.7
Northwest	100.0	12.9	58.6	28.5
North	100.0	15.3	57.7	26.0
Northeast	100.0	13.7	59.0	27.3
Southeast	100.0	18.6	59.3	22.2
Sex and age				
Male (60-74)	100.0	14.4	62.2	23.3
Female (60-74)	100.0	18.7	54.1	27.2
Male (≥ 75)	100.0	13.6	63.6	22.8
Female (≥ 75)	100.0	10.3	75.9	13.8
Marital status				
Never married	100.0	19.7	57.4	22.3
Married	100.0	15.4	58.3	26.2
Separated/divorced	100.0	21.3	61.7	17.0
Widowed	100.0	15.3	63.7	21.0
Retirement status				
Retired	100.0	14.7	61.3	24.0
Not retired	100.0	18.6	58.1	23.3
Living arrangement				
Living alone	100.0	15.6	59.6	12.7
Not living alone	100.0	15.9	60.7	23.4

[a]Not answered

Source: 1978 SNAP Survey of the Elderly, Baltimore County, Maryland

Table 6-4. Activities often enjoyed in spare time (in percents)

Characteristics	Activities							
	Reading	Going to movies, plays or concerts	Going to meetings, clubs	Walks	Cards	Gardening	Hobbies	Playing Sports
Total	65.5	5.1	19.5	29.2	20.9	44.5	42.6	7.7
Area								
Southwest	63.5	2.5	18.5	31.5	18.2	42.9	40.9	6.7
Northwest	72.9	10.0	25.7	27.1	18.6	42.9	42.9	10.6
North	81.0	5.5	19.0	24.5	29.4	42.3	41.7	8.6
Northeast	64.3	8.4	22.4	31.1	22.4	51.2	46.3	8.4
Southeast	57.0	3.2	15.4	26.2	18.1	39.8	40.7	7.2
Sex and age								
Male (60-74)	63.1	5.5	19.9	32.9	20.5	48.1	37.8	13.5
Female (60-74)	68.6	6.3	20.4	29.3	23.2	46.9	47.8	7.2
Male (≧ 75)	59.1	0.0	13.6	25.0	18.2	36.4	27.3	2.3
Female (≧ 75)	63.2	2.9	18.4	23.6	15.5	33.3	42.5	0.6
Marital status								
Never married	68.9	1.6	14.8	37.7	9.8	29.5	42.6	6.6
Married	64.0	5.3	19.7	27.5	23.1	50.6	41.0	9.7
Separated/divorced	76.6	8.5	6.4	42.6	27.7	42.6	40.4	4.3
Widowed	66.0	4.8	21.2	29.0	18.5	37.9	45.0	5.3
Retirement status								
Retired	62.2	4.7	17.1	26.5	21.5	48.4	50.1	6.5
Not retired	66.8	5.9	20.4	30.2	20.6	42.9	39.5	8.2
Living arrangement								
Alone	71.3	5.4	24.2	31.2	20.7	41.1	47.8	6.7
Not living alone	63.4	5.0	17.7	28.5	21.0	45.7	40.7	8.1

Source: 1978 SNAP Survey of the Elderly, Baltimore County, Maryland

6.4

Table 7-1. Proportion of persons who have reported a specific service need by service area (in percents)

Service Needs	Total	Service area				
		South-west	North-west	North	North-east	South-east
Personal needs						
Counseling for personal or family problems	2.5	2.5	1.4	0.6	1.9	5.0
Someone to look after all the time	4.9	4.7	5.7	3.1	4.6	6.0
Someone to check on five times a week	12.4	12.1	11.4	9.4	13.7	13.7
Assistance for routine house-work that one cannot do	13.3	16.3	17.4	12.3	8.2	14.5
Legal assistance or assistance for personal business management	6.0	4.7	8.6	9.2	6.0	5.5
Health care needs						
Medicine that one cannot afford	4.6	4.0	2.9	1.2	3.7	10.2
Nursing care prescribed by a doctor	2.1	1.2	5.8	1.2	0.9	5.1
Physical therapy	4.5	5.4	5.7	1.9	3.5	6.4
Assistance in ADL functioning	4.0	3.0	5.7	4.9	4.0	5.1
Doctor or social worker's review of status	5.1	6.4	2.9	3.0	2.5	8.7
Instruction for learning basic personal skills	3.7	3.4	2.9	1.3	4.7	4.6
Recreational needs						
Participation in planned and organized social, recreational, or group activities	15.2	14.0	15.7	12.9	15.1	19.2
Housing and home needs						
Help in finding a place to live	4.1	4.7	5.8	3.1	1.2	7.4
Assistance for home repairs or yard work	25.1	18.7	27.5	17.9	32.9	28.2
Nutritional needs						
Someone who regularly prepared meals	3.4	2.2	7.1	3.7	2.8	5.0
Employment needs						
Assistance for finding a job	6.8	3.9	8.5	7.3	6.8	10.9
Information and referral						
Information about home security or crime prevention methods	5.4	5.1	6.1	5.6	3.8	8.1
Information and referral services	19.8	22.8	8.6	12.3	17.5	26.8

Source: 1978 SNAP Survey of the Elderly, Baltimore County, Maryland

Table 7-5. Multiple classification analysis of perceived personal care needs

Predictors	Counseling	Constant care	Regular visits	Home-maker	Legal Assistance
Area: Beta[a]	0.08	0.03	0.04	0.01	0.08
Southwest	2.43	4.33	11.41	15.21	4.44
Northwest	1.62	5.24	13.89	17.86	9.11
North	.97	3.45	10.17	12.99	10.18
Northeast	2.05	4.50	13.89	7.89	5.89
Southeast	4.78	5.80	13.51	15.09	5.48
Sex and age: Beta[a]	0.03	0.13*	0.06	0.09	0.03
Male (60–74)	1.98	3.68	10.18	11.98	6.40
Female (60–74)	2.95	2.89	12.52	11.01	6.52
Male (≥ 75)	2.60	9.18	12.81	18.49	4.15
Female (≥ 75)	2.07	9.64	16.43	18.90	5.09
Marital status: Beta[a]	0.04	0.10	0.08	0.14*	0.10
Never married	1.57	3.00	6.07	10.82	8.60
Married	2.64	3.27	10.78	9.07	3.99
Separated/divorced	4.89	0.90	18.70	10.74	3.31
Widowed	2.18	7.10	15.02	19.29	9.05
Living arrangement: Beta[a]	0.03	0.10*	0.17*	0.03	0.01
Living alone	3.31	0.94	21.75	11.59	5.78
Living with others	2.22	5.89	9.06	13.58	6.20
Poverty: Beta[a]	0.12*	0.11*	0.07*	0.03	0.07*
Not poor	1.94	3.86	11.70	12.72	5.57
Poor	8.75	12.51	20.47	16.55	11.62
Grand Mean	2.51	4.58	12.45	13.05	6.09

[a] Beta refers to the net effect of the given predictor variable on a specific need
*Significant at .05 or lower level

Source: 1978 SNAP Survey of the Elderly, Baltimore County, Maryland

Table 7-2. Proportion of persons who have reported a specific service need by age and sex

Service needs	Total	60-74 Male	60-74 Female	≥ 75 Male	≥ 75 Female
Personal needs					
Counseling for personal or family problems	2.5	2.0	3.0	2.3	1.7
Someone to look after all the time	4.9	3.5	3.0	10.2	10.4
Someone to check on five times a week	12.4	7.0	13.6	12.5	19.7
Assistance for routine housework that one cannot do	13.3	9.9	11.4	18.2	23.6
Legal assistance or assistance for personal business management	6.0	4.9	6.7	4.5	6.9
Health care needs					
Medicine that one cannot afford	4.6	4.6	4.4	3.4	5.7
Nursing care prescribed by a doctor	2.1	1.2	1.8	3.4	4.6
Physical therapy	4.5	2.6	5.3	4.5	6.3
Assistance in ADL functioning	4.0	2.9	3.4	4.6	8.6
Doctor or social worker's review of status	5.1	5.2	4.1	6.8	7.4
Instruction for learning basic personal skills	3.7	3.2	5.3	0.0	1.2
Recreational needs					
Participation in planned and organized social, recreational, or group activities	15.2	12.6	18.7	9.3	11.6
Housing and home needs					
Help in finding a place to live	4.1	2.6	4.8	4.5	4.7
Assistance for home repairs or yard work	25.1	19.4	26.1	27.3	32.6
Nutritional needs					
Someone who regularly prepares meals	3.4	2.6	4.2	2.2	2.9
Employment needs					
Assistance for finding a job	6.8	10.1	2.5	13.6	10.9
Information and referral					
Information about home security or crime prevention methods	5.4	5.7	5.2	6.8	4.8
Information and referral services	19.8	19.4	19.9	17.4	21.9

Source: 1978 SNAP Survey of the Elderly, Baltimore County, Maryland

Table 7-3. Proportion of persons who have reported a specific service need retirement status and living arrangement

Service Needs	Total	Retirement Status Not Retired	Retirement Status Retired	Living Arrangement Living alone	Living Arrangement Not living alone
Personal needs					
Counseling for personal or family problems	2.5	3.9	1.9	3.1	2.2
Someone to look after all the time	4.9	5.4	4.5	2.9	5.5
Someone to check on five times a week	12.4	13.8	11.9	24.6	8.1
Assistance for routine housework that one cannot do	13.3	12.7	13.4	16.7	12.0
Legal assistance or assistance for personal business management	6.0	7.7	5.4	7.7	5.5
Health care needs					
Medicine that one cannot afford	4.6	5.3	4.3	5.1	4.4
Nursing care prescribed by a doctor	2.1	3.0	1.8	1.6	2.3
Physical therapy	4.5	5.4	4.3	6.1	4.0
Assistance in ADL functioning	4.0	3.9	4.1	2.5	4.6
Doctor or social worker's review of status	5.1	5.7	4.9	5.8	4.9
Instruction for learning basic personal skills	3.7	4.1	3.5	3.3	4.8
Recreational needs					
Participation in planned and organized social, recreation, or group activities	15.2	15.9	14.9	18.9	13.8
Housing and home needs					
Help in finding a place to live	4.1	4.8	3.9	5.2	3.7
Assistance for home repairs or yard work	25.1	25.9	24.9	33.6	22.2
Nutritional needs					
Someone who regularly prepares meals	3.4	4.7	2.8	3.5	3.3
Employment needs					
Assistance for finding a job	6.8	5.6	7.2	4.5	7.6
Information and referral					
Information about home security or crime prevention methods	5.4	6.7	4.9	7.2	4.8
Informaton and referral services	19.8	22.3	17.9	20.2	19.7

Source: 1978 SNAP Survey of the Elderly, Baltimore County, Maryland

Table 7.4 appears on page 194.

7.4

Table 7-4. Proportion of persons who have reported a specific service need by marital status

Service Needs	Total	Never married	Married	Separated/ divorced	Widowed
Personal needs					
Counseling for personal or family problems	2.5	1.6	2.2	6.4	2.6
Someone to look after all the time	4.9	1.6	4.1	0.0	6.7
Someone to check up on five times a week	12.4	9.8	6.7	23.4	19.9
Assistance for routine housework that one cannot do	13.3	9.9	9.3	10.6	19.7
Legal assistance or assistance for personal business management	6.0	8.2	4.2	4.2	8.5
Health care needs					
Medicine that one cannot afford	4.6	3.3	4.0	8.5	5.3
Nursing care prescribed by a doctor	2.1	0.0	2.2	2.1	2.3
Physical therapy	4.5	3.3	3.3	8.5	6.2
Assistance in ADL functioning	4.0	3.4	3.0	4.2	5.9
Doctor or social worker's review of status	5.1	4.9	4.1	8.6	6.1
Instruction for learning basic personal skills	3.7	3.3	2.1	6.5	5.7
Recreational needs					
Participation in planned and organized social, recreational, or group activities	15.2	10.0	12.5	14.9	19.9
Housing and home needs					
Help in finding a place to live	4.1	3.4	2.6	10.6	5.8
Assistance for home repairs or yard work	25.1	31.7	20.1	10.7	33.4
Nutritional needs					
Someone who regularly prepares meals	3.4	0.0	2.2	6.4	5.0
Employment needs					
Assistance for finding a job	6.8	4.9	6.0	4.3	8.5
Information and referral					
Information about home security or crime prevention methods	5.4	3.3	4.9	10.6	5.9
Information and referral services	19.8	15.0	17.3	42.5	21.6

Source: 1978 SNAP Survey of the Elderly, Baltimore County, Maryland

7.6

Table 7-6. Multiple classification analysis of perceived health care needs

Predictors	Medicine	Nursing care	Physical therapy	ADL Assistance	Professional status review	Basic skills
Area: Beta[a]	0.10*	0.12*	0.07	0.06	0.08	0.04
Southwest	3.78	1.05	5.29	2.44	6.29	3.59
Northwest	2.83	5.67	6.10	5.38	2.81	3.12
North	2.56	1.35	2.21	5.22	4.02	2.39
Northeast	4.12	1.23	3.54	4.40	2.97	4.61
Southeast	9.03	5.22	6.50	4.82	7.52	3.78
Sex and age: Beta:[a]	0.03	0.11*		0.09	0.06	0.12
Male (60-74)	4.75	0.53	3.10	3.15	5.75	4.62
Female (60-74)	4.17	1.92	5.24	3.13	3.83	5.06
Male (≥ 75)	3.73	3.76	4.93	4.50	7.02	-0.19
Female (≥ 75)	6.20	5.38	5.71	8.02	6.88	-0.48
Marital Status: Beta:[a]	0.02	0.04	0.05	0.12*	0.05	0.14*
Never married	3.84	0.29	3.38	4.61	5.41	3.92
Married	4.26	2.71	3.97	1.89	4.16	1.38
Separated/ divorced	5.38	1.46	7.29	5.59	6.42	4.95
Widowed	5.13	1.76	5.54	6.69	6.23	6.87
Living Arrangement: Beta[a]	0.00	0.02	0.01	0.13*	0.00	0.04
Living alone	4.57	1.81	5.02	0.13	4.63	2.61
Living with others	4.62	2.31	4.53	5.45	5.26	4.11
Poverty: Beta[a]	0.32*	0.10*	0.07*	0.07*	0.24*	0.18*
Not poor	2.55	1.75	4.21	3.58	3.54	2.68
Poor	26.73	6.80	9.71	8.32	22.45	15.28
Grand Mean	4.61	2.18	4.66	3.97	5.09	3.71

[a] Beta refers to the net effect of the given predictor variable on a specific need
*Significant at .05 or lower level

Source: 1978 SNAP Survey of the Elderly, Baltimore County, Maryland

194

Table 7-7. Multiple classification analysis of perceived miscellaneous service needs

Predictors	Recreation Participation in activities	Housing Help finding	Repairs Home repairs	Employment Help finding	Nutrition Meal preparation	Information/Referral Crime prevention	I & R[b]
Area: Beta[a]	0.04	0.10*	0.09*	0.11	0.08	0.06	0.11
Southwest	14.21	4.54	27.89	3.60	2.28	5.13	22.86
Northwest	15.50	4.67	29.47	7.89	7.63	6.49	8.52
North	14.76	3.78	19.09	7.44	3.79	5.82	13.64
Northeast	14.42	1.44	20.83	7.20	2.63	3.95	18.52
Southeast	18.52	7.02	28.96	11.55	4.83	7.90	24.70
Sex and age	0.11*	0.03	0.06	0.18	0.04	0.03	0.03
Male (60-74)	14.85	3.37	21.53	10.93	3.58	6.19	21.60
Female (60-74)	18.42	4.46	26.00	2.31	3.84	5.14	18.93
Male (≥ 75)	9.17	4.97	26.78	14.00	2.39	7.29	18.11
Female (≥ 75)	8.40	3.69	28.23	9.70	2.02	4.42	20.59
Marital status: Beta[a]	0.11	0.09	0.12*	0.15*	0.12*	0.05	0.14*
Never married	10.03	3.69	29.87	6.86	0.59	2.84	16.45
Married	12.53	2.51	22.60	3.46	1.72	5.38	16.26
Separated/divorced	11.35	8.76	6.74	8.45	5.73	9.60	40.60
Widowed	20.25	5.86	30.01	11.44	5.87	5.60	23.28
Living arrangement: Beta[a]	0.02	0.02	0.07	0.12*	0.04	0.05	0.06
Living alone	16.55	3.46	29.77	1.60	2.09	7.44	15.82
Living with others	14.73	4.27	26.76	8.71	3.84	4.79	21.36
Poverty: Beta[a]	0.09*	0.16*	0.05	0.01	0.11*	0.04	0.23*
Not poor	14.21	3.11	24.44	6.75	2.76	5.20	17.19
Poor	26.30	14.27	31.89	7.57	10.24	8.93	50.20
Grand Mean	15.21	4.06	25.06	6.82	3.37	5.50	19.88

[a] Beta refers to the net effect of the given predictor variable on a specific need.
[b] I & R = Information and referral service.
* Significant at .05 or lower level.
Source: 1978 SNAP Survey of the Elderly, Baltimore County, Maryland

Table 7-9. Proportion of persons who have reported a specific unmet need by age and sex (in percents)

Service Needs	Total	Age			
		60-74		≥75	
		Male	Female	Male	Female
Personal needs					
Counseling for personal or family problems	2.3	2.0	2.8	2.3	1.1
Someone to look after all the time	1.1	0.3	0.7	1.1	4.0
Someone to check on five times a week	1.1	0.9	1.1	3.4	0.6
Assistance for routine housework that one cannot do	4.3	2.3	4.4	5.7	6.9
Legal assistance or assistance for personal business management	2.7	2.0	3.7	1.1	1.7
Health care needs					
Medicine that one cannot afford	4.6	4.6	4.4	3.4	5.7
Nursing care prescribed by a doctor	1.4	0.6	1.4	2.3	2.9
Physical therapy	3.1	2.0	3.5	4.5	3.4
Assistance in ADL functioning	1.4	0.3	1.8	2.3	2.3
Doctor or social worker's review of status	3.1	2.9	2.3	4.5	5.7
Instruction for learning basic personal skills	3.7	3.2	5.3	0.0	1.2
Recreational needs					
Participation in planned and organized social, recreational, or group activities	10.4	8.6	13.3	8.1	5.2
Housing and home needs					
Help in finding a place to live	3.6	1.7	4.6	4.5	3.5
Assistance for home repairs or yard work	9.6	7.8	11.1	8.0	9.3
Nutritional needs					
Someone who regularly prepares meals	3.2	2.6	4.0	1.1	2.9
Employment needs					
Assistance for finding a job	0.8	0.0	0.9	0.0	2.3
Information and referral					
Information about home security or crime prevention methods	5.4	5.7	5.2	6.8	4.8
Information and referral services	18.3	17.6	19.0	15.1	19.0

Source: 1978 SNAP Survey of the Elderly, Baltimore County, Maryland

Table 7.8 appears on page 196.

Table 7-8. Proportion of persons who have reported a specific unmet service
            need by service area (in percents)

Service Needs	Total	Service area				
		South-west	North-west	North	North-east	South-east
Personal needs						
Counseling for personal or family problems	2.3	2.5	1.4	0.6	1.9	4.1
Someone to look after all the time	1.1	0.7	1.4	0.6	0.9	2.3
Someone to check on five times a week	1.1	1.2	5.6	0.6	0.3	0.9
Assistance for routine house-work that one cannot do	4.3	7.4	5.8	1.2	2.2	3.2
Legal assistance or assistance for personal business management	2.7	2.5	4.3	2.5	3.8	1.4
Health care needs						
Medicine that one cannot afford	4.6	4.0	2.9	1.2	3.7	10.2
Nursing care prescribed by a doctor	1.4	1.0	2.9	0.0	0.9	3.7
Physical therapy	3.1	4.2	1.4	1.9	1.9	4.6
Assistance in ADL functioning	1.4	1.5	1.4	1.8	1.2	1.4
Doctor or social worker's review of status	3.1	3.9	2.9	1.2	1.6	5.5
Instruction for learning basic personal skills	3.7	1.2	0.2	0.2	1.3	0.9
Recreational needs						
Participation in planned and organized social, recrea-tional, or group activities	10.4	11.3	7.1	7.4	8.8	14.2
Housing and home needs						
Help in finding a place to live	3.6	4.7	2.9	2.5	1.2	6.0
Assistance for home repairs or yard work	9.6	9.9	14.5	3.7	10.2	11.4
Nutritional needs						
Someone who regularly pre-pares meals	3.2	2.2	5.7	3.7	2.8	4.5
Employment needs						
Assistance for finding a job	0.8	0.2	1.4	0.6	1.2	0.9
Information and referral						
Information about home security or crime prevention methods	5.4	5.1	6.1	5.6	3.8	8.1
Information and referral services	18.3	22.3	7.2	8.6	15.9	25.0

Source: 1978 SNAP Survey of the Elderly, Baltimore County, Maryland

Table 7-12. Multiple classification analysis of perceived unmet personal
             care needs

Predictors	Personal care services				
	Counseling	Constant care	Regular visits	Home-maker	Legal assistance
Area: Beta[a]	0.05	0.06	0.12*	0.12*	0.07
Southwest	2.45	0.54	1.25	7.24	2.02
Northwest	1.51	1.29	5.82	6.43	4.42
North	0.95	0.73	0.68	1.36	2.95
Northeast	1.99	1.11	0.28	2.02	3.84
Southeast	3.61	2.33	0.88	2.99	0.80
Sex and age	0.03	0.12*	0.07	0.05	0.06
Male (60–74)	1.94	0.30	0.96	2.78	1.98
Female (60–74)	2.71	0.69	1.07	4.28	3.69
Male (≥ 75)	2.49	1.18	3.52	5.78	0.79
Female (≥ 75)	1.44	3.99	0.31	5.77	1.99
Marital status: Beta[a]	0.04	0.06	0.04	0.05	0.06
Never married	1.64	0.31	1.99	2.51	6.95
Married	2.37	0.75	0.74	4.75	2.64
Separated/divorced	5.14	0.04	2.11	0.10	0.91
Widowed	1.93	1.84	1.42	4.00	2.45
Living arrangement: Beta[a]	0.01	0.05	0.02	0.11*	0.01
Living alone	2.59	0.18	0.08	7.98	2.40
Living with others	2.17	1.43	1.22	2.79	2.84
Poverty: Beta[a]	0.13*	0.08*	0.05	0.03	0.15*
Not poor	1.70	0.84	0.95	4.00	1.99
Poor	8.66	4.02	2.87	6.04	10.70
Grand Mean	2.28	1.10	1.11	4.17	2.72

[a] Beta refers to the net effect of the given predictor variable on a specific need
*Significant at .05 or lower level

Source: 1978 SNAP Survey of the Elderly, Baltimore County, Maryland

Table 7-10. Proportion of persons who have reported a specific unmet service need by marital status (in percents)

Service Needs	Total	Marital status			
		Never married	Married	Separated/ divorced	Widowed
Personal needs					
Counseling for personal or family problems	2.3	1.6	2.2	6.4	2.1
Somone to look after all the time	1.1	0.0	0.6	0.0	2.1
Someone to check on five times a week	1.1	1.6	1.0	2.1	1.1
Assistance for routine housework that one cannot do	4.3	3.3	3.0	2.1	6.4
Legal assistance or assistance for personal business management	2.7	6.6	2.5	2.1	2.5
Health care needs					
Medicine that one cannot afford	4.6	3.3	4.0	8.5	5.3
Nursing care prescribed by a doctor	1.4	0.0	1.4	2.1	1.6
Physical therapy	3.1	3.3	2.8	6.4	3.2
Assistance in ADL functioning	1.4	1.7	1.1	2.1	1.8
Doctor or social worker's review of status	3.1	1.6	2.4	4.3	4.3
Instruction for learning basic personal skills	3.7	3.3	1.1	0.3	2.1
Recreational needs					
Participation in planned and organized social, recreational, or group activities	10.4	8.3	8.7	14.9	12.6
Housing and home needs					
Help in finding a place to live	3.6	1.7	2.1	10.6	5.3
Assistance for home repairs or yard work	9.6	10.0	8.7	4.3	11.6
Nutritional needs					
Someone who regularly prepares meals	3.2	0.0	2.2	6.4	4.8
Employment needs					
Assistance for finding a job	0.8	0.0	0.5	0.0	1.4
Information and referral					
Information about home security or crime prevention methods	5.4	3.3	4.9	10.6	5.9
Information and referral services	18.3	11.7	15.7	41.3	20.5

Source: 1978 SNAP Survey of the Elderly, Baltimore County, Maryland

Table 7-13. Multiple classification analysis of perceived unmet health care needs

Predictors	Health care services					
	Medicine	Nursing care	Physical therapy	ADL assistant	Professional status review	Basic skills
Area: Beta[a]	0.10*	0.09*	0.06	0.02	0.07	0.04
Southwest	3.71	0.84	4.10	1.38	3.72	3.54
Northwest	2.77	2.74	1.58	1.58	2.89	3.13
North	2.50	0.19	2.09	1.97	1.86	2.36
Northeast	4.35	1.16	2.02	1.31	1.89	4.58
Southeast	8.81	3.55	4.39	1.36	5.02	3.72
Sex and age	0.03	0.09	0.05	0.07	0.07	0.12*
Male (60-74)	4.56	0.19	1.93	0.27	3.13	4.60
Female (60-74)	4.26	1.44	3.51	1.77	2.24	4.97
Male (≥ 75)	3.67	2.50	4.80	2.26	4.73	-0.17
Female (≥ 75)	6.27	3.45	3.63	2.37	5.44	-0.49
Marital status: Beta[a]	0.02	0.03	0.03	0.01	0.03	0.14*
Never married	3.70	0.27	3.20	1.51	1.78	3.88
Married	4.38	1.67	3.29	1.56	2.88	1.31
Separated/ divorced	5.33	1.47	5.21	1.42	2.55	5.08
Widowed	4.96	1.29	2.75	1.29	3.82	6.88
Living arrangement: Beta[a]	0.00	0.03	0.01	0.01	0.02	0.04
Living alone	4.57	0.85	3.35	1.74	3.62	2.54
Living with others	4.61	1.67	3.09	1.34	2.99	4.08
Poverty: Beta[a]	0.32*	0.14*	0.10*	0.07*	0.20*	0.18*
Not poor	2.58	0.96	2.65	1.20	2.09	2.65
Poor	26.80	6.82	8.72	4.15	14.89	14.83
Grand mean	4.60	1.45	3.16	1.45	3.16	3.67

[a]Beta refers to the net effect of the given predictor variable on a specific need
*Significant at .05 or lower level

Source: 1978 SNAP Survey of the Elderly, Baltimore County, Maryland

Table 7.11 appears on page 198.

Table 7-11. Proportion of persons who have reported a specific unmet service need by retirement status and living arrangement

Unmet service need	Total	Retirement status		Living arrangement	
		Not retired	Retired	Living alone	Not living alone
Personal needs					
Counseling for personal or family problem	2.3	3.6	1.8	2.5	2.2
Someone to look after all the time	1.1	1.8	0.8	1.0	1.2
Someone to check on five times a week	1.1	0.9	1.2	1.0	1.2
Assistance for routine housework that one cannot do	4.3	5.0	3.9	8.0	2.9
Legal assistance or assistance for personal business management	2.7	4.1	2.2	2.6	2.8
Health care					
Medicine that one cannot afford	4.6	5.3	4.3	5.1	4.4
Nursing care prescribed by a doctor	1.4	2.7	1.0	1.0	1.6
Physical therapy	3.1	3.6	3.0	3.5	3.0
Assistance in ADL functioning	1.4	1.5	1.4	1.9	1.3
Doctor or social worker's review of status	3.1	3.3	3.1	4.2	2.8
Instruction for learning basic personal skills.	3.7	1.2	2.5	4.8	3.3
Recreational needs					
Participation in planned and organized social, recreational, or group activities	10.4	11.2	10.0	9.6	10.6
Housing and home needs					
Help in finding a place to live	3.6	3.9	3.5	4.2	3.4
Assistance for home repairs or yard work	9.6	10.7	9.2	13.9	8.1
Nutritional needs					
Someone who regularly prepares meals	3.2	4.7	2.6	3.5	3.1
Employment needs					
Assistance for finding a job	0.8	0.6	0.8	1.0	0.7
Information and referral					
Information about home security or crime prevention methods	5.4	6.7	4.9	7.2	4.8
Information and referral services	18.3	20.8	17.3	18.6	18.2

Source: 1978 SNAP Survey of the Elderly, Baltimore County, Maryland

Table 7-14. Multiple classification analysis of miscellaneous perceived unmet service needs

Predictors	Recreation Participation in activities	Housing Help finding	Repairs Home repairs	Employment Help finding	Nutrition Meal preparation	Information/referral Crime prevention	I & R[b]
Area: Beta[a]	0.07	0.08*	0.08	0.06	0.06	0.06	0.03*
Southwest	11.55	4.58	9.73	0.14	2.25	5.06	22.12
Northwest	7.22	3.06	15.21	1.43	6.04	6.41	6.96
North	8.62	3.12	4.78	0.65	3.72	5.78	10.72
Northeast	8.33	1.29	9.86	1.96	2.57	3.84	16.29
Southeast	2.79	5.42	10.54	1.03	4.35	7.85	22.55
Sex and age	0.11*	0.05	0.05	0.09	0.05	0.03	0.03
Male (60-74)	10.29	2.69	7.73	-0.01	3.49	6.02	19.31
Female (60-74)	12.96	4.32	11.02	0.88	3.62	5.10	15.55
Male (≥ 75)	8.18	4.85	7.96	-0.02	1.23	7.20	15.55
Female (≥ 75)	2.79	2.07	9.21	2.38	1.92	4.36	17.14
Marital status: Beta[a]	0.14*	0.13*	0.08	0.03	0.11	0.04	0.14*
Never married	9.49	2.17	8.88	0.04	0.49	2.81	13.10
Married	6.58	1.59	10.98	0.74	1.60	5.29	14.30
Separated/divorced	13.86	9.24	-0.39	-0.08	5.69	9.37	37.38
Widowed	15.48	5.98	8.66	1.00	5.48	5.55	22.18
Living arrangement: Beta[a]	0.09*	0.05	0.11*	0.01	0.04	0.05	0.07
Living alone	5.80	1.88	14.96	0.66	1.05	7.32	13.69
Living with others	11.96	4.15	7.61	0.73	3.54	6.11	19.72
Poverty: Beta[a]	0.11*	0.16*	0.15*	0.01	0.01*	0.04	0.24*
Not poor	9.35	2.68	8.21	0.74	2.62	5.12	15.34
Poor	21.01	13.22	24.54	1.11	9.07	8.77	49.01
Grand Mean	10.32	3.55	9.56	0.77	3.15	5.42	18.11

[a]Beta refers to the net effect of the given predictor variable on a specific need

[b]Information and referral service

Source: 1978 SNAP Survey of the Elderly, Baltimore County, Maryland

Table 7-16. Transportation barriers by age, sex, marital status and retirement status (in percents)

Characteristics	Total	Yes	No	NA[a]
Sex and age				
Male (60-74) (N=347)	100.0	6.3	93.4	0.3
Female (60-74) (N=573)	100.0	15.0	84.5	0.5
Male (≥ 75) (N=88)	100.0	9.1	89.8	1.1
Female (≥ 75) (N=174)	100.0	21.3	78.2	0.6
Marital status				
Never married (N=61)	100.0	9.8	90.2	0.0
Married (N=636)	100.0	7.9	91.7	0.5
Separated/divorced (N=47)	100.0	25.5	73.3	2.1
Widowed (N=438)	100.0	19.4	80.1	0.5
Retirement status				
Retired (N=843)	100.0	13.0	87.0	0.6
Not retired (N=339)	100.0	12.7	86.4	0.3
Living arrangement				
Live alone (N=314)	100.0	18.2	80.9	1.0
Not living alone (N=868)	100.0	11.1	88.6	0.3

[a]Not answered

Source: 1978 SNAP Survey of the Elderly, Baltimore County, Maryland

Table 7.15 appears on page 200.

7.15

Table 7-15. "Do you have trouble getting around? That is, does lack of transportation keep you from doing things you would like to do?" (in percents)

Transportation problem	Total	Service area				
		South-west	North-west	North	North-east	South-east
Total (N=1182)	100.0	100.0	100.0	100.0	100.0	100.0
Yes (N=153)	12.9	15.0	8.6	9.8	10.2	16.7
No (N=1023)	86.5	84.0	90.0	90.2	89.4	83.3
No answer (N=6)	0.5	1.0	1.4	0.0	0.3	0.0

Source: 1978 SNAP Survey of the Elderly, Baltimore County, Maryland

7.17

Table 7-17. "Does anyone in this household have a car in working condition?" (in percents)

Car available	Total	Service area				
		South-west	North-west	North	North-east	South-east
Total (1182)	100.0	100.0	100.0	100.0	100.0	100.0
Yes (N=950)	80.4	75.6	92.9	84.0	81.7	80.5
No (N=224)	19.0	23.4	7.1	16.0	18.0	18.1
No answer (N=8)	0.7	1.0	0.0	0.0	0.3	1.4

Source: 1978 SNAP Survey of the Elderly, Baltimore County, Maryland

7.18

Table 7-18. Have a car in working condition by selected social and demographic characteristics (in percents)

Characteristics	Total	Yes	No	NA[a]
Sex and age				
Male (60-74) (N=347)	100.0	94.2	5.2	0.6
Female (60-74) (N=573)	100.0	80.8	18.8	0.4
Male ($\geq$ 75) (N=88)	100.0	73.9	25.0	1.1
Female ($\geq$ 75) (N=174)	100.0	54.6	43.7	1.7
Marital status				
Never married (N=61)	100.0	68.9	31.1	0.0
Married (N=636)	100.0	92.6	6.6	0.8
Separated/divorced (N=47)	100.0	63.8	36.2	0.0
Widowed (N=438)	100.0	66.0	33.3	0.7
Retirement status				
Retired (N=843)	100.0	83.5	16.2	0.3
Not retired (N=239)	100.0	79.1	20.0	0.7
Living arrangements				
Living alone (N=314)	100.0	54.8	43.9	1.3
Not living alone (N=868)	100.0	89.6	9.9	0.5

[a]Not answered

Source: 1978 SNAP Survey of the Elderly, Baltimore County, Maryland

Table 7-19. Distribution of car use among <u>respondents with car</u> in household by service area   (in percents)

| Car available | Total | Service area | | | | |
		South-west	North-west	North	North-east	South-east
Total (N=984)	100.0	43.3	54.5	58.3	49.5	43.8
Frequently (N=472)	48.0	24.0	22.7	15.8	26.0	20.0
Occasionally (N=222)	22.6	3.1	1.5	4.3	4.0	7.0
Almost never (N=41)	4.2	29.6	21.2	21.6	20.5	29.2
Never (N=249)	25.2	29.6	21.2	21.6	20.5	29.2

Source: 1978 SNAP Survey of the Elderly, Baltimore County, Maryland

Table 7-20. Distribution of car use among <u>respondents with car</u> in household by sex and age, marital status, retirement status, and living arrangement (in percents)

7.20

Characteristics	Total	Frequently	Occasionally	Almost Never	Never
Sex and age					
Males (60-74) (N=331)	100.0	68.9	23.3	3.6	4.2
Females (64-74) (N=978)	100.0	42.3	21.5	5.2	31.0
Males (≥75) (N=69)	100.0	33.3	40.6	4.3	21.7
Females (≥ 75) (N=106)	100.0	17.9	13.2	0.9	67.9
Marital status					
Never married (N=472)	100.0	55.8	23.3	0.0	20.9
Married (N=222)	100.0	53.3	25.0	4.8	16.9
Separated/divorced (N=41)	100.0	59.4	18.8	3.1	18.8
Widowed (N=249)	100.0	35.5	18.1	3.5	42.9
Retirement status					
Retired (N=696)	100.0	47.7	23.7	4.6	24.0
Not retired (N=288)	100.0	48.6	19.8	3.1	28.5
Living arrangement					
Living alone (N=193)	100.0	60.6	26.4	1.6	11.4
Not living alone (N=791)	100.0	44.9	21.6	4.8	28.7

Source: 1978 SNAP Survey of the Elderly, Baltimore County, Maryland

Table 7-21. "On the average, how many round trips do you make each week for shopping, visiting, work, business, or any other reason? (in percents)

7.21

| Number of trips | Total | Service area | | | | |
		South-west	North-west	North	North east	South-east
Total (N=1182)	100.0	100.0	100.0	100.0	100.0	100.0
0 (N=71)	6.0	6.7	5.7	1.8	6.8	6.8
1-3 (N=544)	46.0	44.0	44.3	36.2	49.1	52.9
4-9 (N=474)	40.1	39.7	42.9	56.4	37.0	32.6
10-52 (N=93)	7.9	9.6	7.1	5.5	7.1	7.7

Source: 1978 SNAP Survey of the Elderly, Baltimore County, Maryland

7.22

Table 7-22. Elderly persons who made varying number of trips each week by selected characteristics (in percents)

Characteristics	Total	Number of trips			
		0	1-3	4-9	10-52
Sex and Age					
Males (60-74) (N=347)	100.0	2.6	34.0	48.7	14.7
Females (60-74) (N=573)	100.0	5.8	46.4	41.5	6.3
Males (≥ 75) (N=88)	100.0	9.1	59.1	28.4	3.4
Females (≥ 75) (N=174)	100.0	12.1	62.1	24.1	1.7
Marital status					
Never married (N=61)	100.0	6.6	50.8	32.8	9.8
Married (N=636)	100.0	3.6	40.7	45.4	10.2
Separated/divorced (N=47)	100.0	4.3	51.1	38.3	6.4
Widowed (N=438)	100.0	9.6	52.5	33.6	4.3
Retirement status					
Retired (N=843)	100.0	5.1	48.6	39.1	7.1
Not retired (N=339)	100.0	8.3	39.5	42.5	9.7
Living arrangement					
Living alone (N=314)	100.0	5.1	47.8	40.4	6.7
Not living alone (N=868)	100.0	6.3	45.4	40.0	8.3

Source: 1978 SNAP Survey of the Elderly, Baltimore County, Maryland

7.23

Table 7-23. "When you go shopping, to the doctor, visit friends, etc., how do you get there?" (in percents)

Mode of transportation	Total	Service area				
		South-west	North-west	North	North-west	South-east
Walking (N=264)	22.3	29.8	15.7	26.4	20.5	10.4
Driving self (N=685)	58.0	52.2	74.3	62.6	63.7	51.6
Driven by others (N=673)	56.9	63.3	51.4	61.3	48.1	56.6
Taxi (N=165)	14.0	18.0	10.0	13.5	10.9	12.7
Senioride/other public agency (N=40)	3.4	4.7	2.9	3.7	2.5	2.3
Bus (N=270)	22.8	37.2	15.7	23.9	13.7	11.7

Source: 1978 SNAP Survey of the Elderly, Baltimore County, Maryland

7.26

Table 7-26. Distribution of those using bus service by age, sex, marital status, retirement status, and living arrangement (in percents)

Characteristics	Total	All	Most	Some	A few	None	Don't know
Sex and age							
Males (60-74) (N=79)	100.0	17.7	17.7	19.0	26.6	15.2	3.8
Female (64-74) (N=194)	100.0	18.0	22.2	19.1	28.4	10.8	1.5
Males (≥ 75) (N=29)	100.0	10.3	27.6	17.2	13.8	31.0	0.0
Females (≥ 75) (N=66)	100.0	12.1	19.7	18.2	27.3	19.7	3.0
Marital status							
Never married (N=18)	100.0	22.2	22.2	16.7	33.3	0.0	5.6
Married (N=173)	100.0	12.7	17.9	22.0	28.3	16.8	2.3
Separated/divorced (N=18)	100.0	27.8	27.8	5.6	33.3	5.6	0.0
Widowed (N=159)	100.0	18.2	23.9	17.0	23.3	15.7	1.9
Retirement status							
Retired (N=278)	100.0	15.8	21.2	19.8	27.0	14.4	1.8
Not retired (N=90)	100.0	17.8	21.1	15.6	25.6	16.7	3.3
Living arrangement							
Living alone (N=110)	100.0	19.1	25.5	16.4	26.4	10.0	2.7
Not living alone (N=258)	100.0	15.1	19.4	19.8	26.7	17.1	1.9

Source: 1978 SNAP Survey of the Elderly, Baltimore County, Maryland

Tables 7.24 and 7.25 appear on page 204.

Table 7-27. Distribution of total population by reasons for not using bus service **7.27**

Reason	Number	Percentage
Total	1182	100
Not convenient/too far	242	20
Does not go where I want to go	35	3
Costs too much	2	0
Buses do not run often enough	24	2
Seats are not available	1	0
Seats are not comfortable	1	0
Routes and schedules not understandable	7	1
Bus stops are not safe	5	0
No protected area to wait for bus	3	0
Don't like/want to ride the bus	147	12
Don't know	19	2
Other	277	23
Not applicable*	419	36

*Includes those who use bus and those who did not answer

Source: 1978 SNAP Survey of the Elderly, Baltimore County, Maryland

Table 7-28. Persons not using bus service by service area (in percents) **7.28**

Reason	Total	Service Area				
		Southwest	Northwest	North	Northeast	Southeast
Total (N=163)	100.0	100.0	100.0	100.0	100.0	100.0
Not convenient, too far from home (N=242)	31.7	22.1	27.5	45.4	29.1	41.3
General dissatisfaction with service (N=97)	12.7	12.2	3.9	13.9	15.4	11.6
Don't like/want to ride the bus (N=147)	19.3	14.9	35.3	22.2	22.5	13.5
Other (N=277)	36.3	50.9	33.3	18.5	33.0	33.5

Source: 1978 SNAP Survey of the Elderly, Baltimore County, Maryland

Table 7-29. Distribution of those not using bus service by sex and age, marital status, retirement status, and living arrangements (in percents) **7.29**

Characteristics	Total	Not convenient too far from here	General dissatisfaction with service	Don't like/ want to ride the bus	Other
Sex and age					
Males (60-74) (N=252)	100.0	29.0	16.7	19.8	34.5
Female (64-74) (N=353)	100.0	31.3	11.6	19.9	37.2
Males ($\geq$ 75) (N=64)	100.0	34.4	10.9	25.0	29.7
Females ($\geq$ 75) (N=95)	100.0	38.9	7.4	11.6	42.1
		16.7		16.7	47.2
Marital status					
Never married (N=36)	100.0	19.4	13.7	20.2	32.7
Married (N=446)	100.0	33.4	9.5	19.0	33.3
Separated/divorced (N=21)	100.0	38.1	10.8	18.1	41.2
Widowed (N=260)	100.0	30.0			
Retirement status					
Retired (N=529)	100.0	33.3	12.5	18.5	35.7
Not retired (N=234)	100.0	28.2	13.2	20.9	37.6
Living arrangement					
Living alone (N=174)	100.0	25.9	14.9	20.1	39.1
Not living alone (N=589)	100.0	33.4	12.1	19.0	35.5

Source: 1978 SNAP Survey of the Elderly, Baltimore County, Maryland

7.24

Table 7-24. Transportation by selected social and demographic characteristics (in percents)

Characteristics	Walking	Driving self	Driven by others	Taxi	Senioride/ other public agency	Bus
Sex and age						
Males (60-74)	19.6	85.0	33.4	4.9	1.7	15.9
Female (64-74)	22.2	53.4	63.5	16.4	3.1	25.8
Males (≥ 75)	29.5	58.0	62.5	14.8	3.4	18.2
Females (≥75)	23.6	19.0	79.3	23.6	7.5	29.3
Marital status						
Never married	32.8	55.7	55.7	18.0	6.6	26.2
Married	19.2	72.2	48.6	8.2	2.0	18.2
Separated/divorced	34.0	51.1	59.6	23.4	10.6	36.2
Widowed	24.2	38.4	68.9	20.8	4.1	27.6
Retirement status						
Retired	23.1	58.2	57.5	14.2	3.9	24.8
Not retired	20.4	57.2	55.5	13.3	2.1	18.0
Living arrangement						
Living alone	29.3	52.5	59.6	19.1	5.7	29.9
Not living alone	19.8	59.9	56.0	12.1	2.5	20.3

Source: 1978 SNAP Survey of the Elderly, Baltimore County, Maryland

Table 7-25. Distribution of those using bus service by service area (in percents)

Number of places	Total	Service area				
		Southwest	Northwest	North	Northeast	Southeast
Total (N=368)	100.0	100.0	100.0	100.0	100.0	100.0
All (N=60)	16.3	21.6	15.0	7.2	14.3	14.8
Most (N=78)	21.2	24.1	25.0	18.8	19.0	16.7
Some (N=69)	18.8	23.5	15.0	13.0	17.5	14.8
A few (N=98)	26.6	25.3	15.0	33.3	33.3	18.5
None (N=55)	14.9	4.9	30.0	23.2	14.3	29.6
Don't know (N=8)	2.2	0.6	0.0	4.3	1.6	5.6

Source: 1978 SNAP Survey of the Elderly, Baltimore County, Maryland

7.25

Table 7-30. "Do you need additional transportation for any of the following reasons?" (in percents)

Transportation needs	Total	Service area				
		Southwest	Northwest	North	Northeast	Southeast
Visiting friends or relatives (N=86)	7.3	8.1	11.4	4.3	6.5	7.7
Recreational or social activities (N=75)	6.3	5.4	7.1	6.1	5.6	9.0
Shopping (N=96)	8.1	10.3	10.3	4.9	5.6	9.5
Doctor, dentist or clinic visits (N=121)	10.2	11.3	11.4	8.0	8.7	11.8
Pleasure trips (N=93)	7.9	7.6	11.4	4.9	5.3	13.1
Going to social service offices (N=57)	4.8	4.9	8.6	1.8	2.8	8.6
Personal business (N=74)	6.3	5.9	8.6	3.1	5.0	10.4
Going to educational programs (N=35)	3.0	2.2	4.3	4.3	1.2	5.4
Going to work (N=16)	1.4	1.0	1.4	1.2	0.9	2.7

Source: 1978 SNAP Survey of the Elderly, Baltimore County, Maryland

Table 7-31. "Do you need additional transportation for any of the following reasons?" (in percents)

Characteristics	Visiting	Recreation Social Activities	Shopping	Health Care Visits	Pleasure	Social Service Visits	Personal business	Educational progress	Work
Sex and age									
Males (60-74)	2.3	1.7	2.0	3.2	3.2	1.7	1.7	0.6	1.2
Female (64-74)	9.1	8.6	9.1	12.7	9.9	5.2	7.7	3.8	1.6
Males (≥ 75)	4.5	3.4	8.0	9.1	5.7	2.3	3.4	2.3	0.0
Females (≥ 75)	12.6	9.8	17.2	16.7	11.5	10.9	12.1	5.2	1.7
Marital status									
Never married	6.6	3.3	8.2	8.2	3.3	1.6	4.9	1.6	1.6
Married	3.3	3.1	4.4	5.8	4.6	2.5	2.8	1.7	0.6
Separated/divorced	21.3	17.0	14.9	19.1	21.3	14.9	14.9	8.5	4.3
Widowed	11.6	10.3	12.8	16.0	11.9	7.5	10.5	4.3	2.1
Retirement status									
Retired	7.4	6.3	8.1	9.7	8.1	4.3	5.8	3.0	0.8
Not retired	7.1	6.5	8.3	11.5	7.4	6.2	7.4	2.9	2.7
Living arrangement									
Living alone	11.8	9.9	13.7	15.0	10.5	6.4	10.2	3.5	2.5
Not living alone	5.6	5.1	6.1	8.5	6.9	4.3	4.8	2.8	0.9

Source: 1978 SNAP Survey of the Elderly, Baltimore County, Maryland

205

7.32

Table 7-32. Distribution of transportation responses by number of functional limitations[a] (in percents)

Number of functional limitations	Have transportation problem	Drive car frequently	Use senior ride	Use MTA	Not convenient to use MTA	Need additional transportation for			
						Shopping	Doctor/ dentist	Work	Visiting friends
None (N=854)	8.7	49.5	3.0	25.8	19.0	6.3	6.7	1.4	5.9
One (N=130)	16.9	26.9	4.6	23.8	16.9	7.7	10.8	1.5	9.2
Two-four (N=134)	28.1	7.3	6.4	10.6	30.1	12.3	23.6	0.0	9.5
Five-seven (N=45)	21.2	1.2	1.2	1.2	23.0	21.8	24.8	1.2	13.2
Eight-ten (N=16)	58.7	0.0	0.0	5.7	26.0	32.6	42.8	11.1	26.9
Eleven or more (N=3)	25.0	0.0	0.0	0.0	0.0	0.0	0.0	0.0	25.0

[a]Functional limitations include limitations in physical functioning as measured by the Activities of Daily Living Scale (ADL) and limitations in performing instrumental activities as measured by the Instrumental Activities of Daily Living Scale (IADL)

Source: 1978 SNAP Survey of the Elderly, Baltimore County, Maryland

8.1

Table 8-1. "Do you have any health or medical coverage?" (in percents)

Health insurance	Total	Service area				
		South-west	North-west	North	North-east	South-east
Medicaid	14.9	9.9	14.3	14.7	16.8	21.7
Medicare "A" only	24.5	28.3	25.7	11.0	30.1	18.6
Medicare "A" & "B"	44.9	48.0	48.6	59.5	37.9	37.6
Blue Cross/Blue Shield	73.5	77.6	74.3	82.8	71.4	62.0
A prepaid health plan	18.4	17.7	21.4	23.9	15.5	18.6

Source: 1978 SNAP Survey of the Elderly, Baltimore County, Maryland

8.2

Table 8-2. Regression of physician visits on predisposing, enabling, and need factors (N=1,182)

Independent variable	Partial regression coefficients in standard form			
	All independent variables	Predisposing factors	Need factors	Enabling factors
Sex	.001	.016		
Age	.003	.053		
Educational level	.033	-.011		
Living alone	.000	-.001		
Married	-.020	-.036		
Retired	.024	.021		
Economic dependency	.010	.073*		
ADL score	-.111*		-.105*	
IADL score	.178*		.171*	
Depression score	.174*		.150*	
Perceived need for services	.117*		.103*	
Transportation barriers	-.074*			.027
Knowledge of services	-.006			-.051*
Social support	.052			.038
Medicaid coverage	-.020			.000
Medicare "A" only	-.000			.015
Blue Cross/Blue Shield	.007			-.011
Prepaid health plan	-.018			-.033
Multiple regression	-.302	.102	.284	.079
R^2	.091	.010	.080	.006

*Significant at .05 or lower level
Source: 1978 SNAP Survey of the Elderly, Baltimore County, Maryland

Table 8-3. Multiple classification analysis of the number of physician visits in a year (N=1182; mean=5.61; R²= 0.162)

Predictors	Mean (Doctor visits)	Adjusted[a] mean	Gross effect[b] (Eta)	Net effect[c] (Beta)
Area			0.08	0.07
Southwest	6.38	6.22		
Northwest	4.09	4.14		
North	5.28	5.71		
Northeast	5.12	5.20		
Southeast	5.65	5.48		
Sex and age			0.09	0.05
Male (60-74)	5.44	5.45		
Female (60-74)	5.24	5.26		
Male (≥ 75)	5.39	5.61		
Female (≥ 75)	7.31	6.43		
Marital status			0.11	0.12*
Never married	4.36	4.40		
Married	4.94	4.89		
Separated/divorced	6.26	6.43		
Widowed	6.69	6.73		
Living arrangement			0.01	0.07*
Living alone	5.78	4.70		
Not living alone	5.55	5.94		
Disability status			0.38	0.37*
No disabling condition	4.11	4.4		
Disabled for 1 or 6 days	6.57	6.59		
Disabled for 7-30 days	9.36	9.23		
Disabled for 31+ days	15.32	15.13		

*Significant at 0.05 or lower level

[a] The average number of physician visits for each subclass of a predictor was adjusted for other four predictors

[b] The gross effect refers to probability of a predictor variable to explain variation in the dependent variable without taking other factors into account.

[c] The net effect refers to the ability of a predictor variable to explain variation in the dependent variable while the effects of other predictors are controlled.

Source: 1978 SNAP Survey of the Elderly, Baltimore County, Maryland

8.3

207

8.4

Table 8-4. Multiple classification analysis of the likelihood of having a physician visit in a year (N=1182; mean = 80.03; R^2=0.04)

Predictors	Proportion of having a doctor visit	Adjusted[a] proportion	Gross effect[b] (Eta)	Net effect[c] (Beta)
Area			0.04	0.05
Southwest	78.82	78.46		
Northwest	80.00	79.10		
North	84.05	84.71		
Northeast	79.05	80.37		
Southeast	80.09	79.25		
Sex and age			0.07	0.07
Male (60-74)	80.12	79.95		
Female (60-74)	78.53	78.55		
Male (≥ 75)	77.27	77.97		
Female (≥ 75)	86.21	86.10		
Marital status			0.04	0.04
Never married	78.69	78.98		
Married	79.40	79.69		
Separated/divorced	87.23	87.98		
Widowed	80.37	79.81		
Living arrangement			0.02	0.03
Living alone	78.98	77.74		
Not living alone	80.41	80.86		
Disability status			0.18	0.18*
No disabling condition	75.90	75.98		
Disabled for 1-6 days	86.21	86.22		
Disabled for 7-30 days	94.12	94.16		
Disabled for 31+ days	96.25	96.34		

*Significant at 0.05 or lower level

[a]The proportion of those who made a doctor visit for each subclass of a predictor was adjusted for other four predictors.

[b]The gross effect refers to probability of a predictor variable to explain variation in the dependent variable without taking other factors into account.

[c]The net effect refers to the ability of a predictor variable to explain variation in the dependent variable while the effects of other predictors are controlled.

Source: 1978 SNAP Survey of the Elderly, Baltimore County, Maryland

Table 8-5. Regression of hospitalization on predisposing, enabling and need factors (N=1182)

Independent variable	Partial regression coefficients in standard form			
	All independent variables	Predisposing factors	Need factors	Enabling factors
Sex	-.007	.011		
Age	-.020	.028		
Educational level	-.033	-.063*		
Living alone	.016	.012		
Married	.000	-.011		
Retired	.026	.023		
Economic dependency	.022	.076*		
ADL score	-.005		-.005	
IADL score	.129*		.127*	
Depression score	.069*		.072*	
Perceived need for services	.088*		.094*	
Transportation barriers	.002			.075*
Knowledge of services	.002			-.035
Social support	.004			.039
Medicaid coverage	-.048			.030
Medicare "A" only	.001			.020
Blue Cross/Blue Shield	-.002			-.026
Prepaid health plan	-.043			-.061*
Multiple Regression	.240			.121
R^2	.060			.014

*Significant at 0.05 or lower level
Source: 1978 SNAP Survey of the Elderly, Baltimore County, Maryland

Table 8-6. Regression of number of hospitalization days on predisposing, enabling and need factors (N=1182)

Independent variable	Partial regression coefficients in standard form			
	All independent variables	Predisposing factors	Need factors	Enabling factors
Sex	.002	.014		
Age	-.071*	.004		
Educational level	-.042	-.075*		
Living alone	-.011	-.021		
Married	.008	-.000		
Retired	-.025	-.030		
Economic dependency	-.019	.037		
ADL score	-.018		-.017	
IADL score	.203*		.185*	
Depression score	.011		.022	
Perceived need for services	.086*		.081*	
Transportation barriers	-.007			.053
Knowledge of services	-.023			.050
Social support	.013			.018
Medicaid coverage	.011			.023
Medicare "A" only	-.026			-.019
Blue Cross/Blue Shield	.006			.022
Prepaid health plan	-.058*			-.075*
Multiple Regression	.258			.114
R^2	.066			.013

*Significant at 0.05 or lower level
Source: 1978 SNAP Survey of the Elderly, Baltimore County, Maryland

Table 8-10. Regression of dental visits on predisposing, enabling and need factors (N=1182)

Independent variable	Partial regression coefficients in standard form			
	All independent variables	Predisposing factors	Need factors	Enabling factors
Sex	.039	.029		
Age	-.104*	-.122*		
Educational level	.209*	.235*		
Living alone	.026	.031		
Married	-.008	-.001		
Retired	.019	.013		
Economic dependency	-.038	-.061*		
ADL score	-.012		.021	
IADL score	-.060		-.154*	
Depression score	-.051		-.074*	
Perceived need for services	.009		.001	
Transportation barriers	-.035			-.074*
Knowledge of services	-.023			.051
Social support	-.033			-.037
Medicaid coverage	-.049			-.073*
Medicare "A" only	.009			-.028
Blue Cross/Blue Shield	.032			.066*
Prepaid health plan	.050			.090*
Multiple Regression	.318	.289	.180	.170
R^2	.101	.083	.032	.028

*Significant at 0.05 or lower level
Source: 1978 SNAP Survey of the Elderly, Baltimore County, Maryland

Tables 8.7, 8.8, and 8.9 appear on pages 210-212.

8.7

Table 8-7. Multiple classification analysis of the likelihood of being hospitalized in a year (N=1182; mean=9.98; R^2= 0.262)

Predictors	Proportion of having a doctor visit	Adjusted[a] proportion	Gross effect[b] (Eta)	Net effect[c] (Beta)
Area			0.07	0.04
Southwest	12.32	11.66		
Northwest	8.57	9.26		
North	6.75	9.25		
Northeast	8.39	8.45		
Southeast	10.86	9.90		
Sex and age			0.06	0.04
Male (60-74)	8.07	8.81		
Female (60-74)	9.60	9.98		
Male (≤ 75)	13.64	14.11		
Female (≤ 75)	13.22	9.90		
Marital status			0.09	0.06
Never married	8.20	8.81		
Married	7.86	9.98		
Separated/divorced	10.64	14.11		
Widowed	13.24	10.22		
Living arrangement			0.02	0.03
Living alone	11.15	8.47		
Not living alone	9.56	10.53		
Disability status			0.50	0.50*
No disabling condition	2.86	2.87		
Disabled for 1-6 days	9.77	9.63		
Disabled for 7-30 days	41.18	40.79		
Disabled for 31+ days	52.50	52.22		

*Significant at 0.05 or lower level

[a]The average number of hospital days for each subclass of a predictor was adjusted for other four predictors

[b]The gross effect refers to probability of a predictor variable to explain variation in the dependent variable without taking other factors into account.

[c]The net effect refers to the ability of a predictor variable to explain variation in the dependent variable while the effects of other predictors are controlled.

Source: 1978 SNAP Survey of the Elderly, Baltimore County, Maryland

Table 8-8. Multiple classification on analysis of the number of days in hospitals in a year
(N=1182; Mean=3.16; R^2=0.192)

Predictors	Proportion of having a doctor visit	Adjusted[a] proportion	Gross effect[b] (Eta)	Net effect[c] (Beta)
Area			0.06	0.04
Southwest	3.36	2.96		
Northwest	2.06	2.45		
North	1.40	2.27		
Northeast	3.37	3.47		
Southeast	4.15	3.96		
Sex and age			0.06	0.03
Male (60-74)	2.66	2.93		
Female (60-74)	2.91	3.04		
Male (≤ 75)	2.66	2.76		
Female (≤ 75)	5.24	4.12		
Marital status			0.09	0.11*
Never married	2.49	2.99		
Married	2.23	1.92		
Separated/divorced	1.40	1.81		
Widowed	4.80	5.13		
Living arrangement			0.02	0.09*
Living alone	2.79	0.92		
Not living alone	3.30	3.97		
Disability status			0.42	0.42*
No disabling condition	0.77	0.87		
Disabled for 1-6 days	1.83	1.60		
Disabled for 7-30 days	10.16	9.89		
Disabled for 31+ days	24.17	24.03		

8.8

*Significant at 0.05 or lower level

[a] The average number of hospital days for each subclass of a predictor was adjusted for other four predictors

[b] The gross effect refers to probability of a predictor variable to explain variation in the dependent variable without taking other factors into account.

[c] The net effect refers to the ability of a predictor variable to explain variation in the dependent variable while the effects of other predictors are controlled.

Source: 1978 SNAP Survey of the Elderly, Baltimore County, Maryland

211

8.9

Table 8-9. Multiple classification of the likelihood of being institutionalized in a year (N=1182; average proportion = 1.27; R^2 = 0.038)

Predictors	Proportion of having a doctor visit	Adjusted[a] proportion	Gross effect[b] (Eta)	Net effect[c] (Beta)
Area			0.04	0.04
Southwest	1.23	1.19		
Northwest	2.86	2.98		
North	0.61	0.89		
Northeast	1.24	1.17		
Southeast	1.36	1.31		
Sex and age			0.05	0.05
Male (60-74)	2.02	1.83		
Female (60-74)	0.70	0.76		
Male (≥ 75)	1.14	1.44		
Female (≥ 75)	1.72	1.76		
Marital status			0.06	0.07
Never married	1.64	2.03		
Married	1.26	0.86		
Separated/divorced	4.26	4.68		
Widowed	0.91	1.30		
Living arrangement			0.03	0.05
Living alone	0.64	0.41		
Not living alone	1.50	1.58		
Disability status			0.17	0.17*
No disabling condition	0.37	0.40		
Disabled for 1-6 days	1.15	1.13		
Disabled for 7-30 days	2.35	2.26		
Disabled for 31+ days	6.25	6.21		

*Significant at 0.05 or lower level

[a]The average number of hospital days for each subclass of a predictor was adjusted for other four predictors

[b]The gross effect refers to probability of a predictor variable to explain variation in the dependent variable without taking other factors into account.

[c]The net effect refers to the ability of a predictor variable to explain variation in the dependent variable while the effects of other predictors are controlled.

Source: 1978 SNAP Survey of the Elderly, Baltimore County, Maryland

Table 8-11. Multiple classification analysis of the likelihood of having a doctor visit in the last year
(N = 1182; Mean = .41; R^2 = .06)

Predictors	Proportion of having a doctor visit	Adjusted[a] proportion	Gross effect[b] (Eta)	Net effect[c] (Beta)
Area				
Southwest	.39	.40	.20	.11
Northwest	.53	.54		
North	.60	.60		
Northeast	.40	.40		
Southeast	.27	.26		
Sex and age				
Male (60-74)	.43	.41	.20	.11
Female (60-74)	.45	.45		
Male (≥ 75)	.34	.32		
Female (≥ 75)	.29	.52		
Marital status				
Never married	.44	.42	.08	.11
Married	.44	.46		
Separated/divorced	.43	.39		
Widowed	.36	.34		
Living arrangement				
Living alone	.42	.49	.01	.09
Not living alone	.41	.38		
Poor				
Not poor	.42	.42	.08	.05
Poor	.29	.32		

*Significant at 0.05 or lower level

[a] The average number of hospital days for each subclass of a predictor was adjusted for other four predictors

[b] The gross effect refers to probability of a predictor variable to explain variation in the dependent variable without taking other factors into account.

[c] The net effect refers to the ability of a predictor variable to explain variation in the dependent variable while the effects of other predictors are controlled.

Source: 1978 SNAP Survey of the Elderly, Baltimore County, Maryland

8.11

Table 8-12. "When was the last time you went to a dentist?" (in percents)

Characteristics			Last time went to a dentist			
	Total	Never	Within past year	1-3 yrs. ago	3+ yrs. ago	NA[a]
Total	100.0	1.8	41.0	13.5	35.4	8.2
Area						
Southwest	100.0	1.5	39.4	13.1	38.9	7.2
Northwest	100.0	1.4	52.9	11.4	22.9	11.4
North	100.0	1.2	60.1	12.3	20.9	5.5
Northeast	100.0	1.9	40.4	15.5	34.5	7.7
Southeast	100.0	2.7	27.1	12.7	45.2	12.3
Sex and age						
Male (60-74)	100.0	2.6	42.7	14.1	34.3	6.1
Female (60-74)	100.0	1.4	44.7	14.1	31.2	7.5
Male (≥ 75)	100.0	3.4	34.1	10.2	48.9	3.4
Female (≥ 75)	100.0	0.6	29.3	11.5	44.8	12.1
Marital status						
Never married	100.0	0.0	44.3	11.5	36.1	8.2
Married	100.0	2.1	44.3	14.3	32.7	6.6
Separated/divorced	100.0	0.0	42.6	17.0	31.9	8.5
Widowed	100.0	1.8	35.6	12.1	39.7	10.7
Retirement status						
Retired	100.0	2.1	41.0	13.4	35.7	7.7
Not retired	100.0	0.9	41.0	13.6	31.8	9.8
Living arrangement						
Living alone	100.0	1.6	42.0	12.7	36.6	7.0
Not living alone	100.0	1.8	40.7	13.7	35.0	8.1

[a]Not answered
Source: 1978 SNAP Survey of the Elderly, Baltimore County, Maryland

Table 9-1. Regression of use of social services on predisposing, enabling, and need factors

Independent variable	Partial regression coefficients in standard form			
	All independent variables	Predisposing factors	Need factors	Enabling factors
Sex	.017	.018		
Age	.087*	.012		
Educational level	-.025	.033		
Living alone	.066*	.080*		
Married	-.012	-.013		
Retired	.023	.031		
Economic dependency	-.053		-.065	
ADL score	-.053		-.060	
IADL score	-.042		-.078*	
Depression score	-.032		-.125	
Perceived need for services	-.081*		.193*	
Transportation barriers	.184			-.015
Knowledge of services	-.046			.311*
Social support	.322*			.038
Medicaid coverage	.006			.010
Medicare "A" only	-.004			.006
Blue Cross/Blue Shield	.024			.032
Prepaid health plan	.051			.038
Multiple Regression	.382	.097	.194	.323
R^2	.146	.009	.038	.104

*Significant at 0.05 or lower level
Source: 1978 SNAP Survey of the Elderly, Baltimore County, Maryland

Table 9-2. Proportion of persons who have heard of the health-related and social services programs by service area

Services	Total	Service area				
		Southwest	Northwest	North	Northeast	Southeast
Health care services						
Visiting nurse association	50.3	54.2	64.3	38.7	51.9	44.8
Hospital social service dept.	25.6	20.9	31.4	20.9	30.1	29.4
Balto. county health dept.	55.1	47.0	60.0	55.2	61.8	58.4
Community health care	18.9	17.7	20.0	12.9	23.0	19.0
Alcoholics anonymous	78.1	71.9	81.4	82.2	82.0	79.6
Balto. county neighborhood health center	38.5	42.1	28.6	23.9	39.1	44.8
Personal services						
Mail alert program	25.1	20.7	30.0	23.9	32.9	21.3
William day care program	11.0	8.1	8.6	17.8	12.7	9.5
Emergency assistance	28.5	23.6	44.3	15.3	36.0	31.2
Senior citizen discount card	71.9	69.2	72.9	79.1	76.7	64.3
Senior aide program	17.7	14.5	18.6	15.3	23.3	16.7
Circuit breaker tax program	56.6	56.2	65.7	42.3	66.5	50.7
Rent supplements to senior citizens	19.9	15.8	18.6	12.9	23.3	28.1
Supplementary security income	29.4	27.3	24.3	18.4	33.2	38.5
Telecare	17.9	16.0	37.1	9.8	21.4	16.3
Employment						
Over 60 counseling and employ-ment service	34.0	33.7	38.6	19.0	41.9	32.6
Retired senior volunteer program	28.0	26.4	28.6	20.2	33.9	28.1
Education						
Community college programs	53.0	58.6	61.4	35.0	57.5	47.1
Library services for seniors	35.9	31.8	44.3	38.7	37.9	35.7
Senior digest	34.4	26.6	42.9	50.3	37.0	30.8

Source: 1978 SNAP Survey of the Elderly, Baltimore County, Maryland

9.2

Table 9-3. Proportions of persons who have heard of the health and social service program by age and sex

Services	Total	Age and sex			
		60-74		≥75	
		Male	Female	Male	Female
Health care services					
Visiting nurse association	50.3	48.7	53.6	34.1	50.6
Hospital social service dept.	25.6	25.4	29.5	14.8	19.0
Balto. county health dept.	55.1	57.6	59.5	38.6	43.7
Community health care	18.9	18.2	20.4	14.8	17.2
Alcoholics anonymous	78.1	80.4	82.7	62.5	66.1
Balto. county neighborhood health center	38.5	43.2	41.5	20.5	28.2
Personal services					
Mail alert program	25.1	27.1	28.4	21.6	12.1
William day care program	11.0	11.2	11.9	6.8	9.8
Emergency assistance	28.5	30.5	30.5	21.6	21.3
Senior citizen discount card	71.9	76.1	74.7	63.6	58.6
Senior aide program	17.7	21.3	18.0	13.6	11.5
Circuit breaker tax program	56.6	73.5	55.7	45.5	31.6
Rent supplements to senior	19.9	23.3	20.9	13.6	12.6
citizens	29.4	35.2	30.2	17.0	23.0
Supplementary security income	17.0	15.3	21.8	13.6	12.6
Telecare	17.9	15.3	21.8	13.6	12.6
Employment					
Over 60 counseling and employ-ment service	34.0	39.2	36.5	25.0	20.1
Retired senior volunteer program	28.0	30.0	30.0	20.5	21.3
Education					
Community college programs	53.0	59.9	57.1	26.1	39.7
Library services for seniors	35.9	40.3	37.7	29.5	24.1
Senior digest		34.3	37.7	25.0	28.7
Nutrition					
Lunch plus	66.8	68.0	70.0	51.1	61.5
Meals on wheels	81.5	80.4	85.0	71.6	77.0
Transportation; senioride	48.1	51.9	49.4	33.0	43.7
Information and referral	39.5	45.5	42.1	27.3	25.3
Recreation: Senior center program	51.1	51.9	57.1	33.0	39.1

Source: 1978 SNAP Survey of the Elderly, Baltimore County, Maryland

9.4

Table 9-4. Proportion of persons who have heard of a program and participated in it

Services	Total	Service area				
		Southwest	Northwest	North	Northeast	Southeast
Health care services						
Visiting nurse association	10.8	10.8	13.3	6.3	13.0	8.5
Hospital social service dept.	6.7	11.4	9.0	2.9	4.0	5.5
Balto. county health dept.	10.8	9.3	7.1	8.8	14.0	10.5
Community health care	3.5	4.1	.0	4.7	4.0	2.1
Alcoholics anonymous	.04	.0	.0	.0	1.0	.0
Balto. county neighborhood health center	14.4	18.0	10.0	15.3	10.3	13.9
Personal services						
Mail alert program	2.9	3.4	4.7	2.5	2.8	1.8
William day care program	3.5	.0	.0	3.4	6.9	3.6
Emergency assistance	5.5	6.2	3.2	3.8	8.4	1.3
Senior citizen discount card	56.3	65.8	64.7	50.3	51.6	47.8
Senior aide program	2.3	3.3	.0	3.4	1.3	2.4
Circuit breaker tax program	40.7	50.4	26.0	24.6	39.0	39.6
Rent supplements to senior citizens	4.6	.0	.0	.0	2.6	14.0
Supplementary security income	5.9	3.5	5.8	3.3	4.5	11.4
Telecare	2.3	3.0	7.6	.0	.0	2.5
Employment						
Over 60 counseling and employ-ment service	4.4	4.3	.0	6.4	4.4	5.1
Retired senior volunteer program	5.9	7.4	.0	9.0	5.4	4.5
Education						
Community college programs	5.9	5.8	9.3	1.7	6.4	5.6
Library services for seniors	19.8	24.6	25.8	17.4	17.0	15.8
Senior digest	37.0	40.7	30.0	39.0	34.4	36.6
Nutrition						
Lunch plus	11.0	9.3	20.3	4.3	12.2	12.2
Meals on wheels	4.6	5.2	5.3	4.8	4.8	2.3
Transportation: senioride	5.9	8.6	4.9	3.8	5.5	4.0
Information and Referral	7.0	4.7	11.8	2.2	8.1	8.8
Recreation: Senior Center Program	17.4	17.7	21.0	17.4	13.3	21.9

Source: 1978 SNAP Survey of the Elderly, Baltimore County, Maryland

217

Table 9-5. Proportion of persons who have heard of a program and who have participated in it

Services	Total	Age and sex			
		60-74		≥75	
		Male	Female	Male	Female
Health care services					
Visiting nurse association	10.8	8.1	9.9	20.0	15.9
Hospital social service dept.	6.7	5.4	6.9	7.7	9.1
Balto. county health dept.	10.8	20.8	12.7	8.8	3.9
Community health care	3.5	3.0	4.2	7.1	0.0
Alcoholics anonymous	0.4	0.0	0.6	1.8	0.0
Balto. county neighborhood health center	14.4	13.2	14.5	26.3	13.7
Personal services					
Mail alert program	2.9	1.0	3.0	15.8	0.0
William day care program	3.5	0.0	5.3	16.7	0.0
Emergency assistance	5.5	5.5	5.0	7.9	5.5
Senior citizen discount card	56.3	53.4	56.8	66.7	55.9
Senior aide program	2.3	2.6	2.9	0.0	0.0
Circuit breaker tax program	40.7	33.1	41.7	51.2	61.8
Rent supplements to senior citizens	4.6	2.4	7.4	0.0	0.0
Supplementary security income	5.9	5.6	5.1	0.0	12.5
Telecare	2.3	3.6	1.6	7.1	0.0
Employment					
Over 60 counseling and employment service	4.4	5.0	3.8	9.1	2.9
Retired senior volunteer program	5.9	4.7	7.5	10.5	0.0
Education					
Community college programs	5.9	6.2	5.5	8.3	5.8
Library services for seniors	19.8	19.0	22.9	14.8	9.5
Senior digest	37.0	34.7	35.8	41.7	46.0
Nutrition					
Lunch plus	11.0	73.1	71.8	87.5	90.0
Meals on wheels	4.6	2.9	4.9	3.2	7.5
Transportation: senioride	5.9	0.5	7.0	10.3	13.2
Information and Referral	7.0	7.4	6.6	4.2	9.1
Recreation: Senior center program	17.4	15.4	15.5	24.1	29.4

Source: 1978 SNAP Survey of the Elderly, Baltimore County, Maryland

Table 10-1. Intercorrelations, means and standard deviations of well-being, need and use indicators

Indicators	1	2	3	4	5	6	7
Number of Physican Visits	1.00	.037	.203	.161	.106	.138	.121
Use of social services			.067	.031	-.060	-.080	-.045
Need				.787	.284	.252	.348
Unmet needs					.179	.231	.275
Physical well-being[a]						.263	.221
Psychological well-being[a]							.103
Social well-being[a]							.100
Mean	5.61	1.42	1.41	.66	.045	.147	.065
Standard deviation	7.99	1.60	1.92	1.88	.208	.354	.246

[a]Dichotomized variable is used: those who had poor well-being status were assigned a score of 1 and others were assigned 0.

Source: 1978 SNAP Survey of the Elderly, Baltimore County, Maryland

Table 10-2. Distribution of frailty[a] by social and demographic characteristics

Characteristics	Low (N=938)	Medium (N=222)	High (N=22)
Total	79.4	18.6	2.8
Area			
Southwest	77.8	20.0	1.5
Northwest	85.7	12.8	1.4
North	82.8	15.9	1.2
Northeast	82.9	14.2	2.7
Southeast	72.4	25.7	1.8
Age			
60-74	81.1	17.3	1.5
(≥ 75)	73.3	23.6	3.0
Marital status			
Never married	82.0	18.0	0.0
Married	83.3	16.0	1.6
Separated/divorced	80.9	17.0	2.1
Widowed	73.1	24.4	2.6
Retirement status			
Retired	79.5	18.2	2.2
Not retired	79.1	20.0	0.0
Living arrangement			
Living alone	77.1	21.0	1.9
Not living alone	80.2	17.9	1.8

[a]Frailty has been grouped into three categories on the basis of mean number of unmet service need and functional impairments. Low refers to having no limitations in physical, psychological or social functioning and a mean unmet service need of less than one; medium refers to having one or two of functional impairments and a mean of 1.28 unmet service needs; high refers having impairments in both psychological and social functioning or in all three areas of functioning and a mean of three unmet service needs.

Source: 1978 SNAP Survey of the Elderly, Baltimore County, Maryland

10.3

Table 10-3. Distribution of selected characteristics by physical, psychological and social well-being status   (in percents)

Characteristics	Physical well-being		Psychological well-being		Social well-being	
	Poor (N=54)	Non-poor (N=1,128)	Poor (N=174)	Non-poor (N=1,108)	Poor (N=77)	Non-poor (N=1,105)
Problem getting needed medical treatment	22.2	5.9	15.5	5.1	26.0	5.2
Have transportation problems	31.5	12.1	27.6	10.4	33.8	11.5
Need health aides (hearing aid, walker, etc.)	14.8	2.9	7.5	2.8	14.3	2.7
Have Medicaid	22.2	14.5	15.5	14.8	24.7	14.2
Have someone who helps with housework, shopping, dressing	87.0	43.3	59.8	42.8	75.3	43.2
Have social security income	9.3	2.1	4.6	0.1	9.1	2.0
Weak social support (1 or less)	14.9	7.1	15.5	6.1	10.4	7.3
Low knowledge of services (recognize less than ten services)	76.2	49.0	64.3	48.0	74.1	48.5
House in deteriorating condition	1.9	.9	1.1	.9	2.6	.8

Source: 1978 SNAP Survey of the Elderly, Baltimore County, Maryland

10.4

Table 10-4. Magnitude of met and unmet needs by physical, psychological, and social functioning status

Magnitude of perceived needs	Physical functioning		Psychological functioning		Social functioning	
	Poor (N=54)	Normal (N=1128)	Poor (N=174)	Normal (N=1008)	Poor (N=77)	Normal (N=1105)
None	11.1	44.0	24.7	45.5	10.4	44.7
Low (1)	9.3	25.4	17.2	25.9	10.4	25.6
Medium (2-4)	42.6	24.4	38.0	23.0	45.5	23.8
High	37.0	6.2	20.1	5.6	33.7	5.9
Total average of perceived needs[a]	3.9		2.6		3.9	
Magnitude of actual unmet needs						
None	31.5	65.5	46.0	67.1	27.3	66.5
Low (1)	27.8	20.4	20.1	20.8	24.7	20.5
Medium (2)	14.8	7.5	12.1	7.1	22.1	6.9
High (3-8)	25.9	6.6	21.8	5.0	25.9	6.1
Total average of unmet needs[b]	1.6		1.3		1.9	

[a]Refers to number of needs reported whether or not these needs are being met with services

[b]Refers to number of needs reported which are not being met with services

Source: 1978 SNAP Survey of the Elderly, Baltimore County, Maryland

220

Table 10-5. Proportion of frail elders who perceived a specific social and
health service need by physical, mental and social functioning
status (in percents)

Need	Frailty in terms of having poor functioning		
	Physically (N=54)	Mentally (N=174)	Socially (N=77)
Personal needs			
Counseling for personal or family problems	1.9	5.2	6.5
Someone to look after all the time	27.8	11.5	24.7
Someone to check on five times a week	31.5	21.9	35.1
Assistance for routine housework that cannot do	55.5	26.4	40.3
Legal assistance or assistance for personal business management	7.4	8.0	9.1
Health care needs			
Medicine that one cannot afford	18.5	12.6	32.5
Nursing care prescribed by a doctor	9.3	7.5	10.4
Physical therapy	22.3	9.7	14.3
Assistance in ADL functioning	35.2	10.9	20.8
Doctor or social worker's review of status	16.7	13.7	23.4
Instruction for learning basic personal skills	o.9	7.5	7.5
Recreational needs			
Participation in planned and organized social, recreational, or group activities	7.4	21.2	14.3
Housing and home needs			
Help in finding a place to live	11.2	9.2	28.1
Assistance for home repairs or yard work	38.9	33.3	39.0
Nutritional needs			
Someone who regularly prepared meals	7.5	5.7	9.1
Employment needs			
Assistance for finding a job	35.2	15.5	22.1
Information and referral			
Information about home security or crime prevention methods	11.1	5.7	11.7
Information and referral services	53.7	33.3	58.4
Average number of perceived needs	3.9	2.6	3.9

Source: 1978 SNAP Survey of the Elderly, Baltimore County, Maryland

221

10.6

Table 10-6. Proportion of frail elders who reported a specific unmet service
need by physical, mental and social functioning status
(in percents)

Need	Frailty in terms of having poor functioning		
	Physically (N= 54)	Mentally (N=174)	Socially (N=77)
Personal needs			
Counseling for personal or family problems	1.9	5.2	6.5
Someone to look after all the time	7.4	2.9	6.5
Someone to check on five times a week	5.6	2.9	1.3
Assistance for routine housework that one cannot do	14.8	10.9	14.3
Legal assistance or assistance for personal business management	3.7	4.0	3.0
Health care needs			
Medicine that one cannot afford	----	----	----
Nursing care prescribed by a doctor	7.4	6.9	9.9
Physical therapy	20.4	8.0	10.4
Assistance in ADL functioning	9.3	3.4	9.1
Doctor or social worker's review of status	9.3	8.0	13.0
Instruction for learning basic personal skills	----	----	----
Recreational needs			
Participation in planned and organized social, recreational, or group activities	7.4	17.8	11.7
Housing and home needs			
Help in finding a place to live	9.3	8.6	15.6
Assistance for home repairs or yard work	11.1	13.8	22.1
Nutritional needs			
Someone who regularly prepared meals	5.6	5.7	9.1
Employment needs			
Assistance for finding a job	3.7	2.9	2.6
Information and referral			
Information about home security or crime prevention methods	----	----	----
Information and referral services	46.3	31.0	54.5
Average number of unmet service needs	1.6	1.3	1.3

Source: 1978 SNAP survey of the Elderly, Baltimore County, Maryland

10.7

Table 10-7. Mean number of physicians' visits and mean use of social and health
services by physical, psychological, and social functioning

Functioning			Mean number of physician visits	Mean number of social services used
Physical,	Psychological,	Social		
N[a]	N	N	4.86	1.48
N	N	P[b]	8.17	1.27
N	P	N	7.60	1.24
P	N	N	10.13	1.73
N	P	P	14.46	1.00
P	P	N	9.90	.54
P	N	P	12.75	1.12
P	P	P	4.44	.67
Grand Mean			5.61	1.42

a=non-poor functioning

b=poor functioning

Source: 1978 SNAP Survey of the Elderly, Baltimore County, Maryland

Index